Essays on Anscombe's *Intention*

Essays on Anscombe's *Intention*

EDITED BY

Anton Ford

Jennifer Hornsby

Frederick Stoutland

HARVARD UNIVERSITY PRESS
Cambridge, Massachusetts
London, England

First Harvard University Press paperback edition, 2014

Library of Congress Cataloging-in-Publication Data

Essays on Anscombe's Intention / edited by Anton Ford, Jennifer Hornsby,
and Frederick Stoutland.
p. cm.
Includes bibliographical references and indexes.
ISBN 978-0-674-05102-7 (cloth : alk. paper)
ISBN 978-0-674-28426-5 (pbk.)
1. Anscombe, G. E. M. (Gertrude Elizabeth Margaret). Intention—Congresses.
2. Intention (Logic)—Congresses.   I. Ford, Anton.   II. Hornsby, Jennifer.
III. Stoutland, Frederick.
B1618.A573   I5834
128'.4—dc22   2010045536

Contents

Preface

This volume of essays originated in two conferences. The first, in September 2008, was held at the Philosophy Department of the University of Uppsala, sponsored jointly by the five-year program *Understanding Agency* centered in Uppsala, and the *Rational Agency* section of the Centre for the Study of Mind in Nature at the University of Oslo. The second was a Lipkind conference at the Department of Philosophy, University of Chicago, held in April 2009 in honor of the fiftieth anniversary of Elizabeth Anscombe's *Intention* (two years late, but such is the way of these things). The Uppsala conference was not specifically devoted to Anscombe's work, its emphasis being on the Aristotelian tradition, but renewed attention to that tradition is surely owed to a revived interest in *Intention,* to which its republication in 2000 by Harvard University Press is both owed and owing. In the event, of the ten papers presented at Uppsala, five were on themes in Anscombe. At the Chicago conference, eight papers were presented, each with a commentary.

Three of the philosophers whose work is included in this collection (McDowell, Müller, and Thompson) presented papers at both conferences; Thompson's paper in this volume is from Uppsala, the papers by McDowell and Müller are from Chicago. The papers by Ford and by Moran and Stone were presented in Uppsala, and the papers by Hornsby, Setiya, and Rödl were presented in Chicago. The papers by Haddock and Laurence were solicited by us as editors. With the exception of the paper by Moran and Stone (Chapter 1 of this volume), all the papers have been revised, some very significantly, and we have divided the task of editing them among us. Chapter 1, originally published as "Anscombe on Expression of Intention," in Constantine Sandis, ed., *New Essays on the Explanation of Action,* Copyright © Richard Moran and Martin J. Stone 2009, is reproduced with the permission of Palgrave Macmillan.

We are greatly appreciative of the support and assistance of many persons in helping to bring this project to completion. For the Uppsala Conference, they include Lilli Alanen, Tomas Eckenberg, Martin Gustafsson, and Frans Svensson. For the Chicago Conference, special thanks are owed to Charles Todd. In addition to giving invaluable help with that, and assisting with the final manuscript of this volume, Todd has prepared an index to Anscombe's *Intention,* which is included here. Lindsay Waters of Harvard University Press was a welcome participant in the Chicago conference, and he has been an enthusiastic supporter of the book. It has been a real pleasure to work with the authors of the papers that follow, and since these include ourselves, in thanking them all, we thank one another.

A.F., J.H., F.S.

Essays on Anscombe's *Intention*

Introduction:
Anscombe's *Intention* in Context

FREDERICK STOUTLAND

Elizabeth Anscombe's *Intention,* published in 1957,[1] is a book of only ninety-four pages, but crafted with great care and wasting no words, it develops a profound, original, and remarkably comprehensive account of intentional action and the concepts that circle round it. It is, wrote Donald Davidson, "the most important treatment of action since Aristotle,"[2] an admiration shared by the authors of the essays in this volume.

That kind of admiration for Anscombe's book has been slow in coming. The book did not fall stillborn from the press, but it was not generally recognized as a work of great philosophical importance. Although written by someone who considered herself an analytic philosopher, it is an obscure, terse, and often puzzling book that is intelligible and useful only to persons prepared to read it with considerable patience and charity. But until recently few were prepared to read it in that way, and it was too easily dismissed as the incomprehensible work of an eccentric genius who was, moreover, a woman.

---

1. Oxford, 1957; 2nd ed., Cambridge, Mass., 2000.

2. On the cover of the Harvard University Press edition of *Intention* (Cambridge, Mass., 2000).

Born in 1919, Anscombe studied Greats at St. Hugh's College, Oxford (1937–1941), and then held a one-year research fellowship there. In 1941 she married the philosopher Peter Geach, who, like herself, was a convert to Catholicism and with whom she had seven children. She was a research student at Cambridge for four years, becoming pupil and close friend of Wittgenstein. In 1946 she joined Oxford's Somerville College and spent the next twenty-four years there, first as a research fellow and then as a tutorial fellow. In 1970 she was named to the Chair of Philosophy at Cambridge that Wittgenstein had held (before him, Moore, and after, von Wright). She retired in 1986 and died in Oxford in 2001.

Her reputation during her long career at Oxford and Cambridge was that of a highly regarded analytic philosopher, distinguished by her close association with Wittgenstein, by her incisive arguments and stimulating lectures, and by the power, if not stridency, of her personality. She was a productive scholar, publishing three books—*Intention, An Introduction to Wittgenstein's Tractatus,* and (with Peter Geach) *Three Philosophers*[3]—and numerous papers, many of which are in the three volumes of her collected papers. Two more volumes of her papers have been published posthumously.[4] These writings expand on her account of action in *Intention,* but they also cover many other topics: ethics, political philosophy, philosophy of mind, epistemology, metaphysics, philosophy of language, and more. She gave numerous lectures around the world and regularly lectured and held seminars at Oxford and Cambridge on an astonishing variety of subjects. She often lectured to Catholic priests and laity on theological topics to which philosophy was relevant. Wittgenstein had named her one of his literary executors (along with G. H. von Wright and Rush Rhees), and she translated and helped edit his central works, above all his *Philosophical Investigations,*[5] her translation of which is now quoted around the world as if it were the words of Wittgenstein himself.

---

3. *An Introduction to Wittgenstein's Tractatus:* London, 1959; *Three Philosophers:* Oxford, 1961.

4. *The Collected Philosophical Papers of G. E. M. Anscombe,* vol. 1: *From Parmenides to Wittgenstein;* vol. 2: *Metaphysics and the Philosophy of Mind;* vol. 3: *Ethics, Religion, and Politics* (Minneapolis, Minn., 1981). The posthumous volumes are *Human Life, Action and Ethics* (Exeter, U.K., 2005) and *Faith in a Hard Ground: Essays on Religion, Philosophy and Ethics* (Exeter, U.K., 2008), both edited by Mary Geach and Luke Gormally. A bibliography of Anscombe's work is in Roger Teichmann's *The Philosophy of Elizabeth Anscombe* (Oxford, 2008).

5. Ludwig Wittgenstein, *Philosophical Investigations,* trans. G. E. M. Anscombe (Oxford, 1953), ix.

In recent years there has been a greatly renewed interest in Anscombe's philosophy, and especially in her philosophy of action. There are a number of reasons for this. Philosophers of a new generation, who are unwilling simply to take the dominant account of action for granted, have sought something different, which they have found in Anscombe. Many are suspicious of analytic philosophy for having come to define itself in terms of distinctive, substantive doctrines (e.g., physicalism), and Anscombe's work, while in the analytic tradition and having many of its virtues, suggests a stance that avoids commitment to those doctrines. Moreover, her work is now sufficiently distant so that it is the subject of historical and scholarly investigation, allowing it to be seen with fresh eyes. Finally, a number of recent publications have made substantial use of her insights, demonstrating how they can alter one's conception of action in the interest of a view that is more coherent and plausible than current reigning orthodoxy.[6]

This renewed interest in Anscombe's philosophy of action has come with a growing appreciation of her status as one of the great philosophers of the twentieth century. The more time passes, the more one is struck by the magnitude of her achievement. Her works in philosophy of action are not only probing and constantly instructive, but they can now be seen to be unified by what Michael Thompson calls her "analytical Aristotelianism."[7] Of course, they remain difficult, and many passages continue to puzzle. But *Intention* has, for many, acquired the status of a classic, and it will be interpreted, exploited, and argued over as classics always are.

No discussion of Anscombe is complete without mention of her Catholicism: if philosophy was the center of her life, Catholicism was its ground. She was not only very devout but expended a good deal of energy in the service of an exceptionally conservative Catholic doctrine rooted in the authority of the church and the pope. Although she did not bend her philosophy to her faith, she used philosophical arguments in defense of it, particularly in defense of Catholic moral teaching. Her defense of that teaching, including her impassioned opposition to abortion, employed traditional Aristotelian theses—for example, that man is an animal and that the soul is the form of the living

6. Perhaps the best example of this is Michael Thompson's *Life and Action* (Cambridge, Mass., 2008). Material from the first part had been published in 1995 and from the third part in 2001, and the manuscript has been circulating for a number of years.

7. Ibid., 6.

body—which she took, along with all her philosophical views, to be entirely consistent with her commitment to Catholicism. Whatever one may think about that commitment, it was an important motivation for her philosophical work that helped relate it to the essential concerns of humanity.

Intention is a case in point. When Oxford University proposed to give an honorary degree to then ex-president Harry Truman, who had ordered the bombing of Hiroshima and Nagasaki, Anscombe opposed it in a speech delivered to her colleagues in which she argued that one may as well honor Genghis Khan, Nero, or Hitler. In Truman's defense, she heard it said that all he actually *did* was to sign his name on a piece of paper, that it wasn't his *aim* to kill innocent civilians, and that his only *intention* was to end the war. This led her to think that it was worth a philosopher's time to explain what it is to intend to do something, and so she decided to give a series of lectures on that topic, which grew into her *Intention*.[8]

1. My main task in this introduction is to situate Anscombe's *Intention* in the context of contemporary philosophy of action. The latter may be said to have begun with Gilbert Ryle's *The Concept of Mind*.[9] Ryle's principal aim was to undermine what he took to be the Cartesian notion of mind, but along the way he said much about action, since he thought the primary aim of the Cartesians was to bifurcate actions into non-observable, "occult" acts of the mind and movements of the body, with the former causing the latter. That is a mistake, he argued: in observing an agent's actions, we thereby observe what he intends, enjoys, hates, desires, which are characteristics of his acting, not its causes. We observe what he is doing or trying to do, not that his body is moving in such and such a way as a result of the contraction of his muscles caused by his will. On Ryle's view, the Cartesians have given us a distorted picture of the mind in large part because they have given us a distorted conception of action.

The next significant event in the development of contemporary philosophy of action was the publication (in 1953) of Wittgenstein's *Philosophical Investigations*. While Ryle had no doubt been influenced by Wittgenstein, their

---

8. See "Mr. Truman's Degree," in *Ethics, Religion, and Politics,* and Mary Geach's "Introduction," in *Human Life, Action and Ethics.*
9. Gilbert Ryle, *The Concept of Mind* (London, 1949).

philosophical methods were quite different, and Ryle made no reference to Wittgenstein in *The Concept of Mind.* However, with Wittgenstein's mature work now widely available to the philosophical community, it soon became influential for many philosophers of action.

The nature of this influence is a complicated story because Wittgenstein wrote rather little about philosophy of action as such. *Philosophical Investigations* consists of numerous remarks that, as he wrote, "concern many subjects: the concept of meaning, of understanding, of a proposition, of logic, the foundations of mathematics, states of consciousness, and other things"[10]— remarks that are relevant to action but do not add up to an account of its nature and explanation. His aim was "to stimulate someone to thoughts of his own," not to write a treatise on action (or anything else), and his influence on philosophy of action, therefore, took many forms. It often involved what he complained of in saying that he prepared *Philosophical Investigations* for publication because his results had been "variously misunderstood, more or less mangled or watered down,"[11] but even when it rested on a better grasp of his work, his remarks were frequently used without regard to their context, and the result was often not what Wittgenstein would have accepted. His work is nevertheless of first importance for philosophy of action. Many philosophers may dismiss his work as obscurantist and irrelevant, but many others regard him as *the* major philosopher of the twentieth century, and more penetrating interpretation of his writing will increase his role in the work of philosophers.

2. Anscombe's *Intention* is the book that definitively established philosophy of action as a distinctive field—the first book in English since Thomas Reid's *Essays on the Active Powers of Man* (1788) that was entirely devoted to that topic. Published only four years after *Philosophical Investigations,* it is, like all her works, much influenced by Wittgenstein, whose writing she understood as well as anyone. Being an original and powerful thinker in her own right, she made substantive use of Wittgenstein's work even while disagreeing with it, modifying it, and referring to it rather seldom. Although there are deep differences between Wittgenstein and Anscombe—in their style of writing,

---

10. Wittgenstein, *Philosophical Investigations,* ix.
11. Ibid., x.

their attitude to the history of philosophy, and the topics about which they wrote—this does not mean that her philosophical views are not deeply indebted to Wittgenstein. She was just the kind of student he wanted—one who was not an acolyte but who would strike out on her own. "I should not," he wrote, "like my writing to spare other people the trouble of thinking."[12]

The other great influence on Anscombe's work is Aristotle. Very many of the key ideas in *Intention* use Aristotelian terminology and assume Aristotle's discussion. I list just some of them: practical reason, the practical syllogism, practical knowledge, the centrality of ends in action, the concept of desire and wanting, human agents as animals, the notion of form, and the idea of something being what it is by its nature. *Intention* is permeated with Aristotelianism, but it is expressed in ways that reflect the influence of Wittgenstein. It is fair to say that Anscombe read Wittgenstein in the light of Aristotle, and Aristotle in the light of Wittgenstein—and then went her own way.

The most immediate result of the publication of *Intention* was a kind of Wittgensteinian school in the philosophy of action, which produced numerous books (among them the "little red books" published by Routledge and Kegan Paul) and papers attacking views similar to those Ryle had attacked, while developing alternatives influenced by their authors' reading of Anscombe and Wittgenstein. Two features characterized this school. One was its focus on "ordinary language"—on what we would or might say (or not say) about action, motives, intentions, desires, explanation, and so on—as the key to understanding action. The other was its contention that since mental states like belief, desire, or intention are connected with their objects not by empirical laws but conceptually, they cannot cause them. That an agent acted intentionally because of a reason does not, therefore, mean that the reason caused her action. Nor can the distinction between an agent's mere behavior and her acting be made in terms of the latter being caused by her reasons for acting. It was further claimed that action as such could not be understood in the impersonal terms of the natural sciences but only in terms of the concepts of ethics, the law, and everyday social life, concepts that are intelligible to the agent herself.

Although the work of this school came to be neglected, indeed disdained, by mainstream philosophers, one can find in it illuminating accounts of

12. Ibid., ix. Those who knew both Wittgenstein and Anscombe maintain that Anscombe's philosophical demeanor was exceptionally like Wittgenstein's.

concepts crucial for the philosophy of action, like state, performance, intention, and desire. Its publications were, however, too often deficient in argument, philosophically thin, and dismissive of alternatives. Moreover, although it took its appeal to ordinary language to be sanctioned by Wittgenstein, that is a dubious claim that certainly was not sanctioned by Anscombe, who at one point in *Intention* rejected an appeal to "what we would say" by contending that "it does not seem to me to matter whether it is incorrect speech or not."[13]

3. There were at that time other philosophers who thought of action from a very different point of view, one that was a legacy of logical positivism.[14] They saw philosophy of action as a branch of general philosophy of science and were primarily interested in the explanation of action. They held that *any* adequate explanation of why phenomena occur, from the collision of meteors to human acts, is *nomological:* it requires a law-like, empirical generalization that connects the phenomenon to be explained with the conditions that give rise to it. This is the "covering law model" of *explanation,* so called because it holds that one phenomenon explains another only if an empirical general law *covers* both of them—that is, only if, given normal conditions, every instance of the first is followed by an instance of the second. It yields the covering law model of *causality* given its assumption that "*c* causes *e*" *means* that, under normal conditions, events of type *c* are followed, as a matter of law, by events of type *e*. Both causality and explanation were regarded as essentially nomological, a view that derived from Hume's conception of causation as requiring constant conjunction.

Applied to human action, this meant that if an agent's belief and desire explain his action, they do so in virtue of an empirical generalization that connects the content of the belief and desire he has on an occasion with the kind of action he performs on that occasion. Thus his wanting to buy a television and believing he should buy one at the appliance store explains his going to the store in virtue of an empirical generalization to the effect that anyone in similar circumstances with that want and belief goes to such a store.

13. Anscombe, *Intention,* 49n.

14. The most important was C. G. Hempel, who wrote, already in 1942, a classic paper on general laws in history: "The Function of General Laws in History," *The Journal of Philosophy* 39 (1942): 35–48.

The main virtue of the covering law model is that, in holding that a belief and desire explain, hence cause, an action in virtue of their content, it yields an intelligible connection between the agent's having a reason for a given action and that reason causing his action. On this view, the generalizations that connect the content of an agent's beliefs and desires with the actions for which they are his reasons are also empirical laws in virtue of which those beliefs and desires explain (cause) his actions. His desire to buy a television and belief that he should do so at the appliance store are both his reasons for going there and essential constituents of a nomological explanation of why he did.

The main difficulty with the model is that the empirical generalizations it requires for explanation are seldom true. An agent may, for instance, be irrational, wanting to buy a television and thinking he can get one at the appliance store but concluding he should go to the men's store. The model can rule that out by holding that explanation in terms of an agent's reasons for action requires that the agent be rational, which this agent is not. But even if he is rational, he may have no money, may be prevented, may change his mind, and so on. The generalization can be restricted by specifying that it holds provided he has the money, is not prevented, does not change his mind, etc., but that undermines the distinction between putting a restriction on the generalization and recognizing that it is false. If it is empirical (as the model requires), it must be possible to falsify it, but if, whenever it appears to be false a further restriction is added to save its truth, it cannot be false, and hence it ceases to be empirical. If we require that it be an empirical claim, it will seldom be true, and if we attempt to save its truth by adding restrictions, it will cease to be empirical.

4. This was the situation when Donald Davidson's "Actions, Reasons, and Causes" was published in 1963. It soon became a widely influential paper and with other papers made Davidson the central figure in philosophy of action for many years. Although these papers were sophisticated, creative, and often brilliant, they were so immensely influential mostly because they appeared at a fortuitous time when there was a standoff between Wittgensteinian philosophers of action and philosophers who defended the covering law model. While the former were often dismissive of alternatives, the latter largely ignored their claims. Davidson was sympathetic to both, his aim being to incorporate important features of the Wittgensteinian point of

view into the philosophical framework underlying the covering law model of explanation and causation. He was particularly impressed by Anscombe's work, and although he is often regarded as wanting to replace an account like Anscombe's with a causal account of action, it would be more accurate to say that he thought Anscombian notions could be integrated with a causal account.

A number of prominent features of Davidson's account derived (as he recognized) from Anscombe. He accepted her view that an account of action must give central place to *intentional* action. He agreed that actions are events that "have parts that are events, and the parts may be discontinuous temporally or spatially,"[15] and that an act has many descriptions under some of which it is intentional, others not. An agent who flips a switch, thereby turning on the light, illuminating the room, and alerting a burglar acts only once, but his act has numerous descriptions, intentional under some but not others. Being intentional cannot, therefore, be a property of an act because if it were, an act would both have and not have the property of being intentional. His claim that "there is an irreducible difference between psychological explanations that involve the propositional attitudes and explanations in sciences like physics and chemistry"[16] is an echo of Anscombe's position.

Perhaps the most striking echo is his contention that "when we ask why someone acted, we want to be provided with an interpretation . . . a new description of what he did, which fits it into a familiar picture. . . . When we explain an action, by giving the reason, we do redescribe the action, [which gives it] a place in a pattern, and in this way the action is explained."[17] He stressed the first-person character of this, holding that we are authoritative about our own actions and reasons in a way that we are not about others', and that first-person authority is not grounded in introspection. He thought that beliefs, desires, intentions, etc., are states not of the brain, but of agents, and that their contents are conceptually connected with actions.

Davidson's aim was to incorporate these Anscombian-derived notions in an account of action that took "the ordinary notion of cause" as its central concept. He wrote that his *Essays on Actions and Events* are "unified in theme

15. Donald Davidson, *Essays on Actions and Events* (Oxford, 1980), 183.
16. Donald Davidson, *Problems of Rationality* (Oxford, 2004), 101.
17. Davidson, *Essays on Actions and Events,* 10.

and general thesis. The theme is the role of causal concepts in the description and explanation of human action. The thesis is that the ordinary notion of cause which enters into scientific or common-sense accounts of non-psychological affairs is essential also to [an account of action]. . . . Cause is the cement of the universe; the concept of cause is what holds together our picture of the universe."[18] These remarks reflect the philosophical commitments that gave rise to the covering law model. Davidson shared the commitments but denied that the model applied to intentional action on the ground that there are no relevant general laws in terms of the contents of an agent's beliefs or desires. His aim was an account of action that construed its explanation as *causal* but, rather than conforming to the covering law model, respected the notion that to explain an action is to interpret or redescribe it so as to fit it in a familiar pattern.

This led him to argue that an explanation of *why* an agent acted intentionally must embody "the ordinary notion of cause." If it does not, it may explain by interpretation and redescription *what* the agent did or *how,* but it cannot explain *why* he did what can be so interpreted or redescribed. To explain that requires reference to events that are causally efficacious of the agent's acting, and hence Davidson's claim that at the core of *any* successful action explanation is an agent's beliefs and desires that are her *primary reasons* for acting. If an agent not only *has* a reason to act but acts *because* of it, she must also have a relevant belief and desire that *causally* explain her acting.[19] He argued further that an event is an action *only* if it is thus explained, such causal explanation being *constitutive* of action.

Davidson held that these points apply in the first instance to an agent's bodily movements, which are her intentionally *moving* her body only if caused by the belief and desire that are her reasons for acting as she does. In a certain sense, moving her body is all an agent does: having moved her hand in an appropriate way, and if things go well, the switch is flipped, the light turned on, and the burglar alerted. The latter describe three events that result from her bodily movements, but they describe only one act—her moving her

18. Ibid., xi.

19. "It is not necessary to classify and analyze the many varieties of emotions, sentiments, moods, motives, passions, and hungers whose mention may answer the question, 'Why did you do it?' in order to see how, when such mention rationalizes the action, a primary reason is involved." Ibid., 7.

hand—in three ways: as her flipping the switch, turning on the light, and alerting the burglar, her acting being intentional under the first two descriptions, unintentional under the third. In moving her body intentionally, she thereby brings about many results that yield further descriptions of what she is doing.

Many Wittgensteinians argued that since the contents of beliefs and desires are conceptually connected with the actions for which they are reasons, they cannot cause them—the so-called logical connection argument. Davidson argued that if what is at stake here is a causal *relation* between events, the logical connection argument is simply confused. A causal relation obtains between particular events, and hence events are causally efficacious no matter how described or how their descriptions are related.[20]

Davidson, however, denied that beliefs and desires are causally *related* to actions on the ground that they are states rather than events. His view is that beliefs and desires figure in causal *explanations,* which do not connect events but sententially structured items—states, facts, situations—and are, therefore, sensitive to how reasons and actions are described. He held, moreover, that there is a conceptual connection between an agent's beliefs and desires and her acting intentionally, but he did not think that rules out a causal-explanatory connection.

Davidson nonetheless made causal *relations* central to his account by contending that to be *causal* an explanation must mention causally efficacious events. He argued that an agent's states of belief and desire causally explain her acting only if they are *associated with* an event that is causally efficacious of her acting. That event might be a change in her belief or desire, her coming to have them, some event not connected with her reasons, or even an event of which she is ignorant.

Moreover, Davidson thought causality was *nomological,* by which he meant that if *c* causes *e,* there is a strict, deterministic law connecting *some* description of *c* with *some* description of *e.* That is not the rejected covering law model because *c* may cause *e* even if the descriptions we use to pick out *c* and *e* occur in no strict, general law. In Davidson's view, only physics has such strict laws, and hence causally related events have physical descriptions and thus are physical. Consequently, events *associated with* the beliefs and desires

---

20. Davidson was not consistent on this, as he held that events are causally related only if they have descriptions that instantiate laws of physics.

that cause agents' acting also have physical descriptions and are physical (though Davidson denied that *states* of belief and desire are physical).[21]

5. The majority of contemporary philosophers accept what has been called the "standard story" of action.[22] That there is a standard story is largely due to Davidson, and he is usually said to accept it. It comes in different versions, however, many of which diverge from Davidson's own view to a greater or lesser extent. What unifies them is commitment to the claim that an agent's acting consists of those events that are her bodily movements caused (in the right way) by the beliefs and desires that are her reasons for acting. What divides them are different ways in which this claim is construed and developed.

Many proponents of the standard story construe it in ways that abandon Davidson's attempt to incorporate Anscombian notions and, in my view, undermine some of the more attractive and subtle features of his own account. Some argue that it is indifferent whether acts are individuated so that a single act has numerous descriptions rather than each description yielding a different act. Some downplay the role of interpretation in explanation of action: they assimilate it to scientific explanation and ignore its first-person character. These people are likely to contend that beliefs and desires explain actions because *coming to have* beliefs and desires is a causally efficacious event. They may then argue not only that one event's causing another entails

21. I have discussed Davidson's philosophy of action at greater length in a paper, "Interpreting Davidson on Action," to appear in a volume on Davidson's work edited by Jeff Malpas (MIT Press, 2011). My discussion there is more sympathetic to Davidson than anything I say in this Introduction. That is partly because I stress different aspects of his work, and partly because I have changed my mind on crucial issues as a result of writing this Introduction.

22. My account of the context of Anscombe's *Intention* is very brief, hence I do not discuss much important work in philosophy of action. But two philosophers who (like Anscombe) rejected the standard story should be given particular mention. J. L. Austin wrote "A Plea for Excuses," "Three Ways of Spilling Ink," and other papers [now in *Philosophical Papers* (London, 1971)] that continue to be notably stimulating and useful. G. H. von Wright published numerous works in philosophy of action that endorsed the covering law account of causality but denied that the account applies to intentional action. His view of the latter, which resembles Anscombe's, is subtle, creative, free from philosophical orthodoxy, and remarkably thought-provoking and instructive. He was also, like Anscombe, a pupil and close friend of Wittgenstein, who was the main influence on von Wright's work but determined neither its content nor its style.

that both have descriptions from physics and hence are physical, but that it is *because* they are physical that they cause actions. That yields for many a physicalist account of mind and action, whereby beliefs and desires are realized in states of the brain and their causal efficacy explained by physics. And now the problem of "mental causation" will arise—whether or how the mental as such has any causal efficacy—a problem that, it may be said, Davidson faces but lacks the resources to resolve.

These are not claims Davidson would accept. His account *requires* that actions are individuated so that a single act has numerous descriptions. He held that although *coming to have* a belief or desire may be *associated* with the belief and desire that causally *explain* an action, the associated event might be distinct from the belief and desire and might be an event of which the agent is ignorant. He did not think events are causally related *because* they are physical but that their being so related *entails* a physical law covering them. Although holding that the mental supervenes on the physical, he denied that the physical *explains* the mental (he insisted that action explanation is distinct from scientific explanation), but held simply that any mental difference entails a physical difference and not vice versa, which is a version of global supervenience consistent with his rejection of physicalism (and dualism). Beliefs, desires, and other mental states are, he held, irreducibly mental states of agents, not physical states of their brains.

Other proponents of the standard story are much more faithful to Davidson's own account but argue that it is incomplete, in particular, in his account of intention. Rejecting his early view that intentions are reducible to beliefs and desires, they emphasize the distinctive role intentions have in constituting action. Michael Bratman, for instance, contends that intentions for the future are distinct from beliefs and desires in being elements in an agent's planning that help coordinate his actions. They are not, therefore, merely results of practical reasoning but are fixed points that help determine the structure of that reasoning. David Velleman argues that causal explanation by beliefs and desires may be sufficient for action that is not full-blooded or "par excellence," but that the latter requires a more complex account than Davidson's of the connection between an agent's intentions and her knowing what she is doing. Indeed, he claims that the aim of knowing what we are doing is constitutive of action.

These attempts to improve on Davidson's account might be seen as steps toward a more Anscombian view, given that Anscombe takes both intention and knowledge of what one is doing to have a far more distinctive role than Davidson. But such steps will not bring success to Davidson's project of combining significant features of her view with his thesis that "the ordinary notion of cause which enters into scientific or common-sense accounts of non-psychological affairs is essential also to the understanding of what it is to act with a reason, to have a certain intention in acting, to be an agent, to act contrary to one's own judgment, or to act freely."[23] The project of blending that thesis—accepted by all versions of the standard story—with Anscombian features faces insurmountable difficulties.

An important symptom of this is that all versions of the project confront the problem of what it is for events to be caused *in the right way* to avoid counter-examples such as Davidson's mountain climber, who desires to unburden himself of the heavy load of his companion's hold on the rope supporting them, and believes he can do so if he loosens his grip. But his grip loosens, not because he loosened it but because his desire and belief so unnerved him that he inadvertently let go of the rope. Although his bodily movements were caused by his belief and desire, they were not his action: they did not cause his movements in the right way.

While I do not believe these accounts have the resources to resolve this problem (as Davidson admitted), the more important point is that the problem should not arise at all for an account that takes significant Anscombian notions seriously. The distinction between action and mere movements is one any agent can make about herself, and while it may occasionally be difficult to apply to others, no theory about causation will help in applying it. The problem is an artifact of Davidson's thesis about the role of causation, and it will cease to be a problem if the thesis is rejected.

6. Davidson's account and all versions of the standard story rest on a number of assumptions that Anscombe would reject. Her rejection of the first comes out in the following: "If one simply attends to the fact that many actions can be either intentional or unintentional, it can be quite natural to think that events which are characterized as intentional or unintentional are a certain natural class, intentional being an extra property that a philosopher must try

23. Davidson, *Essays on Actions and Events*, xi.

to describe."[24] The assumption here, on the part of those whose view Anscombe contests, is that an agent's bodily movements are *essentially* such as to be adequately describable in neurophysiological terms. To be intentional movements—to be an agent's intentionally moving her body—they must possess a property additional to what they are essentially (or naturally). Intentional bodily movements do not, therefore, differ essentially from bodily movements that occur when an agent is unconscious or as a result of disease or manipulation, but only in possessing a transient extra property.

Anscombe claims, on the contrary, that a bodily movement that is an action is not a movement that happens to have some property additional to any of its neurophysiological properties. Being intentional is an *essential* feature of the bodily movements normal agents make in the normal course of their lives. In moving her body intentionally, an agent exercises her active powers, which, although rooted in her being an animal and moving as animals do, are distinctively *human* powers that have become rational and conceptual because of her upbringing. Because moving her body intentionally is natural to her as a human agent, it does not require any special explanation. There may, of course, be an explanation of why she acted in a particular way—why she moved her body as she did—but that will not be an explanation of why her moving it was *intentional*.[25] What may require special explanation is her bodily movements being unintentional—occurring when she is asleep or because she was bumped; resulting from trauma, disability, or brain manipulation; and so on—hence not the result of the exercise of her natural powers.

Anscombe did articulate a *mark* of particular actions being intentional, namely, the *applicability* to them of the question "Why?"—"For what reason?" But no action is intentional *in virtue of* the applicability of that question nor in virtue of its actually being done for a reason. An agent's bodily movements are not intentional *in virtue of* anything that occurs at the time of his moving his body.

The second assumption, intertwined with the first, is that an agent's bodily movements are intentional in virtue of mental factors *external* to those

24. Anscombe, *Intention,* 84. Davidson also rejected this assumption, although not for Anscombe's reasons, and hence their views on this matter are quite different.

25. The term "bodily movement" as used here fits Anscombe's view only if it is understood to include bodily activities that are more than the sum of the bodily movements involved. I discuss this matter in section 7.

movements. It is assumed not only that there is a *distinction* between the physical aspect of an intentional action—the bodily movements, and its mental aspect—its rationality and intentionality, but the two are *separable.* An intentional action is a composite of bodily movements and rationalizing mental causes, both of which are what they are independently of the composite that comes to be at the time of acting.

Davidson assumed this in claiming that an agent intentionally moves her body only if the movements are causally explained by beliefs and desires she has, which, although conceptually connected with the movements, are nonetheless external to them. Other proponents of the standard story contend that an agent's bodily movements are intentional in virtue of the *intention* with which she moves them, which is external to the movements and is their cause.

Anscombe claims, on the contrary, that "an action is not called 'intentional' in virtue of any extra feature which exists when it is performed."[26] Her reason is that since a normal agent's moving her body and the bodily movements involved are *essentially* intentional, they cannot be so in virtue of factors *external* to her moving her body or to the bodily movements—certainly not to external factors that exist only when she moves her body on an occasion. The factors in virtue of which her movements are intentional are not, therefore, their causes.

This claim is suggestive of the Wittgensteinian philosophers' argument that intentions and other mental states cannot cause actions because they are conceptually connected to them. Davidson successfully undermined that argument, but the point here is more fundamental. It is not that such mental states are not suited to causally explain action, but that the mental states in virtue of which bodily movements are intentional are inherent in the structure of what it is to move one's body intentionally and not external to the movements.

Neurophysiological investigation of an agent's bodily movements do not, therefore, investigate the physical *part* of her intentional movements—intentional movements do not have such parts—but *abstract* their purely physical aspect and develop an account of that alone. The investigation remains targeted on the agent's intentional movements, however, because reference to them enables identification of the bodily movements from which the purely physical aspect is abstracted. The situation is different for movements resulting from disease or manipulation because they have no such mental

26. Anscombe, *Intention,* 28.

aspect, which is a reason neurophysiological investigation is so often directed at them.

The third assumption is that explanatory reasons for action must include events or states that are causes of the action for which they are reasons. Although Davidson thought that some reasons interpret or redescribe actions and are in that sense internal to them, he held that they explain why an agent acted only if they are connected to primary reasons—beliefs and desires external to the action—that causally explain it.

This assumption comes with a monolithic conception of causation that Davidson endorsed in referring to the crucial role of "*the* ordinary notion of cause," which assumes there is only one such notion. Davidson thought that all causal explanation presumes event causation, that the latter does not come in different kinds, and that events are causally related only if they can have descriptions that instantiate laws of physics. Causal explanations are at bottom, therefore, matters of event causation that is nomological, deterministic, and not varying in kind.[27]

Anscombe rejected this monolithic conception of causation and explanation. Her view implies a distinction between internal and external explanation of action. *Internal* explanation involves the role of intention in the structure of action, illustrated with her example of the man who moves his arms up and down with the intention of operating the pump in order to fill the water supply to poison the inhabitants of the house. That is the story of *what* the man is doing, but it includes explanatory claims. His moving his arm up and down is explained by his intention to operate the pump, and that is explained by his intentionally filling the water supply, which he does because he intends to poison the inhabitants. The man's intentions play explanatory roles internal to his overall action of poisoning the inhabitants, thereby constituting that whole action and its sub-parts as intentional.

An *external* explanation of his action would specify his reason for performing the *whole* action—for poisoning the inhabitants.[28] This explanation, if external, has no role in *constituting* his action as intentional because it *presumes* that it is (already) intentional. An agent's belief and desire may explain

27. This is consistent with his claim that causal explanation of action in terms of reasons is irreducibly different from explanations in the physical sciences. [See Donald Davidson, *Truth, Language, and History* (Oxford, 2005), 282.] That claim is true of the explicit structure of a Davidsonian explanation of action, which rests, nevertheless, on the assumption that the force of such explanation requires event causation.

28. The line between internal and external is not sharp and not always clear, but it is there.

why she performed an intentional act but they do not *as reasons* explain unintentional movements of her body. Since such explanation is external, it can be *causal.* Anscombe never explicitly asserted that, but it is consistent with her rejection of a monolithic conception of cause and explanation. She held that event causation comes in many kinds, depending on the kind of object involved, something she expressed in terms of "causatives"—verbs like "crush," "scrape," "cut," "push," and "fold." These verbs denote different kinds of events that presume the involvement of different kinds of objects. She denied that such causes necessitate their effects or involve general laws. She also thought reasons are much more extensive than beliefs and desires and hence that explanations of an agent's intentional actions are very diverse. Many of her explanations of action are in a significant sense causal explanations, although not in the sense that is crucial to the standard story.

The fourth assumption concerns the knowledge an agent has of her own acting and of her reasons for her so acting. Davidson admitted a distinctive first-person knowledge of the contents of one's own beliefs, desires, and intentions—hence of (what he took to be) one's reasons for acting—that is not based on evidence, observation, or introspection, and in his later writings he gave an intriguing account of that knowledge. But he did not extend such knowledge of the reasons for which one acts to acting itself, and he did not, therefore, put knowledge of what one is doing at the center of his account of intentional action or stress its distinctively practical character.

Anscombe made practical knowledge essential to acting intentionally, and she gave a distinctive account of it, contrasting it with theoretical or speculative knowledge. She revived Theophrastus's distinction between a mistake in performance and in judgment and gave a central place to Aquinas's claim that "practical knowledge is 'the cause of what it understands', unlike 'speculative' knowledge, which is 'derived from the objects known'." Some proponents of the standard story attempt to incorporate these points in their account of action but they overlook her claim that the "cause of what it understands" is not efficient but *formal* cause, and they require such significant changes in Anscombe's notion of practical knowledge that it loses its distinctive character.

7. What is at stake in this controversy may be put in terms of a contrast between two different pictures of how we are related to our world. In the Davidsonian

picture, the fundamental relations human beings as such—as knowing the world and acting intentionally in it—have to the world are causal. We know the world because it affects our senses and thus causes us to have various perceptual beliefs that constitute knowledge of the world if they are internally coherent. We know the objects and events in the world, not directly but through their causing beliefs in us that are about them. Our acting in the world is similarly indirect. We act when our beliefs and desires cause bodily movements that cause events outside our body. The movement of our fingers causes the switch to flip, which causes the light to go on, and so on. Whatever we do in the world is the causal result of moving our bodies and limbs, and hence we might intentionally move them without intentionally doing anything in the world beyond our bodies.

Anscombe's picture is different. The knowledge we gain through perceptual experience is of the world directly without the mediation of beliefs: the causal relations that underlie such experience enable it to be direct rather than constitute it as indirect. Action is also direct. To act is not to have one's bodily movements caused by one's beliefs and desires; it is to exercise the power to move one's body directly and intentionally. Further, to exercise that power is not primarily to *cause* events outside one's body; it is to perform actions that extend beyond one's body and its movements. Walking, running, eating, drinking, pounding, skiing, greeting, writing—ordinary bodily activities all—do not consist of bodily movements plus events they cause; they *are* our moving our bodies in ways that extend beyond them. We can run or walk only on a surface, that is, only in a world outside ourselves that also acts on us. We can eat or drink only by eating or drinking something that is edible or drinkable. To use a hammer is not to cause it to move, and to ski is not to cause skis to move: those are extended bodily movements. All these bodily activities require that the bodily movements occur as constituents of a structured activity that is more than the sum of the movements.

The Davidsonian picture has its roots in the Cartesian revolution, which conceived of the physical world as consisting only of what plays a role in the new physics, a physics purified of the teleological, intentional, and normative terms of Aristotelian physics. The physical consists, that is, of the particles and forces of an ideal physics, which as such have neither conceptual structure nor motivational and evaluative significance. Whatever is not physical in this sense is mental, which Cartesians conceived of as whatever takes place within ourselves so that we are immediately aware of it. The Cartesians were, therefore, dualists, in contrast to the physicalists, who argued either that there are no such mental items or that they can be reduced to the physicalist.

Davidson had a sophisticated view of the physical and the mental as two irreducibly different kinds of descriptions (or properties). He held that this mental–physical dualism had no ontological significance, his view being ontological monism. But he denied that his monism was physicalist because although all events have physical descriptions, many of them also have mental descriptions. He also denied that he was a dualist on the ground that the mental is not a domain of inner states of which we are immediately aware. He was, nevertheless, a Cartesian about the essential nature of the physical world: it consists of a vast network of physicalistically describable events devoid of conceptual structure and without motivational or evaluative significance. The relation of agents to the world is, therefore, only causal, and events are describable in mental terms only in virtue of their causal relations to agents.

Anscombe's conception of the physical world is not physicalist, and hence her conception of agents, which she took to be physical beings, is not physicalist either. This allows the relations of agents to their world to be much closer and richer than causal relations. Both agents and world can, of course, be described physicalistically, but these descriptions do not characterize the nature of world and agent—what it is to be a world or to be an agent. Agents are at least animals, and the relation of non-human animals to their world— their environment—is not merely causal either. It is the nature of animals to eat, drink, fight, hunt, copulate, reproduce: how they do so is partly innate, partly a result of their environment that shapes these activities, and is in turn shaped by them. Their world is not just particles and forces; it is food and drink, allies and enemies, mates and offspring, which are not mere causes of their activities but what it is their nature to respond to as the kind of beings they are.

The world of human beings is richer because we have by nature new kinds of powers that enable new kinds of activities, and hence our world is now one of language, art, institutions, agriculture, factories, tools, machines, buildings, highways, and so on. Indeed, Anscombe wrote that "It belongs to the natural history of man that he has a moral environment."[29] These are features our world acquired in the distant past but they are now part of the nature of

---

29. Anscombe, *Faith in a Hard Ground,* 224. Compare Wittgenstein in *Philosophical Investigations,* §25: "Commanding, questioning, storytelling, chatting, are as much a part of our natural history as walking, eating, drinking, playing." See also §415.

the world into which we were born, which made us what we are with the powers we have, which in turn enable us to reshape that world. Our relation to such a world is not merely causal; the nature of the world to which we respond as agents does not depend on how it is affecting us or how we are affecting it at some moment of time. Nor does the nature of our acting depend on its cause and effects at the time of our acting.

Various aspects of Anscombe's picture were shared by other philosophers who sought to undermine the Cartesian picture, like Heidegger, Dewey, Merleau-Ponty, and Wittgenstein.[30] Any account that is consonant with the Anscombian picture will, however, face formidable resistance because the other picture remains dominant among philosophers in the analytic tradition in the shape of physicalism, which presumes and supports the Cartesian picture. Although Davidson denied being a physicalist, his account is surely receptive to it, and many proponents of the standard story have developed a physicalistic account of action and criticized Davidson for not being physicalistic enough. To accept the main features of Anscombe's account is, therefore, to be outside current philosophical orthodoxy, as Anscombe herself always felt she was, even in the heyday of Wittgensteinianism. This means not that her account is eccentric, prescientific, or philosophically outré, but that it is the work of a fiercely independent thinker who was not a captive of the assumptions that have framed philosophical orthodoxy for so long, and who did not fear developing an alternative account that went against this orthodoxy. The essays in this book do not aim at creating a new orthodoxy but at making accessible a great work and exhibiting its power to illuminate the nature of action and its explanation.[31]

8. The primary task of the authors of the essays in this volume is to undertake the painstaking exegesis required for an adequate interpretation of the subtle

30. Although it is unlikely that Anscombe ever read John Dewey, her general outlook is remarkably similar to his naturalism, which presumes "nature" in the natural history (Aristotelian) rather than the physicalist sense. Dewey denied that he was "a materialist as to matter" (*Experience and Nature* [Chicago, 1926], 74). He also claimed that naturalism ruled out supernaturalism, but that is an independent point.

31. I am most grateful to Anton Ford and Jennifer Hornsby, my coeditors, and to Lilli Alanen, Martin Gustafsson, and Anselm Müller for the numerous suggestions, criticisms, and advice they have given me in the writing of this Introduction, most of which I have followed.

claims and intricate arguments in Anscombe's *Intention.* Her work is difficult to understand not only because it is terse, subtle, and complex but also because its depth and originality require reading it without preconceptions as to what is true, acceptable, or relevant. The task, beyond exegesis, is to assess the strength of her arguments, suggest ways in which they might be improved, and develop criticism of competing views.

There are three essays about the overall form and aim of Anscombe's *Intention.* In the first, Richard Moran and Martin Stone discuss the central theme of Anscombe's book—her view of the nature of intention and its relation to action. Anton Ford follows with an account of three relations a species might have to a genus, an account that supports Anscombe's rejection of the received view of the central task of philosophy of action, namely, to characterize the distinctive properties that distinguish intentional action from mere actions or events. Jennifer Hornsby argues that, in spite of surface similarities, Anscombe's overall account of action differs profoundly from Davidson's.

There follow five essays about Anscombe's view of knowledge without observation. John McDowell discusses Anscombe's view of our knowledge of the position and involuntary movement of our own limbs, contending that her view is that such knowledge is neither theoretical nor practical, but a distinctive third kind. Adrian Haddock, Kieran Setiya, and Michael Thompson consider, from very different points of view, Anscombe's conception of the practical knowledge we have of our own actions. Sebastian Rödl discusses her account of practical knowledge by considering its relation to Kant's view of ethical knowledge.

The final two essays consider Anscombe's view of reasons for action. Anselm Müller criticizes her for not giving backward-looking motives (e.g., revenge, gratitude, pity) a sufficiently central role in practical reasoning, while Ben Laurence argues that her conception of reasons for individual actions can be smoothly extended to joint (collective) actions.

Although there are many topics in *Intention* that are not discussed in these essays, taken as a whole they provide an illuminating account of most of the main concerns of Anscombe's book. Those who find it difficult to know what to make of her book or how it can contribute to current discussion of philosophy of action should find these essays particularly useful, while those who recognize its stature but struggle with claims they find puzzling and obscure should be helped toward seeing their point. Although these essays are surely not the final word on Anscombe's *Intention,* they make a significant contribution to understanding and appropriating its insights.

Summary of Anscombe's *Intention*

FREDERICK STOUTLAND

What follows is a summary of the main themes of Anscombe's *Intention*. It may make things easier for those who have not yet read the book, and for those who have it may remind them of the course of its argument. (The numbers in brackets are page numbers in *Intention*.)

Anscombe begins *Intention* with the claim that the concept of intention has three divisions: expressions of intention ("I am going to open the window"), actions as intentional ("I am opening the window"), and intentions with which actions are done ("I am opening the window with the intention to cool the room"). She insists that there is only one sense of "intention" and explains how the concept covers a spectrum from pure intending through acting with an intention to having acted intentionally.

She begins with expression of intention, which is a kind of prediction—an estimate of the future—that is practical rather than theoretical. Both kinds are about the future (not about mental states) and may use the same words; both have truth value and can be justified or contradicted. But an intention is expressed by an agent whose description of the future he justifies not by evidence, but by reasons for acting. Anscombe then asks how we can tell what someone's intention is, arguing that, although his intention can "remain a

purely interior thing" (she is no behaviorist), the first place to look is not into
the contents of his mind (as Cartesians argue) but to "what physically takes
place, i.e. what a man actually does" [9], which is his intentional action—the
second division above. That is the place to look since "The greater number of
the things which you would say straight off a man did or was doing, will be
things he intends" [8], which he himself also knows.

What then distinguishes actions (that Anscombe takes to be events) that
are intentional from events that are not? Her first answer is that they "are the
actions to which a certain sense of the question 'Why?' is given application;
the sense is of course that in which the answer, if positive, gives a reason for
acting" [9]. As it stands, this is circular: the relevant sense of "Why?" and of
"reason" are the same. If we say that the relevant sense of "reason" is the one
we give for sending for a taxi (an action) rather than for giving a sudden start
(a mere movement), we simply take for granted the notion of action we want
to clarify.

The key thing lacking is the commonsense idea that to act intentionally is
to know what you are doing, since the "Why?" question is not applicable if one
says "I was not aware that I was doing that." But the relevant kind of knowledge is not based on evidence or observation; it must be "knowledge without
observation." There are, however, other things than our own actions that we
know without observation: the position of our own limbs, for instance (since
usually nothing *shows* us their position), as well as certain involuntary movements (like the reflex kick when the doctor taps your knee). We also know
without observation what Anscombe calls "mental causes," which may produce actions, feelings, or thoughts. If asked, "Why did you jump like that?"
you may answer, "I saw such and such at the window and it *made me jump.*"
You know straight off what made you jump; no evidence or observation is
necessary to conclude that was the cause—a mental cause.

Anscombe discusses mental causes not because of their intrinsic importance but because they are a counter-example to the Humean conception of
cause and because of their contrast to motives, which are also typically known
without observation. "A very natural conception of 'motive' is that it is what
moves (the very word suggests that)—glossed as 'what *causes*' a man's actions
etc. And 'what causes' them is perhaps then thought of as an event that brings
the effect about" [18]. On her view, this does not characterize motives but
mental causes. While the former "may explain action . . . that is not to say
that they 'determine', in the sense of causing, actions," and, moreover, unlike

mental causes, motives need not involve what went on in my mind and issued in the action.

Anscombe supports this by an account of three kinds of motives. The first are *backward-looking motives*—revenge, gratitude, remorse, pity, and so on—so called because "something that *has happened* . . . is given as the ground of an action or abstention that is good or bad for the person . . . at whom it is directed" [20]. (Revenge because he killed my brother, gratitude because he helped me out, and so on.) The second are *motives-in-general,* which put actions in a certain light by interpreting or redescribing them. The third are *forward-looking motives*—intentions that describe future states of affairs (expression of intention). She says about the first kind of motive that it is distinct from a mental cause because the agent "conceives it as something good or bad, and his own action as doing good or harm [22]. She says about the third kind that "when the question 'Why?' about a present action is answered by a description of a future state of affairs, this is already distinguished from a mental cause just by being future" [23].

What Anscombe means by "cause" in this discussion is obscure. She had earlier written that "It will hardly be enlightening to say: in the case of the sudden start the 'reason' is a cause; the topic of causality is in a state of too great confusion" [10]. But she later put the question, "Is this a reason or a cause?" which suggests that it must be one or the other, although she also writes that we "often refuse to make any distinction at all between something's being a reason, and its being a cause of the kind in question" [23]. We may ask what distinction it is that we refuse to make. Here she apparently thinks of "cause" as denoting events that are causally efficacious but do not thereby explain the events they cause, whereas "reason" denotes explanatory factors with an evaluative dimension that are taken to justify actions. Although she thinks there is often no point in making this distinction, there is in "full-blown" cases like the distinction between revenge (a motive) and the thing that made one jump (a mental cause). "Roughly speaking, it establishes something as a reason if one argues against it . . . in such a way as to link it up with motives and intentions" [24].

Anscombe discusses reasons and causes here and there in *Intention* without a clear thesis emerging, but in later works she articulates a number of claims about causality that are implicit in *Intention* and should be used in articulating her account of action. (See her *Metaphysics and the Philosophy of Mind,* especially "Causality and Determination".) Thus she denies that causes necessitate their effects or are grounded in generalizations, and she argues that we can *observe* instances of causality, which are as varied as the kinds of objects and events involved. She continues to deny that motives and intentions are causes of action (certainly not efficacious event-causes), but she emphasizes the causal nature of actions themselves, arguing that many action verbs *are* essentially causal. Words like "scrape," "push," "wet," "carry," "eat," "burn," and "hurt" denote actions as causing—they are "causatives." Their nature is to bring about effects but not to be caused by bodily movements because they *are* bodily movements of various kinds and hence various kinds of causing.

Anscombe now gives a more informative account of what distinguishes intentional actions from other events. They are actions to which a certain sense of the question "Why?" applies, as follows. The question has that sense if the answer mentions a motive: past history, an interpretation (redescription) of the action, or something future. It does not have that sense if the answer is that "I was not aware I was doing that" or "I observed that I was doing that," or "if the answer is evidence or states a cause, including a mental cause" [24]. It is not refused application even if the agent answers that he acted for no reason ("I was just doodling"), "any more than the question how much money I have in my pocket is refused application by the answer, 'None'" [25]. It also applies if the answer is "no particular reason," provided we can make sense of a man who so acts—for example, spreads out his green books all over the roof of his house. The answers to the special question "Why?" therefore go beyond reasons for action; that question "can now be defined as the question expecting an answer in this range" [28].

Anscombe defers until later the important question of why the "Why?" question applies to certain events and not others. She argues here that it cannot be because those events have an "extra feature" acquired at the time of acting. We cannot add a feature to mere bodily movements to make them into actions or subtract a feature from actions to turn them back into mere bodily movements. She follows this with an intricate argument that no actions would be intentional if there were no such thing as further intention in acting. If our only reasons for acting were motives or if the only answer to the question "Why?" were "I just am," it would be insignificant whether or not an action is intentional. We must be able to answer the "Why?" question by reference to what we intend to do but may not now be doing intentionally.

This clarifies the continuity between acting intentionally and expression of action for the future, and she now turns to the intention *with which* one acts. While this may also mention something future, it requires that we be able to understand the agent's believing that what she mentions will be brought about by the action about which she is being asked "Why?" "Brought about" here means that if I do P with the intention to Q, then Q "is supposed to be a possible later stage in proceedings of which P is an earlier stage" [36]. The notion of *intention with,* therefore, is the key to the internal teleological structure of an action.

She discusses this in terms of her ingenious example of the man who moves his arms up and down, thereby pumping poisoned water into the water supply, with the intention of killing the evil inhabitants of the house, in order to get better people in power. "What," she asks, "is this man doing? What is *the* description of his action?" [37]. The first answer is *any* true description of "what is going on, with him as subject," from generating substances in his nerve fibers to helping to get a better life for everyone. What he is doing intentionally, however, is more limited and is defined in terms of the right kind of answer to the question "Why are you now X-ing?" which will have several right answers. The question "Why are you moving your arms up and down?" may have (at least) the following answers: "I am pumping," "I am filling the water supply," "I am poisoning the inhabitants of the house," "I am helping to get better people in power."

The last represents a break from the others because it is less what I am doing than what I will do (or want to do): it expresses an intention for the future, an intention *of* the action, rather than an intention *with which* I am acting (though the break is not sharp). The others have what she calls an A-B-C-D order. Not only does B-C-D give an answer to why I am A-ing, but C and D give answers to why I am B-ing (namely, with the intention of C-ing and D-ing), and D gives an answer to why I am C-ing (namely, with the intention of D-ing). Moreover, A, B, C, and D are all descriptions of the same action: in saying *why* I am acting, I am also saying *what* I am doing, and vice versa. "There is one action with four descriptions, each dependent on wider circumstances, and each related to the next as descriptions of means to end" [46].

Anscombe thinks that all actions have a similar kind of teleological structure (sometimes simpler, sometimes more complex), which consists of various phases of what a man is doing, ordered as in her example: a man A-ing with the intention of B-ing and B-ing with the intention of C-ing, and so on. It is in general indifferent whether we say: he is A-ing with the intention of B-ing; A-ing in order to B; in A-ing he is B-ing; the reason he is A-ing is that he intends to B; the reason he is A-ing is that he is B-ing (the reason he is pumping is that he is filling the water supply). The structure of an intentional action is, therefore, itself an explanatory structure. In asking why a man is X-ing, the first answer will refer to what he is doing in X-ing—to the explanatory reasons internal to his acting. This is why Anscombe's examples of acting are normally expressed as present-imperfect, expressing what the agent is doing but may not get done rather than what he has done. This permits the equivalence between "He is A-ing with the intention of B-ing" and "The reason he is A-ing is that he is B-ing" because a man may be B-ing even if he never B's. He can be pumping with the intention of filling the water supply and hence pumping because he is filling the water supply, even if he fails to fill it.

Intentions are clearly not functioning here as inner states that are causally efficacious of action. Pumping with the intention of filling the water supply *is* pumping in order to fill the water supply, which means both pumping and filling are intentional. This raises complications Anscombe discusses that I shall omit, but it does not mean there is no place for interior acts of intention. The latter, however, are rarely sufficient to determine what one does intentionally, nor should we conclude that only the agent can know what he intends. Whenever intention is in question, "outward acts are 'significant' in some way" [49].

Anscombe now returns to "knowledge without observation," asking how it can apply to intentional actions described as more than moving one's body. She argues that it *does* so apply, that one can have knowledge without observation of what one is doing, hence what is happening, beyond one's body—knowledge that is necessary if what one is doing is intentional. She denies that such knowledge is only of one's intentions or bodily movements so that the rest of one's action is known by observation as the result of what one intends. On the contrary, "The only description that I clearly know of what I am doing may be of something that is at a distance from me" and hence not a description of my intention or bodily movements. We must, therefore, admit that in some sense "I do what happens," and this is what she calls "practical knowledge" [53].

To show how this can be, she introduces the well-known example of the man using a shopping list in a store. If the list and what he buys do not agree, the mistake is not in the list but in his performance—in his buying the wrong things. But if a detective makes a record of his buying and his list is wrong, the mistake is in the record—in his judgment, not his action. This suggests a distinction between knowledge by observation, which is what the detective has if his list is correct, and knowledge "in intention," which is what the man has if he buys according to his list. The crucial point is that these are not two ways of knowing what the facts are but two distinct kinds of knowledge. The detective's knowledge is *contemplative* (theoretical, speculative) knowledge of what is the case; the man's knowledge is *practical* knowledge of what he makes to be the case.

To understand the latter we must, she writes, understand "practical reasoning" ("practical syllogism"), on which I shall be very brief (hence not very informative). She contends that theoretical and practical knowledge do not differ in subject matter but in the use to which the structure of the reasoning is put. Theoretical reasoning aims at true belief and practical reasoning at good (desirable) action. The starting point of practical reasoning is something wanted, its aim is action, but the reasoning does not *mention* (describe) either the agent's wanting or his acting. Its premises mention *what* he wants (not his wanting it) but assumes that he actually *wants* it; its conclusion mentions what he should do to get what he wants, but given his actually wanting it, it results in his *acting* in accordance with the premises.

At this point she discusses at some length reasons for acting that are external to the teleological structure of actions themselves. The distinction between what is internal and what is external to that structure is not sharp, but in general her concern here is not with the "Why?" *in* an action but with the "Why?" *of* an action, in particular with how the series of "Why?" questions comes to an end with an answer that rules out a further "Why?"—with an answer that cites what we may call "ultimate reasons."

The focus of her discussion is on the concept of *wanting*: what is its nature, whether there are limits to what an agent can intelligibly want, how it is connected with pleasure, whether one always wants something as desirable, and whether there are *final* things that we want. By "wanting" she does not mean "the prick of desire at the thought or sight of an object" [57] or idle wishes or hope. She thinks of it as what we conclude when we deliberate on what to do—"that is what I want to do"—which may not be something we desire or find pleasant. "The primitive sign of wanting [in this sense] is *trying to get*," exemplified even in animals: "There are two features present in wanting; moving toward a thing and knowledge (or at least opinion) that the thing is there" [69]. This is more complicated in human beings but many animals are sufficiently similar to enable us to ascribe intentions to them.

I skip over these topics to return, as she does, to practical knowledge, about which she has intricate views that have led to considerable debate over what we have practical knowledge *of.* That clearly goes beyond our own intentions to include our intentional actions described as more than bodily movements. In putting this as "I do what happens," she means that I can know without observation things that happen in the world because I make them happen, but many find this paradoxical and it is not obvious exactly what she means by it.

One example she gives is of a man directing the building of a house he cannot see and gets no reports on. His knowledge of how the building is going is not theoretical since it is based not on observation or evidence but on his giving precise orders that result in the workers' building it in the way and sequence he directs. His knowledge is practical, since if he is wrong about what the house is like at a certain time it is because his orders were not followed, not because he misperceived or lacked evidence. His knowledge does not depend on his judgment but on his orders being carried out as he directed. They might not be carried out, of course, in which case he lacks both practical and theoretical knowledge of the house. But if his orders are followed, he has practical knowledge of the building of the house, though not theoretical knowledge (perhaps he has plausible belief) since that requires evidence or observation he does not have.

The most plausible claim about that of which an agent has practical knowledge is what he is presently doing, something that may in many cases remain incomplete. He is, for instance, intentionally filling up the water supply, of which he, therefore, has practical knowledge, even if the water flow is, unknown to him, interrupted and he does not get it filled. This case contrasts with one in which, unknown to the agent, the pipe is broken and the water spills out on the ground; in this case he does not have practical knowledge of his filling the water supply because he is not doing that at all. He is, however, intentionally pumping the water, and of that he does have practical knowledge.

Even if practical knowledge is limited to acting that does not require completion, the question remains how it is possible to know even that without observation. This question now merges with the question raised earlier: Why does the "Why?" question that distinguishes intentional actions apply to certain events and not others? Her answer to these questions yields one of the most profound aspects of her account of action.

The reason the "Why?" question applies to certain events is that the *description* of those events presumes the applicability of the question. There are events whose description "is a type of description that would not exist if our question 'Why?' did not. It is not that certain things, namely the movements of humans, are for some undiscovered reason subject to the question 'Why?'" [83]. That is no more the case than that certain marks on paper are for some undiscovered reason subject to the question "What do they say?" "It is of a word or sentence that we ask 'What does it say?' and the description of something as a word or sentence at all could not occur prior to the fact that words or sentences have meaning. So the description of something as a human action could not occur prior to the existence of the question 'Why?' simply as a kind of utterance by which we were *then* obscurely prompted to address the question" [83]. It is of human actions that we ask "Why?" in the relevant sense, but the description of the movements of humans as human actions could not occur independently of there being intentional actions. It is of the nature of actions to be intentional, and if they are not, they are defective.

This means that the descriptions of many things that go on in the world— things that happen beyond our bodily movements—are descriptions employing concepts of human actions—for example, "building a house" or "writing a sentence on a blackboard." They are "descriptions of happenings which are directly dependent on our possessing the *form* of description of intentional actions" [84]. Some may be descriptions of happenings that can only be intentional, for example, "greeting," "buying," "selling," "telephoning." Others are descriptions that may or may not be intentional, like "offending," "kicking," "dropping," "intruding," but which are connected in significant ways with descriptions that do bring in intentions. It is the existence of such descriptions of events that accounts for why the "Why?" question applies to them.

"Intentional" does not denote an extra feature of events but a *form of description* of events. "Event" is the genus of which "intentional action" is a species, not a species in the sense in which "wooden house" and "brick house" are species of "house," but in the sense in which "living body" and "dead body" are species of the genus "animal body." "Being alive," we might say, is a form of description of animal bodies; it is not an extra feature but rather determines the kind of descriptions we can apply to bodies that are alive. (Anscombe calls them "vital descriptions".) It is also presumed in calling something a "dead body," for such a body must have *been* alive: it is of the nature of a body to be living, and it is defective if it is not. A form of description resembles an Aristotelian category—a way of being—and is suggestive of Frege's distinction between concept and object. The distinction between intentional action and mere events, like Frege's distinction, is neither logical in the syntactical sense nor empirical; it rather determines what we can say about (the form of descriptions we can apply to) the relevant items (which is related to the notion of a category in Aristotle and Kant).

Anscombe writes about the intentional form of description that "Events are typically described in this form when 'in order to' or 'because' (in one sense) is attached to their description" [85]. Thus an agent's kicking is described in the intentional form as "She is kicking in order to open the door," which means her kicking is intentional. Descriptions that are necessarily intentional ("telephoning," "slinking") are in this form without adding "in order to" or "because." Descriptions in this form do not apply to inanimate events but they may apply to nonhuman animals. We can say of a cat that "it is stalking a bird in crouching and slinking along with its eyes fixed on the bird and its whiskers twitching" [86]. *We* can describe the cat that way, but the cat, of course, knows nothing of descriptions.

This means that "a great many of our descriptions of events effected by human beings are *formally* descriptions of executed intentions"; it is, that is to say, their nature to be so. A consequence of this is that "surprising as it may seem, the failure to execute intentions is necessarily the rare exception." That is not true of longer-term goals one might like to achieve (wealth, fame, happiness), but it is "necessarily the rare exception . . . for a man's performance in its more immediate descriptions not to be what he supposes" [87]. *That* is what answers the question of how it is possible to have practical knowledge, to know without observation what one is doing because one is doing it. She writes, citing Aquinas, that "Practical knowledge is 'the cause of what it understands', unlike 'speculative' knowledge, which 'is derived from the objects known.'" It is the *formal* cause in that "without it what happens does not come under the description—execution of intentions" [88]. "It is the agent's knowledge of what he is doing that gives the descriptions under which what is going on is the execution of intention" [87].

Anscombe concludes *Intention* with reflections on the distinction between the voluntary and the intentional and returns to expressions for the future. The discussion of the latter reinforces her point that there is only one concept of intention, not three—"To a certain extent the three divisions of the subject . . . are simply equivalent" [40]—but it is a concept that is as complex as, indeed a reflection of, the structure of action itself.

I

Anscombe on Expression of Intention: An Exegesis

RICHARD MORAN

MARTIN J. STONE

Of course in every act of this kind, there remains the possibility of putting this act into question—insofar as it refers to more distant, more essential ends. . . . For example the sentence which I write is the meaning of
the letters I trace, but the whole work I wish to produce is the meaning of
the sentence. And this work is a possibility in connection with which I
can feel anguish; it is truly *my* possibility . . . tomorrow in relation to it
my freedom can exercise its nihilating power.

> Jean-Paul Sartre, *Being and Nothingness,* trans. Hazel Barnes, 74

There might be a verb with the meaning: to formulate one's intention in
words or other signs, out loud or in one's thoughts. This verb would not
be equivalent in meaning to our "intend."

There might be a verb with the meaning: to act according to intention;
and this would also not mean the same as "to intend."

Yet another might mean: to brood over an intention; or to turn it over
and over in one's head.

> Ludwig Wittgenstein, *Remarks on the Philosophy of Psychology,*
> vol. 1, trans. G. E. M. Anscombe, §830

1. The Problem

Anscombe begins her monograph *Intention* by recalling three familiar contexts
in which, as she says, we "employ a concept of intention" (§1):[1]

---

1. G. E. M. Anscombe, *Intention,* 2nd ed. (Cambridge, Mass.: Harvard University Press,
2000).

(Case 1) Someone says "I'm going to walk to the store": An *expression of intention,* she says.

(Case 2) Someone is walking (or has walked) to the store: An *intentional action.*

(Case 3) "Why are you walking to the store?"—"To get some milk": The question seeks—and the answer provides—the *intention with which something is done.*[2]

This isn't philosophy yet, only its raw material. Anscombe will shortly suggest the need for a philosophical investigation by intimating that we have trouble seeing how it is *one* concept of intention that finds application in these cases.[3] This setup seems straightforward, yet on closer inspection someone might understandably object: "What an odd mix of cases!" The first case is a type of act (viz., one of speaking), and, as such, an instance of the second. Doubtless, when performed, it is also done with some further intention (case 3). So there is overlap here. But apart from this, it might be wondered: Why should *expression* of intention appear in an initial division of the subject at all? Sure, we put "a concept of intention" to work in this context. But we put "a concept of emotion" to work in speaking of someone's expressing emotion; and *that* seems unlikely—save in a world described by Borges—to head the opening divisions in a book called "Emotion."

In general, that "expressions of φ" will be pertinent in studying a psychological concept φ isn't simply to be taken for granted. Exceptions would include those concepts taken up in performative verbs, where (e.g.) to command or promise *is* to formulate something in words, to give it expression. But that to intend isn't a performative is seen among other ways in this, that we *can*

2. Or a "further intention in acting." These divisions play a structuring role in Anscombe's discussion. They explicitly appear at p. 1 (statement of the headings), p. 9 (the transition from "expression of intention" to "intentional action"), p. 40 (the unity of the three divisions), and p. 90 (return to "expression of intention for the future"). They are also drawn on elsewhere in Anscombe's discussion.

3. "Where we are tempted to speak of 'different senses' of a word which is clearly not equivocal, we may infer that we are in fact pretty much in the dark about the character of the concept which it represents." *Intention,* 1. In this essay we approach Anscombe's ambitions in *Intention* in light of her sense of why the concept of "intention" calls for philosophy at all. The answer evidently refers to a submerged unity in our otherwise familiar employments of "intention." What makes these all cases of (non-equivocal) "intention" does not immediately appear.

speak of expressions of it, though not of a command;[4] and from this point of view, it seems doubtful that "expressing an intention" has any greater claim to pertinence than, say, "brooding over an intention" or "concealing an intention," and so on. Yet this is Anscombe's first sentence: "Very often, when a man says 'I am going to do such-and-such,' we should say that this was an expression of intention" (p. 1). Anscombe does not pause here to explain why she draws attention to "expression," but instead turns to distinguishing two different uses to which (e.g.) "I am going to fail in this exam" might be put—either (1) an expression of intention, or (2) the speaker's estimate of her chances, a prediction (p. 2).

Distinguishing expressions of intention from predictions suggests that the two were liable to be confused. So it is in fact a particular sort of "expression" that comes up here, a verbal statement of fact. To explain, *we* express ourselves, and our states and attitudes express *them*selves, in a variety of ways—through what we do and say, and through how we do these things. Since we are thus bound to be expressing things continuously, a central distinction in this area will be between expression in the *impersonal* sense (the manifestation of some state or condition) and expression in the *personal* sense (the intentional act of one person directed to another).[5] Evidently, Anscombe is thinking of the personal sense, for her examples are all imperfect statements of fact ("I'm going to . . .")[6]—items that can do double duty for predictions—notwithstanding that intentions are, it would seem, expressed in other ways as well. "It would seem": In fact, in a passage occurring just after the opening, Anscombe will be found denying that intentions, in contrast to other states of the person, are *ever* impersonally expressed (p. 5). (The meaning of this strange and unintuitive doctrine will occupy us in much of this essay.)

To say that Anscombe has inherited this focus on "expression" from Wittgenstein, though correct, is obviously not the sort of explanation needed here.[7] And in truth, if her idea were merely to locate the topic of intention by remembering some main uses of "intention," Anscombe would seem to be

4. Compare *Intention*, 5.

5. On this distinction, see Richard Moran, "Problems of Sincerity," *Proceedings of the Aristotelian Society* 105 (December 2005): 341–361.

6. Or future statements of fact—e.g., "Nurse will take you to the operating theatre," 3.

7. With Anscombe's discussion of expression of intention versus prediction, compare, e.g., Wittgenstein, *Philosophical Investigations*, trans. G. E. M. Anscombe (Oxford: Basil Blackwell, 1953), 224.

forcing something here, for we don't really "very often" speak of "expression of intention" in characterizing what people say. Philosophical purposes aside, we don't generally speak this way unless the context gives special consequence to the distinction between the two kinds of expression—for example, in the law, which sometimes asks whether an intention (e.g., to take possession) has been *expressed* (the personal sense), and not merely whether it was evident under the circumstances to others.

What, then, is the meaning of Anscombe's initial emphasis on "expression"? We aim to show the work this notion is performing throughout *Intention*. But the background to this task is that Anscombe's first division—expression of intention—seems incongruous. It seems to belong only to a very different catalogue of divisions, one featuring such items as symptoms or indications of intention, or intentions that are disguised or merely passively revealed; or perhaps in a catalogue of speech-acts—expressions of belief, predictions, commands, promises, etc.

Consider now that rather strange and unintuitive passage. "Expression" recurs emphatically here, in the form of a claim, made by Anscombe, that while non-human animals (brutes) have intentions, they don't express them:

> Intention appears to be something that we can express, but which brutes (which, e.g., do not give orders) can *have,* though lacking any distinct expression of intention. For a cat's movements in stalking a bird are hardly to be called an expression of intention. One might as well call a car's stalling the *expression* of its being about to stop. Intention is unlike emotion in this respect, that the expression of it is purely conventional; we might say linguistic if we will allow certain bodily movements with a conventional meaning to be included in language. Wittgenstein seems to me to have gone wrong in speaking of the 'natural expression of an intention' (*Philosophical Investigations* (§ 647). (p. 5; emphasis in original)

Someone might read past this unhindered, because they might understandably take Anscombe's point to be merely the anodyne one that brutes do not tell us of their intentions (i.e., express them in the personal sense). But that can't be her point, for clearly what this passage is after is a contrast between intentions and states of emotion with respect to their possibilities of expression ("Intention is unlike emotion in this respect . . ."). That anodyne rendering would undo the contrast, for the natural behavior of brutes does express emotion (or so Anscombe allows), yet brutes do not tell us of their emotions either. So Anscombe's point is best represented—as she herself represents it—like this: There is no such thing as the natural expression of intention, as there is of emotion; the expression of intention is always conventional or linguistic. This is not essentially—but only by application—a point about nonhuman animals. Anscombe might also have said (she should be committed to saying), "The natural behaviour of human beings is no 'expression' of *their* intention either." But the question is, why not? Why say this? The problem which emerges here, beyond Anscombe's making "expressions" one of the topic's divisions, is what the relevant notion of "expression" might be, such that it has no application to the intentions manifested by an agent's stalking movements, while still finding purchase on the nonverbal manifestations of other states like emotion.[8]

The solution to both problems involves seeing Anscombe's emphasis on "expression"—and more generally her explanation of intention "in terms of language" (p. 86)—as part of a distinctive strategy for elucidating the unity of the uses of intention. We'll call this strategy one of immediate elucidation, and we'll contrast it with "connective strategies." An immediate elucidation exhibits the divisions of intention as inflections of a single form. It thereby also helps reveal how the unity of "intention" has become linguistically submerged, hence lost to a philosophically unassisted view. To explain this, however, it seems best to begin by recalling the shape of a prominent strand in contemporary, post-Anscombian philosophy of action, since connective strategies appear to be the main ones, or the only ones, imagined there.

2. Background: The Transformation of *Intention*

A familiar homage says that many action theorists follow Anscombe at least in (1) associating acting intentionally with acting for reasons, (2) treat-

---

8. A similar claim—though perhaps on different grounds—is made by Keith Donnellan, "Knowing What I am Doing," *The Journal of Philosophy* 60, no. 14 (1963): 401–409 at p. 409. But Anscombe's passage is obscure, even by Anscombian standards. The term "expression" is idiomatically multivalent enough to embrace Wittgenstein's talk of natural behavior as "expressions" of intention. So it is hardly obvious that what Anscombe wishes to deny must be the same thing Wittgenstein is asserting. Further, Anscombe herself, turning to the question of "how . . . we tell someone's intentions," will point out that intentions are often legible in someone's behavior: "You will have a strong chance of success [at this] if you mention what he actually did or is doing" (7–8). This only makes more pressing the question of what could be at stake in her denial that natural behavioral manifestations of intentions are proper "expressions" of it. See sections 5–6 below.

ing the topic of intention as comprised of this and at least two other divisions ("intending to act" and "intention with which"), and (3) requiring philosophy to explain how these notions are connected. This account of the influence of Anscombe's work is only *roughly* correct, however. A sign of inexactness is just the way her first division (expression of intention) is apt to be remembered—as here, e.g., by Donald Davidson, in recounting his own theory:

> [Earlier] I believed that of the three main uses of the concept of intention distinguished by Anscombe (acting with an intention, acting intentionally, and intending to act), the first was the most basic. Acting intentionally, I argued . . . was just acting with some intention. That left intending, which I somehow thought would be simple to understand in terms of the others. I was wrong. When I finally came to work on it, I found it the hardest of the three; contrary to my original view, it came to seem the basic notion on which the others depend; and what progress I made with it partially undermined an important theme . . . —that "the intention with which the action was done" does not refer to an entity or state of any kind.[9]

Losing reference to "expression," Anscombe's first division has become "intending to act"—a hard notion for action theory, as Davidson avers, partly because, being potentially free of any contamination by action, it seems to refer to an as yet unanalyzed state of mind. Moreover, given the general drift here—an organization of "intention" around a distinction between worldly events and autonomous mental states—one might understandably speak of just two main Anscombian divisions. Thus, Michael Bratman:

> We use the notion of intention to characterize both people's actions and their minds. Thus, I might *intentionally* pump the water into the house, and pump it *with the intention* of poisoning the inhabitants. Here intention characterizes my action. But I might also *intend* this morning to pump the water (and poison the inhabitants) when I get to the pump this afternoon. And here intention characterizes my mind. (p. 1) . . . Our common sense psychological scheme admits of intentions as states of mind; and it also allows us to characterize actions as done intentionally, or with a certain intention. A theory of intention must address both kinds of phenomena

---

9. Donald Davidson, "Introduction," in *Essays on Actions and Events* (Oxford: Oxford University Press, 1985), xiii.

and explain how they are related. A natural approach, the one I will be taking here, is to begin with the state of intending to act. (p. 3)[10]

And Bratman distinguishes this approach from that of other theorists as follows:

> Instead of beginning with the state of intending to act [some theorists] turn immediately to intention as it appears in action: [they] turn directly to acting intentionally and acting with a certain intention. . . . This is, for example, the strategy followed by Elizabeth Anscombe in her ground-breaking monograph, *Intention.*[11]

On this reception of Anscombe, the question naturally arises: Which is the more "basic" notion of intention? For Bratman, as for Davidson, it is "intending to act," though in analyzing this state Bratman goes boldly (where Davidson had gone only reluctantly) beyond mere "desire" and "belief" to a much richer psychology of states, one more adequate to the complexities of action.[12] The significance of this development will come in for interpretation later on.[13] What matters for the moment, however, are only two apparent

---

10. Michael Bratman, *Intention, Plans, and Practical Reason* (Cambridge, Mass.: Harvard University Press, 1987), 1, 3. Bratman's footnote attributes this distinction between "mind-" and "world-" characterizing uses of intention to Anscombe.

11. Ibid., 5. See also H. L. A. Hart, "Intention and Punishment," in *Punishment and Responsibility* (New York: Oxford University Press, 1968), 117: "Intention is to be divided into three related parts. . . . The first I shall call 'intentionally doing something'; the second 'doing something with a further intention,' and the third 'bare intention' because it is the case of intending to do something in the future without doing anything to execute this intention now."

12. "Reluctantly": Compare Davidson, "Intending," in *Essays on Actions and Events,* 88. If reasons, conceived as belief/desire pairs, seem adequate to explaining what it is to act intentionally, they appear immediately hopeless when it comes to "intending to act." One main problem is that the familiar conflicts that are present among an agent's desires seem intolerable when it comes to her intentions; intentions seem to "commit" the agent in a way that mere desires do not. This and other difficulties with belief/desire psychology in the theory of intention are discussed by Bratman in *Intention, Plans, and Practical Reason.* On the apparently commissive aspect of "intending," see Bratman's discussion at 4–5, and our discussion *infra,* section 6.

Davidson's reluctance, as opposed to Bratman's boldness, will comprise only a superficial difference here, for the reluctance is only about recognizing "intention" as a *sui generis* state of mind (one not "ontologically reducible" to beliefs and desires: see Davidson, "Intending," 88, 83). Both take for granted, however, the explanatory framework described in this section.

13. See Davidson, "Intending," 144, 146, 161–162.

commonplaces heard in these passages: first, that "intending to act" is *some* state of mind; and second, that action theory should explain how this state is related to "intentional" as it characterizes things in the "world"—what people do or cause to happen. We call the framework comprised by these points Transformed Anscombe *(TA)*.

The steps leading from Anscombe to *TA* might be thought of as follows:

1. Noting that Anscombe sometimes calls her first division "expression of intention *for the future*," and sensing perhaps that the invocation of "expression" is not essential here, the latter term is (understandably) factored-out, leaving "intention for the future" ("prior-intention" or "intending to act") as the item Anscombe meant to distinguish.[14]

2. The effect of this—and perhaps one of its motivations too—is to give the list a new sharpness. For occupants of the new category—e.g., someone's intention to fly to Boston next week—seem, as such, to be neither intentional acts nor (supposing the agent hasn't yet done anything to realize her intention) any intention in acting. Naturally, such an intention may be taken up—or become present in some way—in her flying to Boston, and in the intention with which she does other things, like packing her suitcase.[15] But it need not be. For she may change her mind, or something may interrupt her plans, and then her intention to fly to Boston will remain "pure."

3. Given the possibility of "pure" intending, it becomes hard to see how this category could fail to designate a mental state, attitude, or disposition of some kind.[16] So the divisions of "intention" now take shape around the philosophical polestar of the division between mind and world: two notions of intention find purchase only where there is behavior causing things to happen; a third refers to a mental state, attitude, or disposition which, though in some way present in such behavior, is also abstractable from it and capable of existing on its own.

4. The theoretical elucidation of "intention" is now apt to be organized around two tasks: (1) an analysis of "intention," conceived as a (poten-

---

14. We shall generally use "intending" or "intention to act" for this category.

15. "It would be astonishing if that extra element were foreign to our understanding of intentional action." Davidson, "Intending," 88; and see 89: "There is no reason not to allow that intention of exactly the same kind is also present when the intended action eventuates."

16. See Davidson, *Essays on Actions and Events,* xiii, and "Intending," 87–88.

tially "pure") mental state or attitude, and (2) an explanation of the other behavior-dependent applications of "intention" in terms of (1). Theorists are of course apt to disagree about how to carry out these tasks: what other mental states or attitudes are entailed by intention, whether some reduction—ontological or otherwise—is possible, and the relation between the relevant state of intending and intentional action, are familiar points of controversy.

5. Generally, in *TA:* (A) an event is an action when it is intentional under some description; (B) an action meets this requirement when it is done for reasons; (C) this means it is susceptible to a form of rationalization (a special sense of "He did it *because* . . ."); and (D) such rationalizations elucidate action through a movement from inner to outer: from the agent's beliefs, desires, or other states to something happening outside him. (Whether either such a movement or its explanation is—in some previously recognized sense—a causal one is another hub of controversy.)

From within this framework, what differentiates Anscombe is commonly thought to be the "methodological priority" she gives to intention as it appears in action and—curiously, as she doesn't discuss this—her denying that the relation between the mind and action sides of the rationalizing "because" is a causal one.[17] Bratman in fact portrays Anscombe as accepting everything in (5), with one qualification: her view of whether "intending" is an independent psychological state (not reducible to appropriate desires and beliefs) cannot be made out because she says too little about this state.[18]

This story of progress within a single framework of action theory has its obvious satisfactions. Nonetheless, a distortion is present when the contemporary theorist credits Anscombe with having discerned the starting points of *TA,* as described here. This comes out in the following puzzle: while Anscombe does contemplate intending in its putatively "pure" or unworldly form—

A man can form an intention which he then does nothing to carry out, either because he is prevented or because he changes his mind: but the

---

17. See Bratman, *Intention, Plans, and Practical Reason,* 5–6. Anscombe says almost nothing in *Intention* about whether action explanations mention causes, save for an occasional suggestion that the relevant notions of "a cause," and "causal" would have to be made clearer for us to understand what this question is about. See e.g., §§5 and 9–11.

18. Bratman, *Intention, Plans, and Practical Reason,* 7.

intention itself can be complete, although it remains a purely interior thing (p. 9)

—she offers, as Bratman observes, almost no account of it. In fact, returning late in the book to her first division, Anscombe merely remarks briefly that what has been "said about intention in acting applies also to intention in a proposed action" (p. 90). Here a large gap in her account must appear from the contemporary point of view: How can her previous teachings about intentional actions, things done, simply now "apply" to an intention in a proposed action, conceived as something which may remain "a purely interior thing"?

By *TA*'s lights, Anscombe's previous remarks cover 5A–D. Beyond identifying the central case of intentional action with action for a reason, they explain how when an agent so acts he has a further intention, which often furnishes a wider description of what he is doing—and related matters. But surely some further explanation of "intention in a proposed action"—and not merely an application of these doctrines—was needed, even by Anscombe's standard of compression. For we can't understand, say, "an agent's intention to fly to Boston next week" merely on the anemic basis of an agent's having a reason to do as much, however this notion is analyzed.[19] Among the problems, there is the common fact that the agent may simultaneously have a reason *not* to fly to Boston without it being the case that she both intends to fly to Boston *and* intends not to. Intentions apparently stand open to contradiction in a way which mere reasons do not. Since what has been said about intention "in action" thus seems insufficient to cope with intention "in a proposed action," the question arises: Having distinguished these notions of intention, why would Anscombe omit any significant analysis of the latter?

Two answers appear in the literature. *First,* no reason: Anscombe simply does not discuss intending, leaving it to us. This seems implausible: one should really choose between making Anscombe the founder of the Three Divisions and having her omit to discuss the first—the combination amounts to philosophical malpractice. *Second,* her reason is behaviorist: she thinks we will grasp how to explain intending as some function or complication of intentional action, which she takes to be more basic. This too is implausible: Are we really to suppose that Anscombe (a student of St. Thomas, after all)

19. Nor can we understand this on the basis of the agent's having done something for such a reason (say, bought a ticket); for, by hypothesis, the intention in question may remain pure, the action merely proposed.

seeks, with the behaviorist, to solve intellectual problems by collapsing spirit into nature?

Significant internal difficulties block the attribution of behaviorism, in any case. Anscombe's forthright talk of intention as "a purely interior thing" is one difficulty. Her pivotal remark that what was said about intention in acting "applies also to intention in a proposed action" is an even greater one. For a genuine behaviorist doesn't talk that way. He doesn't say that his account of (e.g.) pain-behavior *applies also* to pain! The words "applies also" evidently say that a distinctive kind of unity is available here: that which consists in seeing a group of items as falling under—or engaging application of—a single idea, form, or pattern. In contrast, what the behaviorist needs to say at this point is that the relevant mind-characterizing notions can be analyzed or explained *in terms of* other items. Otherwise put, the behaviorist is someone trafficking in the divisions emerging from *TA*. His problem is therefore to connect the different notions of "intention" through a strategy of explanatory extension; and, in this at least, he will differ from other contemporary theorists only in taking for secondary those notions which they take for basic. But in whichever direction it runs, such a connective explanation will be something different from what Anscombe appears to contemplate: an apprehension of the divisions of intention as instances of a single form.[20]

This explains why the best evidence of behaviorist sympathies in *Intention* is bound to be inconclusive. For the best (of the thin) evidence must be what Anscombe says just after mentioning the possibility of pure intention:

> This conspires to make us think that if we want to know a man's intentions it is into the contents of his mind, and only into these, that we must enquire; and hence, that if we wish to understand what intention is, we must be investigating something whose existence is purely in the sphere of the mind; and that although intention issues in actions, and the way this happens also presents interesting questions, still what physically takes place, i.e., what a man actually does, is the very last thing we need consider in our enquiry. Whereas I wish to say that it is the first. (p. 9)

"Some say A then B, but I say first B then A." No doubt there is a genuine issue of starting points here, of what is to be modeled on what. Anscombe's

---

20. Compare, *Intention*, 84: "The term 'intentional' has reference to a *form* of description of events" (Anscombe's emphasis).

remark will suggest behaviorism, however, only to someone already sure of the theoretical options: either the application of "intention" to what people do will have to be explained in terms of its use to characterize a state of mind, or vice versa. There is another possibility, however. Say that Anscombe's aim is to exhibit the unity of intention directly, by subsuming the three divisions under a single form. Once properly in view, it should be possible to see what this form applies to, without further complication. On this reading, "First B . . ." says only that one doesn't come to see what formally unites the "interior thing" with "intention in acting" by asking first what properties characterize someone's psychological state as one of intending; it is rather *in action* that the genus comes most perspicuously into view. While this might prove an unsatisfying thesis about intention, it isn't exactly novel to suggest that members of a kind have asymmetrical powers of exhibiting it. If you want to see why bad arguments are arguments, for example, it is best to start by examining the valid kind, this being more basic. Or, again, successfully murdering is more basic than attempting the same. To see what kind of wrongdoing unites these, it seems best to start with the infringement of someone's right in the completed act; from here one can discern the wrong in the more attenuated case, without the aid of the sorts of theories that would have to say (starting at the other end) that, e.g., the wrong in every act of murder is "really" only that of someone's intention to murder, plus some causal assistance from the world. Similarly, on the present thesis, what kind of entity or state this is—*intending* to write the word "action"—will best be exhibited in the performance of writing the word "action."[21] This needn't incur any commitment to the behaviorist's denials.

---

21. One feature of this analogy seems worth highlighting. Someone who, endeavoring to understand "wrongful," started with the case in which it characterizes an agent's *plan* would find himself having to connect this to other cases through a story about such a plan bringing about—"in the right way" of course—a situation in which a different, world-involving notion of wrongful finds application (e.g., to another's loss or injury). (And he might feel puzzled over how applications of the world-involving notion of "wrongful"—e.g., wrongful injury—could involve a greater degree of culpability, given the fortuitous role that factors beyond the agent's control are bound to play in this extended story; but this is a distinguishable problem.) Starting at the other end, one sees what makes a plan wrongful by seeing what happens when it succeeds. This doesn't occlude the possibility of causal explanations, but it suggests that the unity of the divisions can and perhaps must be grasped before they get under way.

In support of this: Anscombe speaks of "intention in a proposed action" (where *TA* is apt to write "intending" or "future-directed intention"). Her point is that the distinction in question here is one between two intentions *in action*—items sharing an underlying structure or form, but differing in their positions along a spectrum of presence. On this view, a future intention to write the word "action" is structurally a variant of writing the word "the action"; it is distinguished only by its remoteness, by the intended intervention being, as it were, not yet present. This will need further development: just what Anscombe takes this common structure or form to be—the one best exhibited by intention in present action—remains to be articulated. But it shouldn't be difficult to guess that the answer will have something to do with the attention she gives to her special question "Why?" This is evidently the central "device" (p. 80) in her "non-connective" explanation of the unity of intention. It also goes hand in hand, as will become plain, with her emphasis on "expression of intention."

Here, however, we reach ahead. To summarize, the divisions of "intention" being connected in *TA* aren't, on their face, Anscombe's divisions. One can of course ask why Anscombe omits discussing intending, and offers little analysis of this putative state at just the point—intention in a proposed action—where analysis seems needed. But this problem might also be turned around. Despite the standard homage, few theorists actually find much use for Anscombe's first heading, at least as she inscribes it. Reading them, one would never suspect that "expression of intention" figured centrally in her discussion.

3. Why "Expression": Three Clues

Turning back to the problem of the prominence of "expression" in Anscombe's initial setup, we find two explicit clues in *Intention:* (1) ignoring the expression of intention in favor of what it is an expression *of* is apt to lead to wrong notions: e.g., psychological jargon about "drives" and "sets"; reduction of intention to a species of desire, i.e., a kind of emotion; or irreducible intuition of the meaning of "I intend" (pp. 5–6); and (2), it is also apt to obscure just how different expressions of intention are from paradigm cases of expressions of states of mind.

(1) Anscombe's reference to Wittgenstein's discussion of "I was going to . . ."—a "pure" intention again, only the time for action is past—pinpoints at least one "wrong notion": viz., that the truth or assertability of "I'm going

[was going] to φ" consists in some occurrent words, images, sensations, or feelings.[22] Against this: a person's emotions, desires, or drives may lead in contrary directions without hint of irrationality; not so their intentions. In addition, one can have an intention over a period of time (e.g., to see a friend) while seldom thinking of it; and, in recalling an intention, whatever "scanty" mental items memory presents as having occurred "do not add up to"—they aren't necessary or sufficient for—having that intention. (Nonetheless one can easily enough recall what one was going to do—one simply gives the words which express it.)[23] All this suggests that (unlike, e.g., "I have an itch" or "It feels like going down in a lift"), "I intend to . . ." neither reports an experience-content nor requires an experiential vehicle. To adapt a remark of Anscombe's adapting a remark of Wittgenstein's: No experience could be an intention, because no experience could have the consequences of intending.[24]

(2) Considering such paradigm cases of the "expression" of an experience or state as "Ouch!" "I'm in pain," or "Foiled again!" it might be said: someone who tells us what they are going to do isn't in *that* way "expressing" an intention; they aren't simply venting. Indeed, "I'm going for a walk" no more looks like a communication about the speaker's inner state than does, say, her belief that the store closes at 8:00, as expressed by means of an appropriate declarative sentence. Only in special cases does an expression of belief aim to inform us about the *speaker*—i.e., when it is about her. So too, when someone (actively) expresses an intention, Anscombe says, they give us information—right or wrong—about what is going to happen. (Of course, biographical facts will get passively expressed or manifested as well.) Herein lies a point of likeness with predictions: An expression of intention such as "I'm going for a walk" is true or false according to whether the speaker goes for a walk.[25]

22. See Wittgenstein, *Philosophical Investigations,* §§629–660 (esp. 635, 645–646), 216–217; Wittgenstein, *Zettel,* ed. G. E. M. Anscombe and G. H. von Wright, trans. G. E. M. Anscombe (Oxford: Basil Blackwell, 1970), 44. Anscombe alludes to this discussion on p. 6 of *Intention.*

23. For a related discussion, see Anscombe, "Events in the Mind," in *Metaphysics and the Philosophy of Mind: Collected Papers,* vol. 2 (Oxford: Basil Blackwell, 1981), esp. 57–61.

24. Compare, *Intention,* 77, on the absurdity of accepting both the empiricist idea of pleasure as an impression of some kind and seeing it as "quite generally the point of doing anything." Anscombe is adapting *Philosophical Investigations,* §218: "Meaning is not a process which accompanies a word. For no process could have the consequences of meaning."

25. Compare, *Intention,* 92: "Nor can we say: But in the expression of intention one isn't saying anything is going to happen! Otherwise, when I had said 'I'm just going to get up', it

Hence, like a prediction, it can serve to give someone direct knowledge of what is going to happen.[26] It is not a mere indication of the speaker's psychic condition.

These considerations—in brief, the dissimilarity of intention to a psychic state on the model of emotion—do suggest some motivation for Anscombe's emphasis on "expression," for a personal "expression of intention" clearly makes a kind of claim, and has consequences, recognition of which will serve to place intention outside this model. But without more, these points suggest that Anscombe's peculiar emphasis might be only a dispensable device for avoiding certain philosophical errors—"particular dead-ends," as she calls them (p. 6). To see why these points do not go far enough, remember that the personal expression of belief is also to be understood as presenting a proposition of fact (an answer to the question "What did he/you say?"); it too is no mere indication of mental goings-on. Yet, presumably, this isn't likely to suggest that "expressions" will be a main division in studying belief; that wrong notion, should it arise, could simply be dealt with directly. Why then—apart from the proactive avoidance of errors—should "expressions" figure as one of the main divisions of the topic of intention? That was the problem (see section 1 of this essay), and the problem remains.

The main clue needed here must evidently concern features of intention that are special to it, and that therefore generate a special problem. And there is such a clue, in the low-level linguistic facts that suggest divisions of the topic in the first place. What matters most is just that applications of "intention" *are* spread along a spectrum extending from what is, naïvely speaking, "in the mind" to what is "in the world." Picturing a line, on the far left will be found pure intentions, defined as cases in which the agent intends to do something but hasn't yet done anything else in order to do that. Moving rightward, the agent has more worldly deeds to show for his intentions: if he is described as φ-ing or as intending to φ, then, at this point, it will be correct to say that

---

would be unreasonable later to ask 'Why didn't you get up?' I could reply: 'I wasn't talking about a future happening, so why do you mention such irrelevancies?'" On Anscombe's account, an expression of intention *differs* from a prediction in not being founded for the speaker on evidence or observation, as well as in the particular notion of "mistakenness" we apply in connection with it.

26. "Direct": i.e., knowledge not merely on the basis of an inference from how it is with the speaker. Compare, *Intention*, 3: "Nor does the patient normally *infer* the information from the fact that the doctor said that; he would say that the doctor *told* him."

he is also doing various things in order to φ, or because he intends (wants, aims) to φ. At the far right, his performance is fully unfolded and finds description in the past tense: "He φ-ed" (or "He has φ-ed") will now be true, and not merely—what holds anywhere between these end points—"He was φ-ing." The special problem, as all agree, is that of exhibiting the unity of the notions of intention that appear here.

This progressive structure has no parallel in the case of emotions, desires, or beliefs. Generalizing this contrast, we may say: It begins to specify what is meant by a "state" to note that the progressive form of the relevant verb— e.g., "to believe," "to be hungry," "to be taller than"—isn't used. To join a subject to such a verb, no grammatical discriminations of progressive versus perfected aspect ("was φ-ing" vs. "φ-ed") are needed, only those of tense; and there is always a good inference from the present ("X is hungry . . .") to the perfect ("X was hungry . . ." said at some future time). States, in short, are *static;* and this exhibits, by way of contrast, two related features of the spectrum of uses of intention.

First, with anything an agent does, there are, in principle, any number of purposive sub-parts—i.e., things he must do *in order to* do that. This is because his performance *takes time:*[27] it may be done quickly (taking little time) or slowly, and we can mark its progress—and thereby distinguish further points in our spectrum—by speaking of someone's "just starting to φ," "being nearly half-way done," "just finishing up," and so on. Performances *unfold:* they involve a diminishing future and a swelling past of what the agent needs to do in order to do, or has done, what he is doing. States, in contrast, merely go on for a time, without unfolding: e.g., no one will be found slowly desiring a drink, or almost finished being the tallest boy scout, even if his desire is soon to be quenched or others are about to grow.[28]

Second, the intentional object of "He intends . . ." is given by a performance verb ("to φ"), so that if someone intends to φ, then what fits this notional "state" of his is another performance to which the spectrum of the concept of intention in principle applies (viz., his φ-ing, or his Z-ing in order

27. See Michael Thompson, "Naive Action Theory," in *Life and Action* (Cambridge, Mass.: Harvard University Press, 2008). Our presentation of the spectrum of intention owes a general debt to Thompson's essay.

28. On the contrast between states and performances (and taking time versus going on for a time), see A. Kenny, *Action, Emotion and Will* (London: Routledge and Kegan Paul, 1963), chap. 8, to which we are indebted here.

to φ), and not, apart from this, any extensionally equivalent state of the world. Hence the object of the attitude of intention is another intention or a performance, whereas what makes a belief true (or satisfies a desire) can be propositionally rendered, and is only in special cases characterizable through another application of these same concepts: Not all beliefs are about other beliefs, as not all desires could be merely for other desires. And whatever their causal contribution to a particular action, beliefs and desires do not come to serve as qualifications of the action itself (e.g., as "beliefish" or "desirous").

Here, then, it looks as if "intention" earns its literal, archaic sense—a "stretching forward"—for it is structured as action itself is. Not that this is surprising: it is location on a spectrum of unfolding action that fits an event to be described using concepts of intention in the first place;[29] the kind of thing an intention is is to be explained in terms of a concept that applies throughout the spectrum. Anything this wasn't true of—which didn't characterize both a person's attitude as well as the object of that attitude—wouldn't be our (i.e., a) concept of intention. Anscombe asks:

> Would intentional actions still have the characteristic 'intentional', if there were no such thing as expression of intention for the future, or as further intention in acting? I.e. is 'intentional' a characteristic of the actions that have it, which is formally independent of those other occurrences of the concept of intention? (p. 30)[30]

And she answers: "This supposition [that intention only occurred as it occurs in 'intentional action'] . . . carries a suggestion that 'intentional action' means as it were 'intentious action' . . . that an action's being intentional is rather like a facial expression's being sad." This remark traces the consequences of losing the unity of the concept of intention across its different contexts: cut "intention" loose from its unfolding on a spectrum, consider it only as a qualification of action, and "intentional" becomes "intentious," essentially the name of a state, like sad or angry. By the same token, if TA has recently tended to

---

29. The use of intention which arises in considering how to understand a speaker (especially when the speaker is absent, e.g.,—"the author's intention") would appear to call for separate treatment, as it does not involve a notion of unfolding action. In light of this case, it appears that Anscombe's divisions are neither exclusive nor exhaustive.

30. Anscombe is exploring here the disabling consequences of isolating one her divisions—intentional action—from the others. However, her overall point is more general: Other distortions would arise from the isolation of any of the divisions.

discover that an adequate account of action must go beyond states of "having reasons" conceived as propositional belief-desire pairs, what it has caught sight of may be structurally expressed like this: No psychology will afford the right materials for explaining action that does not make use of a concept that applies throughout the spectrum of unfolding action, and which thus has the same internal complexity as actions themselves.

This said, the image of a performance as a line touching points of "pure" and "perfected" intention is to be taken with a grain a salt. What is represented here is not a performance, but only the kind of thing a performance is, its structural possibilities. A few disclaimers will help to bring the spectrum into clearer focus:

- First, no implication arises that every action touches the right-most point. To the contrary, as J. L. Austin observed, a mark of any action is its exposure to the risk of failure or incompleteness.[31] No inference is available from the progressive ("He is φ-ing") to the perfect ("He φ-ed").
- Likewise, no implication arises that every action begins at the left-most point. Not all intentional action is the execution of a prior intention. Many intentions—e.g., to roll out of bed in the morning, to change speed according to traffic—never exist apart from the things one does.
- Third, where there are pure intentions, no implication arises that they precede acting, except relative to some descriptions of the action in question. To illustrate, someone may have now a pure intention to build a tree house, but only—as is likely—because he is already under way with something else of which building a tree house is a part or phase: e.g., he is raising his kids to enjoy the outdoors, or improving the property before he sells it so he can retire and finish writing his novel.
- Likewise, no implication arises that, in achieving the right-most point, there remains nothing virtual or pure about what the agent is doing. To illustrate, even after our agent's intention to build a tree house has become impure, the point arrives where he forms (what is now) a pure intention to buy lumber; failure on this score will mean he never builds a tree house, and perhaps never does the things of which this was a part.

31. See J. L. Austin, "A Plea For Excuses," in *Philosophical Papers,* ed. J. O. Urmson and G. J. Warnock (Oxford: Clarendon Press, 1961).

• From the above, it appears that wherever "purity," as defined here, is used to characterize intentions, it must be possible to apply the term in the same sense to actions themselves. Consider how it is with our agent who, far along in building his tree house, forms an intention to drive in a nail to fasten two boards together. At the moment, his intention is a "pure" one, for he has taken a break and lies on the grass. What is this agent, with his nail- and plank-regarding intentions, now doing? Well, among other things, it would be correct to say he is building a tree house (he has been at it since winter), only, at the moment, this *action* of his remains pure, for he is not now doing anything in order to do that. Any action of significant duration is apt to have moments of pure intending and pure acting among its innumerable parts.

Notice that our agent's nail-regarding intention may at present be pure (just like his action of building a tree house), though his intention to fix together two boards is impure (he has placed them next to each other)—all this, notwithstanding that hammering the nail, fixing the boards, and building a tree house are, as Anscombe teaches, the same action under different descriptions. So although pure intending comprises the left-limit case, and perfected action the right-limit one, this does not entail that what the person purely intends to do isn't, under a wider description, an action that is already under way and uncertain of completion. Davidson's own example of a pure intention—writing the word "action"—illustrates the point: I have formed this intention because I'm already engaged in writing a sentence, and this with a view to writing a book, the second in a series, and so on. Further, once we are able to locate impure intentions in this way—by enlarging the frame of pure ones—it should naturally be possible also to find pure ones within impure ones, for the principle is the same.[32] If there is a tendency to think of action in terms of a one-way sequence, beginning with intending and moving through acting to having acted—i.e., as something beginning in the mind

32. Thus, someone writing the word "action" may have a pure intention, at this moment, to write the letter "c." But asking why they intend to write "c" will disclose this intention to be grounded in an action already under way: the pure intention to write "c" stands to writing the word "action" (once they have begun on the "a") as writing the word "action" does to writing the sentence "An intention can exist . . ." and so on. So pure intentions are everywhere. But that is because actions, under way but not yet completed, are everywhere; such actions are their grounds.

and ending in a state of the world—an illusion is present that perhaps arises from the philosopher's focus on unmotivated or point-like actions (the lifting of a finger) strangely abstracted from the *vita active*.

Now, returning to the question of Anscombe's divisions, we venture the following thesis. What makes the phrase "expression of intention" look like an outlier in her list—its reference to speech—is also what allows it to stand as a natural example of each division, and thus, in a sense, to subsume the entire list:

> (Case 1) Someone says "I'm buying some shoes": An expression of intention for the future (perhaps even a pure one).
> (Case 2) Someone says "I'm buying some shoes": An intentional act (e.g., when the speaker is asked *what* he is doing).
> (Case 3) Someone says "I'm buying some shoes": A further intention in acting (e.g., when this is the answer to the question "Why are you walking out the door?")

Not that this is unexpected, as if "expression of intention" should somehow be proprietary to the special case of pure intending. The spectrum of intention—which exhibits that as a limit case—already suggests this wouldn't be so. And consider the linguistic facts: one who offers, e.g., "I intend to take the train to Boston tomorrow" (a pure intention, let us suppose) might also express themselves thus: "I *am* taking the train to Boston—tomorrow." And having begun to pack, they might explain what they are doing by reference to the partial presence of that larger performance—"I'm taking the train to Boston"—but they might also revert to the notionally "psychic" explanation: "I intend to take the train to Boston." If any of these are "expressions of intention," surely all must be.

The principle of this linguistic sharing of labor is seen, according to Anscombe, when the use of the progressive is denied:

> The less normal it would be to take the achievement of the objective as a matter of course, the more the objective gets expressed *only* by 'in order to'. E.g. 'I am going to London in order to make my uncle change his will'; not 'I am making my uncle change his will'. (p. 40)

Likewise, the less normal it would be to take the achievement as a matter of course, the more the objective ("in order to ϕ") gets expressed with "because" followed by a proposition which couples the performance verb (to φ) with some overtly psychic form ("I intend . . . ," "I want . . . ," "I plan . . . ," etc.): "I am going to London *because I intend* [*want, will try, etc.*] to make my uncle change his will." Where ordinary language demands them, such "psychic" expressions are markers of absence or remoteness in an unfolding perfor- mance. But in this, they are exactly like the idiomatic use of the simple pro- gressive ("I am φ-ing"), which itself always conveys imperfect aspect, incom- pleteness, and the risk of failure (only to a different degree). All expressions of intention, then, are such as to explain action by locating it within a larger action-in-progress. Where "psychic" markers of remoteness are available, however, we can expect the use of the simple progressive to be correspond- ingly confined to a narrower range of cases exhibiting relative presence or proximity.[33]

This explains a critical remark of Anscombe's. After (1) connecting the no- tion of intentional action to the applicability of a special question "Why?" and (2) showing how an answer can furnish terms for a wider description of what an agent is doing (i.e., just when the question has the right sense), and (3) not- ing that this leads, chain-wise and eventually, to "a break," to an act-description characterizable, on account of remoteness, only as something the agent is now *going* (or—we may add—intending, wanting, planning, etc.) to do, she writes:

> I do not think it is a quite sharp break. E.g. is there much to choose [i.e., in answer to why someone is putting on the kettle] between 'She is making tea' and 'She is putting on the kettle in order to make tea' [and, we may add, "She *intends* to make tea"?—our note]—i.e. 'She is going to make tea'? Obviously not. (p. 40)

The implication of this is that the notionally mind-characterizing uses of intention differ from the others only in articulating a greater degree of re- moteness or uncertainty. That is, they continue—at a different point in the spectrum—the same form of explanation that was most perspicuously seen in the earlier links of the chain: essentially, the fitting of an action into a larger, presently incomplete whole. Call this the teleological structure of ac- tion: Action is the kind of thing that rationalizes its sub-parts (those actions done "in order to" do it). As Michael Thompson has argued, this suggests

33. See Thompson, "Naive Action Theory," on the "openness" of the progressive, and see also Kevin Falvey, "Knowledge in Intention," *Philosophical Studies* 99 (2000): 21–44, esp. 26.

that it is fundamentally intentional actions-in-progress which explain actions, and that it is only on the basis of this primitive structure—an action as a space of reasons—that a more sophisticated development becomes possible: viz., the joining of a psychic expression with a performance verb to create an etiolated form of the same structure in the interest of articulating relative non-presence, remoteness, or uncertainty.[34]

In support of this, it bears remembering that the psychological items under consideration are someone's intending, planning, or wanting *to do something* (to φ) and not, say, someone's wanting or desiring *that* something or other happen or be the case. The progress noted earlier in *TA* toward more committed or articulated psychological states (beyond belief and desire) was just the recognition that only states of mind having a role in the unfolding of action itself—which means only "states" subject to qualification (i.e., to placement on the spectrum) as "pure/impure"—can effectively explain action by reference to the agent's attitudes.[35] But this just means that such states—intending to φ, planning to φ, etc.—inherit through their objects (a performance-form: to φ) the distinctive teleological structure characteristic of intentional action. And this suggests that no matter how rich a psychology we employ, we do not attain to an understanding of the behavior-characterizing uses of "intention" on the basis of relation to a psychological state, except by helping ourselves to a notion of a "state" informed by a prior understanding of the concept of intentional action (as in intending or planning *to do something*).

To summarize: "I intend (plan, want, etc.) to make tea" expresses the same incompleteness of action seen—at earlier points in the chain of answers, where achievement is more "a matter of course"—in the use of a performance verb by itself: e.g., "Why are you boiling water?"—"I'm *making* tea." "And why are you making tea?"—"I *intend* to serve the guests." Hence all such psychic forms are performance modifiers: insofar as they are employable in action-explaining answers to the question "Why?" they express forms of be-

34. Thompson, "Naive Action Theory."

35. Michael Bratman's master term—planning—fits the bill of particulars here. Unlike beliefs and (appetitive) desires, plans are wholes which rationalize their sub-parts, can be pure or impure, take a performance from as their object ("I plan to φ"), are subject to the question "Why?" in the relevant sense ("for what purpose?"), can be commanded ("Plan to be there at 4:00!"), and so on. Planning, in short, shares in the structure of action. Nothing this wasn't true of would even seem to be a good candidate for an intention-explaining psychological state.

ing on-the-way-to-but-not-yet-having φ-ed, of already stretching oneself toward this end. So expressions of intention "for the future" are variations on a common theme: They are structurally of a piece with the simple progressive, only further to the left on the spectrum, where they permit a more refined articulation of the imperfection—an agent's being committedly under way—informing all action explanation. In expressing imperfection, they are just like any other suitable answer to the question "Why?" whether this be a declaration of what one will do, a description of what one is currently doing, an account of the intention with which one is doing something, an explanation of what one desires or is trying or endeavoring to do, or—think of Anscombe's shopping list (p. 56)—a specification of what one is to do. The logical relations between these expressions of intention aren't themselves very important. As a matter of ordinary language, they admit of no exact relative placement on the spectrum, though they are of course open to the stipulations of the philosopher whose purposes require more precision.

4. Expressions of Intention: The General and the Special Use

Conceived as an answer to the question "Why?" "expression of intention" is clearly a capacious notion (any item on the spectrum can be represented as such an answer),[36] and it is this capaciousness (the power to exhibit what is structurally common to any use of intention) that recommends "expression of intention" for Anscombe's purposes. On this conception, there could be no question of finding out what an expression of intention is by first investigating the properties that characterize a psychological state as one of intention, as if the powers this state might have to rationalize what someone does might then remain open for investigation. Anscombe's focus makes us take things the other way around: What can and does count as an agent's "expression of intention" is determined by its availability to enter into an elucidative account of action (fitting it into a whole-in-progress), its suitability, in other words, to be given to another who asks what is going on. An intention is whatever can be given to another in an expression suited to play this role.

36. The instructive exception to this is the right-limit case, which, by definition, does not express imperfection and hence does not enter into action-explanation: e.g., in answer to "Why?" never the past-perfect (I φ-ed), but only the past progressive (I was φ-ing).

The special problem addressed by this account arises from the tendency for the continuity of uses of "intention" to get disguised: "Intend" looks like a state (like "believe") and this sets the problem of its connection to "intentional" as applied to things getting done. Indeed, by at least one criterion, "to intend to φ" should designate a state, since an inference from the present ("He intends to φ") to the perfect ("He intended to φ") does hold, and since, unlike a performance, intending to φ does not—notwithstanding the colloquial use of the progressive—take time.[37] On the other hand, the fact that "intending" (like any psychic verb put to employment in explaining action) takes a performance form rather than a proposition as its object seems to mark a decisive difference. This is related to two features of "intending," which would make it quite special among states, but which are commonplaces of performances. First, we can ask "Why?" (for what purpose, with what intention) someone intends to φ, just as we can ask this about action itself. (All intentions are like actions in this way: they are explained by—and they explain—other actions and other intentions.) Second, intending to φ, being thus something voluntary, is subject to being commanded, like any action.[38]

Taking it that such differences are what matter (and not what label one applies), we propose the following account of the significance of "expression of intention" for Anscombe.

First, although Anscombe quickly leaves her first division ("expression of intention for the future") aside until later, a distinctive form of verbal exchange remains a pervasive feature of her exposition: "Why are you lying there?"—"I'm doing Yoga"; "Why did you pump water this morning?"—"To poison that lot, don't you know?"; "Why worry about them?"—"Those people have strangled the country long enough, I intend to get the good people in." All of the positive answers in such interrogations are "expressions of intention," not just the last answer (an intention for the future):

---

37. See the previous discussion in section 3.

38. This is sometimes missed because there is no imperative form ("Intend to φ!"). However, nothing is easier than making someone's intention—e.g., to return the book—the object of a command: one simply orders them to return the book. It might be objected that, were intending really an etiolated form of performance, it ought to be possible to command someone to "intend to return the book" in perfect purity, i.e., "Plan to return the book, but don't actually return it!" But the answer to this is that it is also impossible to command someone "to go ahead with returning the book without actually returning it." Intending to φ stands to the progressive φ-ing just as φ-ing (or doing things in order to φ) stands to successfully φ-ing or having φ-ed: none can be commanded apart from the others.

If a description of some future state of affairs makes sense just by itself as
an answer to the ["Why?"] question, then it is an expression of intention.
But there are other expressions of the intention with which a man is doing
something: for example, a wider description of what he is doing. For example, someone comes into a room, sees me lying on a bed and asks 'What
are you doing?' The answer 'lying on a bed' would be received with just
irritation; an answer like 'Resting' or 'Doing Yoga', which would be a description of what I am doing in lying on my bed, would be an expression
of intention. (pp. 34–35)

So "expression of intention for the future" is one species of a common genus,
that of positive or action-elucidating answers to the special question "Why?"
Recall the role of that question. It provides a definition of an "intentional
act" in terms of the applicability of a question to which the agent can always
give some knowledgeable response. Given this, it should be possible to see
that "expression of intention" (in the wide, generic sense) works to exhibit the
unity of the three, initially disparate-seeming divisions. This is just what Anscombe says:

To a certain extent the three divisions of the subject made in §1, are simply
equivalent. That is to say, where the answers 'I am going to fetch my camera' [*expression of intention for the future*], 'I am fetching my camera' [*intentional act*] and 'in order to fetch the camera' [*further intention in acting*]
are interchangeable as answers to the question 'Why?' (p. 40)[39]

On this account, the unity of the divisions lies both in the applicability of the
question "Why?" to the material of each, and in the suitability of each to itself rationalize action—i.e., to figure in an agent's answer to the question
"Why?" asked about something else he is doing (in the present example, his
going upstairs). That is, the unity of the divisions is seen in the fitness of their
corresponding linguistic expressions—"I'm going to ϕ," "I'm ϕ-ing," ". . . in
order to ϕ"—to provide elucidatory responses in a special interrogation of the
agent.

"Expression of intention" thus finds a narrower and a broader use in *Intention*: narrower, as one of the headings—"expressions of intention for the
future"—which brings the topic provisionally into view; more broadly, as the
genus—comprised of answers to the question "Why?"—which formally unites
the three divisions. This way of putting things seems to reverse Anscombe's

39. The italics are our notes.

better-known formula, according to which an intentional action is one *subject* to the question "Why?" But the possibility of such reversal is implicit in the chainlike structure of what Anscombe calls "the ABCD form" (p. 45), whereby a positive answer to the question "Why?" is itself the description of an intentional action, and, as such, subject to that question. Starting, then, with an intentional action, we can move forward along the chain by interrogating the action—"Why?" For just when this question has the relevant sense, positive answers to it are themselves expressions of the agent's intention.[40] But, starting from the same point, we can also move *backwards* along the chain, by remembering that an action, suitably described, is something which can be an agent's *answer* to the question "Why?" (i.e., asked about something else he is doing). Anscombe's ABCD form thus pictures intentional action as both ground and grounded, *explanans* and *explanandum,* something both subject to, and responsive to, a distinctive interrogation. And this is represented by saying that the unity of the three divisions lies in their fitness to appear in "expressions of intention" in the generic sense: answers to the question "Why?"

Summarizing, Anscombe's basic idea—her general strategy for discharging the explanatory task set in §1 of *Intention*—is this: (1) the applicability of the relevant question "Why?" is what marks anything out as an *expression of intention* (p. 90); (2) any expression of intention thus *subject* to the question "Why?" is fit also to *answer* a serially related question "Why?"; and (3) the unity of the trinity—intention in a proposed action, intention in a present action, and intentional action—is seen in this, that each is capable of being represented in an "expression of intention," furnishing an answer to a question "Why?" Thus represented (as answers in the interrogation of action), the three divisions are generally interchangeable: usually, "there isn't much to choose between them" (p. 40).

5. "In Terms of Language"

At this point, a contemporary action theorist might still ask: Why define intentional action "in terms of language" (p. 86)—a chain of questions "Why?" Obviously, the content of such exchanges—e.g., "Why are you lying on the

---

40. The relevant sense of the question "Why?" and the fact that positive answers to it are themselves expressions of intention, are mutually defining notions for Anscombe.

bed?"—"I'm doing Yoga"—might always be exhibited, apart from the inter-
rogative context, in a variety of ways, e.g., "A is lying on the bed because she
is doing (she intends/wants to do) Yoga." Such actions can and do take place
without anyone making any speeches![41] Wouldn't it be less obscure to factor
out references to questions and answers, and speak instead of intentional action as (e.g.) "action for a reason"? "Expression of intention," in that case,
needn't get any special emphasis.

One answer to this challenge lies simply in the fruitfulness of Anscombe's
expository procedure in revealing unity in the otherwise diverse materials of
action (cf. p. 80). Still, confidence in this procedure would improve if it became clearer how the specifically linguistic representation of intention really
is an aspect of the thing represented. A further answer might run: "Intentions, like other conditions of the person, may intelligibly be attributed only
insofar as they are publicly expressed." True enough. But Anscombe's expository procedure involves "expressions" of a quite special sort, those suited, we
may now say, to be a person's answers to a question addressed to him. No one
will be tempted to think of "expressions" in this sense as the only or canonical way in which various other conditions of the person get revealed. Is there
a reason to think that intention is different?

Return to that strange passage concerning animals (see section 1). Here
Anscombe does appear to say that intention is different in this respect, and
she even pauses to correct Wittgenstein on this point. Wittgenstein had
written:

> What is the natural expression [*Ausdruck*] of an intention?—Look at a cat
> when it stalks a bird; or a beast when it wants to escape. ((Connection with
> propositions about sensations.))[42]

But this "goes wrong," according to Anscombe: The expression of intention
"is purely conventional" or "linguistic." Animals thus "have intentions" but,
lacking language, don't *express* them.[43] What makes this proposition strange is
that while Anscombe (1) recognizes that intentions are manifest in nonverbal

41. Compare, *Intention,* 80: Like Aristotle's "practical reasoning," the "order of questions
'Why'? can be looked at as a device which reveals the order" in the diverse materials of action.
But Anscombe also points out: it is "as artificial as Aristotle's [construction]; for a series of
questions 'Why?' . . . with the appropriate answers, cannot occur very often."

42. Wittgenstein, *Philosophical Investigations,* §647.

43. This point appears twice in *Intention:* 5, 86–87.

behavior without further gloss;[44] and (2) allows the term "expression" application to the natural manifestation of other states (like emotion); she nonetheless (3) challenges Wittgenstein on this point: An animal's behavior isn't any *expression* of its intention. Taking it that "expression of intention" is a device for exhibiting the unity of "intention," this further problem is raised here: Is there a way of seeing Anscombe's Proposition—

> AP: There is no such thing as the natural (only the linguistic) expression of intention—

as informative rather than merely stipulative? A positive answer would make clearer how the representation of intention "in linguistic terms" comes, so to speak, with the matter itself.

To begin with, however, a few words about what this question is *not*.

As was said, questions concerning an animal's capacities aren't essential here. We are familiar in the human case with the distinctions—expression versus other indications, natural versus conventional expressions—invoked by Anscombe. Among us, there are both verbal and non-verbal expressions of fear, for instance. So if the expression of intention is purely linguistic, then it must be true of the man, and not just of the beast, that the movements of stalking a prey (or catching it and hauling it back to camp, etc.) aren't to be considered "expressions" of intention, notwithstanding that these movements make intentions manifest. Anscombe's point applies to all animals if it applies to any.

Similarly, questions concerning whether non-linguistic creatures can be credited with having intentions at all remain bracketed here. Negative judgments might seem to support Anscombe's linguistic procedure, since they often derive from a focus on the formation of plans or standing intentions—cases in which the basis for attributing intentions must go beyond natural behavior.[45] But not all intentions are standing ones or the result of making

---

44. See p. 8: "If you want to say at least some true things about a man's intentions, you will have a strong chance of success if you mention what he actually did or is doing." If intentions were not so legible, their personal expression would lack much of its point. Such expression gives another warrant to expect behavior of a certain describable shape, and this implies a general capacity to recognize another's behavior, when the time comes, as satisfying (or frustrating) those expectations.

45. See, e.g., Hampshire, *Thought and Action* (London: Chatto and Windus, 1959), 97–98. Relatedly, it is sometimes said that only linguistic creatures initiate action by deciding on it from among a range of alternatives. And, no doubt, we speak of "decisions," just where someone has, in effect, answered a question, or resolved their intentions against the background of other prospects. But these points are moot here, for the reasons explained in the text.

plans. And Anscombe's challenge to Wittgenstein, in any case, does not concern some purer type of standing intention, but just the immediate intentional action of the cat stalking the bird. To speak of "expression" in this case would be as inapt—she says—as calling "a car's stalling the expression of its being about to stop." Unobvious as this thesis is, it expresses no skepticism about the car's *being* about to stop, or about the engine evincing this fact. Likewise, Anscombe nowhere denies (rather, she consistently asserts) that the structures of action uncovered in her investigation apply beyond the human world (pp. 86–87).

Finally, it is worth noting that Anscombe's remarks on animals run contrary to recent arguments that enlist one of her ideas—viz., that actions are intentional "under a description"—in recommending the conclusion that neither intentions nor propositional attitudes are possible for creatures without a language. Davidson writes:

> One can intend to bite into the apple in the hand without intending to bite into the only apple with a worm in it. . . . The intensionality we make so much of in the attribution of thoughts is very hard to make much of when speech is not present. The dog, we say, knows that its master is home. But does it know that Mr. Smith (who is his master) or that the president of the bank (who is that same master), is home? We have no real idea how to settle, or make sense of, these questions.[46]

The intentionality of intentions does suggest that the capacity to recognize intentions in others is exclusive to the talking creatures, or those who interpret the talk of others. But if a creature does not recognize intentions, must it therefore have none of its own?[47] Notably, Anscombe insists that whatever may be "language-centered" in her account, and whatever the role of particular descriptions in delineating the intentional aspects of action, we do discern intentions in non-talking creatures:

> It sounds as if the agent had a thought about a description. But now let's suppose that a bird is landing on a twig so as to peck at bird-seed, but also that the twig is smeared with bird-lime. The bird wanted to land on

46. Davidson, "Thought and Talk," in *Truth and Interpretation,* 63.

47. Indeed, Michael Tomasello's reading of the empirical research on non-human primates defends just this position: While brutes have intentions, they fail to recognize intentions—and hence to distinguish ends from means, and both from the upshots of what is done—in others. See *The Cultural Origins of Human Cognition* (Cambridge, Mass.: Harvard University Press, 2001).

the twig all right, but it did not want to land on a twig smeared with bird-lime. . . . Landing on the twig was landing on bird-lime—we aren't considering two different landings. So, if we form definite descriptions, "the action (then) of landing on the twig", "the action (then) of landing on a twig with bird-lime on it", we must say they are definite descriptions satisfied by the same occurrence, which was something that the bird did, but under the one description it was intentional, under the other unintentional. That the bird is not a language-user has no bearing on this.[48]

We say the bird is intentionally landing on the twig (but not on the lime-twig) because we can see that "landing on a twig to peck at bird-seed" answers to purposes the bird is assumed to have, whereas "a twig smeared with lime" does not, even though we are talking about one and the same twig. We seek a description that makes what the bird did comprehensible within what we know the bird is seeking. A reference to the agent and its good does operate as a constraint here, but this needn't be a reference to the agent's psychology narrowly conceived, i.e., to what is thought or said. Rather, we apply the descriptions under which the creature's action is intentional, without supposing that the creature has such descriptions "in mind."

In sum, various questions concerning the attribution of intention to animals don't shed light on Anscombe's strictures on what an expression of intention can be. What could be at stake for her in refusing to apply the innocuous-sounding phrase "the natural expression of intention" both to humans and other animals? That is the nub of the problem.

6. What Natural Indications Can't Do: Contradiction, Commitment, Impugning the Facts

One possibility should be ruled out. Anscombe had better not be found saying that by "expression" she simply means expression in the personal sense. From this it would of course follow that animals do not express intention, for to *express* intention (or anything else) you've got to use language. But this

---

48. Anscombe, "Under a Description," in *Metaphysics and the Philosophy of Mind*, 208–219. This is in further explanation of her remark in *Intention*, 86–87: "We certainly ascribe intention to animals. The reason is that we describe what they do in a manner perfectly characteristic of the use of intention concepts: we describe what *further* they are doing *in* doing something. . . . We do this although the cat can utter no thoughts, and cannot give expression to any knowledge of its own action, or to any intentions either."

would be mere stipulation.[49] Against this, let it be clear that anyone can call non-verbal manifestations of intention "expressions" if they like—what to call things isn't the question. The question is what distinction Anscombe seeks to mark by refusing application of "expression" to natural manifestations of intention.[50] It looks like the answer must be: some distinction between the verbal and non-verbal manifestation of (1) intention on the one hand, and of (2) emotion (and other states) on the other. But what distinction? If a creature's stalking its prey is not to be considered an *expression* of intention, the interest of this thesis—what raises it above empty stipulation—must derive from a distinction we recognize here.

But there *is* a distinction to recognize here: Between natural behavior which manifests intention and the overt verbal expression of intention, there exists a gap in logical powers, without parallel in the case of emotion or other states.

To explain, it seems natural to speak contrastingly of natural *and* conventional "expressions" of, say, fear, precisely because, in this case, conventional expression can take up or perform the same work as natural expression—there is no gap. Otherwise put, the contrast (natural/conventional) is at home within a space of common functions, where verbal expression continues

49. This is just what is happening, according to Donald Gustafson, one of the few commentators to notice the problem. Concerned mainly to defend Wittgenstein, Gustafson criticizes Anscombe for overlooking this: "That a person's face has a determined look, while it does not imply that *he* expressed determination in the sense that his saying he is determined does so, is [nonetheless] an expression of determination or a determined expression." "The Natural Expressions of Intention," *Philosophical Forum* (Boston) 2 (Spring 1971): 299–315. The implication must be that *AP* joins no issue, since the impersonal sense in which Wittgenstein is asserting that the stalking cat expresses an intention isn't the personal sense in which Anscombe would be denying it. This resolution comes at the cost of making Anscombe incoherent, however; for if her point were merely that animals don't express their intentions in the personal sense—i.e., don't tell us of them—then she ought to have said the reverse of what she does: intention is *just like* emotion in this respect, for animals don't tell us of their emotions, or of their hopes and fears, either.

50. In point of fact, ordinary usage gives *AP* some support. One can express one's intention to turn right by making a hand gesture (since this is a "bodily movement with a conventional meaning": p. 5); but someone who begins to turn right is not "expressing an intention" to do so, even though that same movement might express his determination or his fear, and even though it may make his intentions (e.g., to turn right, to confuse the enemy, etc.) apparent to an observer. We need to see more clearly, however, what distinction language is harboring here.

(while also enhancing and rendering more precise) the same functions more primitively available by natural means.[51] The other's frightened look and his "I'm afraid" can convey the same thing—his fear. This isn't to say that natural expressions of fear are *given* to another or meant to inform him. But conventional expressions of fear aren't always *given* either.[52] When they are, however—and this is what matters here—what they overtly convey is what might also be read in the speaker's non-linguistic behavior. Verbal expressions of intention, in contrast, do not ever stand in for intentional behavior in this way. Certainly it would be wild to suggest that they are "learned as a substitute" for intentional behavior—one point subserved by the phrase "natural expression" as applied by Wittgenstein to emotions and sensations.[53] And as Wittgenstein himself notes, there isn't any distinctive behavioral repertoire of intentional action, as there is of emotional states and feelings.[54] No, the relation between verbal expressions of intention and intentional behavior is different from the relation between (e.g.,) verbal expressions of fear and natural fear-behavior. It is this: When an intention is verbalized, it specifies the performance to which the agent is committed in the future, or in which he is already engaged, and that performance may then be judged *correct* or *mistaken* in light of what is expressed.

So Anscombe is right to mark a difference here. Rather than standing in for performances in either a logical or developmental sense, expressions of intention have a force that no bit of natural behavior could have. Specifically, they make contradictable claims, and they require that something else one does then be regarded as correct or mistaken. Of course, we can sometimes see directly that someone is naturally barking up the wrong tree—say, merely running the brush along the wall when they mean to be painting the room yellow. But here it is important that we grasp a particular description of what

---

51. Of course, numerous states of the person—e.g., a dull throbbing in one's right knee; a slow, spreading fear in the pit of one's stomach—are manifested only in creatures who have the linguistic means to differentiate and report them. So conventional expression goes beyond natural expression. But the present point isn't that conventional expression *only* deputizes for what is already expressible by non-verbal behavior, only that it sometimes does.

52. Cf. Wittgenstein, *Philosophical Investigations,* 189.

53. Cf. ibid., §242; Wittgenstein, *Zettel,* §545.

54. See Wittgenstein, *Remarks on the Philosophy of Psychology,* vol. 2, trans. G. E. M. Anscombe (Oxford: Basil Blackwell, 1980), §179: "There is no cry of intention"—i.e., as there is a cry of pain, joy, grief, etc.

they are doing or intending to do, one which a human being could give in answer to the question "Why?"[55]

To develop the implications of this, a number of contrasts, so far mainly implicit in our discussion, may now be made more explicit. The upshot is that a number of related features—contradictability, claiming, commitment, and the impugning of performances—can be seen to make intention fit for a notion of "expression" that lacks a non-linguistic counterpart.

1. *Intentions are contradicted by other intentions.* Midway through the book, Anscombe asks, "What is the contradictory of a description of one's own intentional action?" She answers:

55. Even God's intentions, insofar as they are not expressed but merely revealed by history, do not impugn anything. For example, the regularity of the seasons does not afford a basis—as a verbal expression would—for regarding unseasonable rain as a divine mistake. See Anscombe, "Rule, Rights and Promises," in *Ethics, Religion and Politics: Collected Philosophical Papers,* vol. 3 (Oxford: Basil Blackwell, 1981), 99: "God himself can make no promises to man except in a human language."

The point of Anscombe's denying that an incipient course of action *expresses* intention (as a face or tone of voice expresses anger) might be approached another way, by considering what might serve to distinguish impersonal "expressions" from other signs or indications of a person's state. As Anscombe elsewhere remarks, "A man could be said not to have given expression to his anger at all—he merely brought it about that the man who had offended him was ruined or hanged." "Pretending," in *Metaphysics and the Philosophy of Mind: Collected Philosophical Papers,* vol. 2 (Minneapolis: University of Minnesota Press, 1981), 88. According to this, an expression is not a mere sign or indication, but what exactly is the difference? It seems correct to say: an expression allows for the possibility of retaining the concept in cases where what is expressed is absent; a mere sign or indication does not. Thus, we may say that the relation "X expresses Y" excludes cases in which the truth of the statement depends on the truth or actuality of Y. To illustrate: ruining him is not an expression of anger, for it is not anger which is expressed at all unless the person really is angry. In contrast, if X expresses Y, then Y is itself present in the expression X, as e.g., anger is present in the angry furrows in the face, whatever the person's state of mind. Hence it is possible to be surprised that (e.g.) a face expresses anger (e.g., since this person has no cause for complaint), whereas—since a person's action only manifests an intention to do what they are really doing or intending to do—there can't be any surprise that a bit of behavior manifests an intention to do such-and-such. Considered apart from their verbal expressability, intentions are sunk in facticity. This is why Anscombe suggests an analogy between the movements of the cat (as a basis for attributing intentions) and the car's stalling engine. Just as the engine's behavior indicates that the car is going to stop only if the car *is* going to stop, so the movements of the cat indicate only what it actually goes on to do.

> The contradiction of 'I'm replenishing the house water supply' is not 'You aren't, since there is a hole in the pipe', but 'Oh, no, you aren't' said by someone who thereupon sets out e.g., to make a hole in the pipe with a pick-axe. And similarly, if a person says 'I am going to bed at midnight', the contradiction of this is not: 'You won't, for you never keep such resolutions', but 'You won't, for I am going to stop you'. (p. 55)

To contradict an expression of intention is intentionally to oppose the act that the agent declares herself to be engaged in—i.e., what the agent is intent *upon*—rather than to assess the agent's states, dispositions, or other conditions affecting the likeliness of performance. Verbal expressions of emotions and desires can also be contradicted, of course, but what is denied, in that case, is the claim that the speaker *has* the item in question. Contradicting an agent's expression of intention to ϕ, in contrast, leaves no doubt—indeed, it presupposes—that she has the intention.

2. *Like a belief, the expression of intention makes a claim upon the world.* From (1), it follows that when Anscombe speaks of "expression of intention" as something that can be true or false, this means a true or false claim about what one is doing or will do, not a good or a bad indication of one's state of mind. Herein lies the aspect of intention that leads some theorists to see it as a kind of belief. If an ordinary assertion ("The train just left") is one canonical form of the expression of belief, its contradiction is the denial of what is claimed ("No, it hasn't left yet"), not the denial that this expression manifests the speaker's state of mind. Expressions of both belief and intention make claims that can be countered by the denial that things are or will be as they are declared to be.

3. *Yet, unlike a belief, the expression of intention can impugn what one does.* Against this background, Anscombe distinguishes an expression of intention, not only in terms of the applicability of the question "Why?" (p. 90), but also, initially, in terms of the impugning of performances:

> If I don't do what I said, what I said was not true. . . . But . . . this falsehood does not necessarily impugn what I *said*. In some cases the facts are, so to speak, impugned for not being in accordance with the words, rather than vice versa. This is sometimes so when I change my mind; but another

case of it occurs when, e.g., I write something other than I think I am writing: as Theophrastus says, the mistake here is one of performance, not of judgment. (pp. 4–5)

Putting this in terms of the previous point concerning contradiction, we may say: To contradict a prediction (or other expression of belief) is merely to deny a proposition of fact; to contradict an expression of intention is also to oppose what someone is *doing* or will do. This specifies a discontinuity between expressions and mere behavioral "indications" of intention. Anything that serves to indicate something (like the animal's intention to escape) will itself be the thing faulted or impugned when it fails to conform to what was putatively indicated. Where there is a clash between an indicator and what it purports to indicate, it is the indicator that stands to be corrected.

4. Practical knowledge: Expressions of intention are distinguished by the possibility of "mistakes in performance" and not otherwise by their "direction of fit." The last point touches on a larger theme of Anscombe's: No statement will count as an expression of intention unless it expresses "practical knowledge." If, for example, the speaker says, "I'm going to crush the snail" (or "I am crushing the snail") on the basis of his observation of forces impelling him to move, then this is no expression of his intention. Now in speaking of expressions of intention as expressing practical knowledge, Anscombe might be taken to mean, in part, that the fit between such knowledge and what is known runs in the opposite direction than it does in cases of belief. This comes out when the speaker is not in fact doing what he takes himself to be doing. Here, if the speaker's words are an expression of intention (rather than, e.g., a prediction), then the mistake will lie not in what the speaker thinks or says, but in what he is doing ("the mistake here is one of performance not of judgment").[56]

Understandably, then, an enduring legacy of Anscombe's monograph is the idea of "direction of fit." The only disappointing aspect of this legacy is that the phrase "direction of fit" doesn't actually occur at its source—and for good reason: while any talk of "knowledge" must find room for application of an idea of fit or accord, the fit present in cases of practical knowledge (or

56. For more on the notion of practical knowledge, see Richard Moran, "Anscombe on 'Practical Knowledge,'" in *Agency and Action,* ed. J. Hyman and H. Steward (Cambridge: Cambridge University Press, 2004), 43–68 (Royal Institute of Philosophy Supplement: 55).

absent in cases of its failure) isn't simply a matter of reversing the priority between the same two items which figure in cases of speculative knowledge; practical knowledge involves a distinctive class of items known. Unsurprisingly, then, Anscombe's distinction bears little resemblance to the contemporary one between the functional roles of belief and desire, defined in terms of different directions of fit between such states and "the world." Instead of "two directions," Anscombe speaks of a difference between a mistake in *what was said* and a mistake *in performance*.

What turns on this? Three things:

(A) *From expression of intention to desire.* The "fit" that concerns Anscombe involves conformity between an expression of intention—something said—and what the person actually does. In the contemporary functionalist account, by contrast, the focus is no longer on verbal expressions, but on states of belief and desire, the later being defined by the requirement of the world (or "the facts") conforming to fit *it* rather than vice versa.

(B) *From action to "the world."* With this shift in focus from intentions to desires goes naturally a transformation in how the other side of the relation—the world—is understood as well. When Anscombe speaks of "the facts [being] . . . impugned for not being in accordance with the words," the facts in question are someone's performance. But in the contemporary account, instead of a "mistake in performance"—an action characterized as needing correction—we are referred to some state of the world itself (e.g., the absence of the cool drink I am longing for) that is to be altered, made to conform to the state of desire.

(C) *Disappearance of the notion of "mistake."* With the foregoing shifts in the nature of the *relata* (a person's state rather than his statements, this state's relation to some state of the world rather than to the person's actions), the idea of "mistake" or "correction" disappears from the analysis. For there is no mistake on anyone's part, mine or God's, when something I desire is out of reach; and the facts comprising this aspect of the world are in no way *impugned* by my desire or its expression. Rather, my having this desire simply means, other things being equal, that I will strive to alter these facts in order to satisfy my desire.

Given this, it is perhaps easy to see why the contemporary functional account of desire, in terms of "direction of fit" between a person's state and the world, does not appear in Anscombe, though it is widely attributed to her. Very simply, it is difficult to see how we are to apply normative notions to either item. In contrast, the application of "mistake" to actions and statements—things done and said—remains straightforward: these are the very things to which notions of mistake, correction, rightness, etc., primarily apply.[57]

5. *Commitment.* Various theorists have seen in intentions a form of "commitment," even though "I'm going to . . ." is not a performative utterance, and the relevant notion of commitment is different from promissory commitment. (Anscombe's denial that there are natural expressions of intention would be straightforward if expressions of intention *were* performatives, speech-acts dependent on conventional means.) But although expressions of intention are not performatives, there is nonetheless a sense in which all intentions involve performances: from (1) above—to contradict an intention is to oppose an agent's action—it follows that an agent's expression of intention is itself a kind of engagement to act, not a mere revelation of his state of mind. (Contradiction is symmetrical.) *Self*-contradiction in intentions exhibits the same pattern. If my intention to fly to Boston conflicts with my intention to stay home this weekend, this is not because these two intentions characterize my state of mind as one that dooms me to some frustration whatever happens (as happens with conflicting desires). It is rather that I engage myself in both doing and not doing the same thing.

The way even pure intentions involve commitment is thus perhaps best understood in terms of the commissive aspect of action itself. Consider someone now engaged in writing the word "action." *That* is how someone who merely intends to write the word "action" is also engaged: he stretches himself toward the act, awaits himself in its successful completion.[58] The structure of intending to act, this is to say, is that of a performance, and, as such, something continuous with intentional action itself.

57. The source of the phrase "direction of fit" as attributed to Anscombe seems to be Mark Platts, *Ways of Meaning* (London: Routledge and Kegan Paul, 1979), 256–257. The transformation of her idea is already complete in this short passage, which re-writes her original thought about the relation between an expression of intention and what the person does as a claim about the relation between a state (desire) and the world: "Miss Anscombe, in her work on intention, has drawn a broad distinction between two kinds of mental state, factual belief being the prime exemplar of one kind and desire a prime exemplar of the other [Anscombe, *Intention,* §2]. The distinction is in terms of the direction of fit of mental states with the world."

58. See Luca Ferrero, "Intending and Doing" (manuscript), which stresses the active quality of such "waiting" (monitoring for interferences, commitment of resources, etc.) in the usual case.

Of course, an intention for the future may be cancelled, blocked, or otherwise never realized. Hence an objection arises here. What sort of "commitment" is it that can be unilaterally rescinded by the agent, without penalty, simply by a change of mind?[59] This argument proves too much, however. If it implies there is no sense of "commitment" independent of obligation, it will follow that even someone now doing X—say, conducting a war in a foreign country—hasn't committed himself to anything, for this action may also be cancelled or blocked at any stage before its perfection. The completion of any extended action requires the agent's continuing assent; as Sartre puts it, there always remains the possibility of "putting [the] act into question."[60] So the fact that an agent may change his mind doesn't distinguish the commissive quality of pure intending from those paradigmatic commitments that are his temporally extended actions. Remembering the idea of spectrum at work here, we therefore affirm that a good analogue of "intending" can be found in someone's doing something.[61]

Less metaphorically, the point is just that intention in a future action does not differ fundamentally from intention in (a present) action, or from intentional action. All alike, as Anscombe taught, are fit to be taken up in "expressions of intention," conceived as answers to the question "Why?" All alike are engagements of agency, and enter into the structure of commitment, contradiction, and impugning which characterizes performances as opposed to paradigmatic "states." All involve an agent stretching toward a describable future which is not-yet.[62]

To summarize: with the verbal expression of intention a discontinuity with natural manifestation arises, and it is this that Anscombe seeks to mark.

59. See Davidson, "Intending," 90.

60. See the opening quotation from Sartre, *Being and Nothingness,* trans. Hazel Barnes (New York: Citadel Press, 1964), 37.

61. Or better, their "being *engaged* in doing something": the word "engaged" straddles the sense of (1) doing something and (2) being committed—in a non-promissory sense—to doing something.

62. We agree with Ferrero's conclusion (see note 51 above) that intending is a kind of performance that is continuous in structure with intentional action, so that to intend to φ to is be (already) engaged in φ-ing. As Ferrero puts it, "Future directed intending is not a truly separate phenomenon from either the intending in action or the acting itself. Ultimately, all intentions are in action, or better still, in extended courses of action."

Such expressions introduce something new: a characterization of what one is doing—what larger action one's actions are part of or toward which they are aimed. Expressions of intention are thus "world-directed," but not just in the way that expressions of states like belief or hope are: they make possible the application of the notion of "mistake" to performances, and they express practical commitments.

7. Homage Revisited

We conclude with: (1) three overlapping ways of making more precise the necessity of representing intention in terms of its verbal expression, and (2) a comment on one prominent theme.

(1) *First,* it might be said that only verbal expressions of intention exhibit the responsiveness of the person to the special question "Why?" This question may apply to the bird pecking at the lime twig as much as to the man putting on his coat. The man, however, is in a position not only to answer the question, but also to refuse it application in a given formulation, as when he says that, as described in *those* terms, he was not aware he was doing *that.* (The bird is not expected to play any role in refusing application to the question "Why?") Both acknowledging and refusing application of a certain question "Why?" are part of the agent's understanding of his action as goal directed. Refusing one application of the question makes the agent subject to some other application of it. ("If you weren't intentionally sawing the last plank of oak, then what *were* you doing? What did you *take yourself* to be doing?") The answer to such a question *gives the terms* in which the action is to be seen as intentional (the point of the activity, the good of it, what is being pursued). The role of the refusal of application to a particular "Why?" question marks the fact that an action will have conditions of success or failure only as described in certain ways and not others. In answering this question, an expression of intention spells out the aim that some piece of behavior is guided by and to which the person is seeking to conform the rest of his action (i.e., the larger actions in Anscombe's ABCD structure). Aims have a linguistic structure in this sense, that the objects we handle in the world (and the movements we make in handling them) are multiply describable, and only a fraction of these descriptions will be relevant to what makes the results something aimed for.

Second, only when intention is not merely indicated, but verbalized as a statement of what one is doing, do we see how its expression could be something in light of which a performance might be mistaken or corrected. For only a statement—a claim upon the world established independently of the regularities it seeks to track—could be in a position to impugn the facts. The content of an expression of intention will have to be conventionally or linguistically determined if it is to serve as an independent standard of this sort.

Finally, only a verbal expression of intention can directly display the unity of "intention" as it occurs in "intending to X" and "an intentional action." What is needed here is essentially the notion of expression we see at work in the description of *what* one is doing as, e.g., replenishing the water supply. When it comes to human actions, "the description of what we are interested in is a type of description that would not exist if our question 'Why?' did not" (p. 83).

Developing this formula, we might say: For every answer to the special "Why?" question there is a complementary answer to a special question "What?" applied to someone's performance. That is, because "intentional" applies to action itself (and not just to something in the mental history of the agent causing action), a true and positive answer to the question "Why?" tells us not merely why some event is taking place, but also *what* is happening, in terms of an action being performed. Thus, building on Anscombe's remark that there isn't "much to choose between [the answers] 'She is making tea' and 'She is putting on the kettle in order to make tea'—i.e., 'She is going to make tea,'" we might add: there often isn't much to choose between the *questions* "Why are you messing about with the kettle" and "What are you doing messing about with the kettle?" The answer to either question will be an expression of intention in the sense canvassed here in terms of the predicates of "contradictability," "commitment," "world-directedness," and "mistake in performance." That the concept of intention applies across the performative spectrum, on the one hand, and that the answer to the special question "Why?" tells us also *what* is happening, amount here to the same thing. In action, the What appears together with—is already made for—an answer to the question "Why?" This serves to distinguish action from other phenomena in nature, where the identification of <What is to be explained> is independent of how its interrogation in terms of "Why?" may turn out.[63]

---

63. In this connection, see recent work of Pamela Hieronymi, where actions as well as attitudes are not only understood as embodying reasons, but more specifically where the relevant notion of "reason" is the more articulated one of "a consideration that bears on a *ques-*

(2) Anachronistically put, Anscombe shows what is at best optional in the contemporary view that we understand what intention is only by asking what the mental state of intending is and how it could causally contribute to the production of intentional action. In place of this, she stresses the conceptual unity of a certain trinity: a single concept at work along a spectrum of cases, including "pure" intending, intentions in action and intentional action. There is irony in the fact that one of her aims was to break up the sense of sharp distinctions among the divisions she is credited with having discerned. There is also a danger that recognition of this point will involve attributing to Anscombe the thesis that "intention" isn't a mental state at all, as happens in the behaviorist reading. But what Anscombe denies is only that we understand how to apply the notion of a "state" here, on the basis of its application in other contexts like those of belief and desire.

In fact, *TA* inches toward the same conclusion, for its more recent discoveries might be represented like this: No psychology will afford the right materials for explaining action that does not make use of a concept which applies throughout the spectrum of unfolding action, i.e., which has the same internal complexity as action itself. Intuiting this, it becomes natural, within the framework of *TA,* to seek an enhanced psychology of states, one which might include such items as intending, planning, or even believing or wanting in some special sense. No doubt there are such states of mind, in the anodyne sense that human agents do intend, plan, want, etc. But the point to

---

tion," as distinct from the more primitive one of "a consideration in favor of" (which might apply equally to considerations in favor of *having* some belief as well as to considerations in favor of its truth). In "The Wrong Kind of Reason," *The Journal of Philosophy* 102, no. 9 (September 2005): 437–457; and "Controlling Attitudes," *Pacific Philosophical Quarterly* 87, no. 1 (March 2006): 45–74, the appeal to the applicability of a certain range of questions as constituting the action or the attitude is motivated in part by reference to Anscombe's "Why?" question.

The systematic unity of action's "What?" and "Why?" might be thought of as Anscombe's central theme. She shows that: (1) An expression of *what* an agent is doing characterizes an intentional action only insofar as there is an answer to the question of *why* she is doing it (in the relevant, reason-involving sense); (2) positive answers to the interrogation *why* themselves characterize *what* the agent is intentionally doing (at least up to the point where use of the progressive gets linguistically denied); and (3) any expression of *what* an agent is doing is itself the answer to a question *why,* directed at something else she is doing.

grasp is that *leading* one's sense of the psychological materials needed (for connecting the various uses of intention) is a prior understanding of what intentional action is. To make that understanding explicit was Anscombe's problem.

To elaborate, suppose the contemporary action theorist inspired, by the felt necessities of his material, to introduce a special psychological state called "intending" or "planning" (call it X-ing: the name doesn't matter). His avowed task is to analyze it and to explain the behavior-involving uses of intention on the basis of their relation to it. But if X-ing is even to seem to be fit for this employment, it had better admit of internally nested relations (parts and wholes) of the sort exhibited in explanations like:

- "A is X-ing to φ because he is ψ-ing" (A is planning to buy lumber because he is building a tree house: the "state" of X-ing explained in terms of a larger whole of action.)
- "A is X-ing to φ because he is X-ing to ψ" (A is planning to buy lumber because he is planning to build a tree house: the "state" of X-ing explained by reference to a different occurrence of X-ing, one directed upon a wider description of the action.)
- "A is φ-ing because he is X-ing to ψ" (A is getting his car keys because he is planning to buy lumber: an action explained by reference to the "state" of X-ing.)

The nature of the pressure to endow action theory with an enhanced psychology of states can be represented concisely, in Anscombe's terms, like this: However we wish to understand the relevant action-theoretic state of X-ing, it ought to be the sort of thing about which it makes sense to ask "Why?" (i.e., for what purpose) one is X-ing-to-do-something, and to answer this by reference to other things one is X-ing-to-do or other things one is doing. And of course, the expression of this "state" will have to partake of the structure of contradiction, action-characterization, and correction of performances (as identified through X-characterizing descriptions).

"Intending" and "planning," in idiomatic employments, do fit this special bill of requirements. But, as our discussion should make clear, that is because the basic psychological item needed must be: X-ing *to do something*. That is, X-ing, whatever it is, must inherit through its object (a performance), just the distinctive structure characteristic of intentional action. And as Anscombe's problem was just to make that basic structure explicit, this suggests a route by which *TA*—after discoveries about the enhanced psychology of states it requires—might at length pay a more unqualified and accurate homage to Anscombe.[64]

64. A special thanks to Mathew Boyle and Doug Lavin for a series of conversations about action at the Garden of Eden in Boston, and for their comments on an earlier draft; to Jonathan Lear, Candace Vogler, and Constantine Sandis for their comments on an earlier draft; to David Velleman, for his comments at the 2006 Central Division APA, and to members of workshops at the University of Chicago, the University of Pittsburgh, the University of Southern California, and Uppsala University, where this paper was discussed. An earlier version of this essay appeared in Constantine Sandis, ed., *New Essays on the Explanation of Action* (New York: Palgrave Macmillan, 2009); reproduced with permission of Palgrave Macmillan.

2

Action and Generality

ANTON FORD

1. Methods and Division

Among the events of the natural world, the actions of a human being are thought to be somehow special. But what is it that makes them so? The standard approach to this question proceeds by a method of division. Because certain things that happen are the fruit and flower of the human will, while others clearly are not, philosophers tend to first distinguish an "action" from a "mere event." And because certain actions, though they spring from the will, do so only indirectly, or directly but imperfectly, a second distinction is frequently drawn between that which is action in a qualified sense—because it is unintentional, or idle, or addictive, or subconscious, or weak-willed, or compelled by force, or what have you—and that which is action unqualifiedly, or action par excellence.

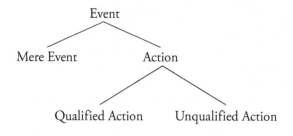

When confronted with these canonical divisions, it is common to suppose that the primary task of the philosopher of action is to hound down the differentiae—to say what an event must be, over and above being an event, in order to be an action, or to say what an action must be, in addition to being an action, in order to be an action in the full and proper sense.[1]

Indeed, some such thought is implicit in a question that was famously posed by Wittgenstein: "What is left over if I subtract the fact that my arm goes up from the fact that I raise my arm?"[2] Wittgenstein's question appears to be concerned with the first of the two now familiar divisions, but it is easily redeployed in connection with the second: "What is left over," one might also ask, "if I subtract the fact that I raise my arm from the fact that I raise it *intentionally*—or *whole-heatedly*, or *autonomously*, or *freely?*" Of course, the idea of subtraction entails the idea of a corresponding addition. So Wittgenstein's question appears to assume a certain conception of what it is to be an action, according to which an action is, as it were, the arithmetic sum of an event and something else. On the model of, for example, this equation: $7 + x = 12$, we are led to imagine this one: *event* + y = *action,* and also, by extension, this one: *action* + z = *intentional action.*[3]

There is reason to think that in Wittgenstein's own opinion, the question he posed was deeply misguided, in which case he sought to expose it as such, and not to inaugurate a program of research.[4] Be that as it may, his question has come to serve as a ritual starting point for the prevailing sort of account in the philosophy of action—the sort of account associated with Donald

1. For an especially clear example of this, see J. David Velleman, "Introduction," in *The Possibility of Practical Reason* (Oxford: Clarendon Press, 2000).

2. Ludwig Wittgenstein, *Philosophical Investigations,* trans. G. E. M. Anscombe (Oxford: Basil Blackwell, 1953), §621.

3. Someone noticing Wittgenstein's reference to "facts" might be led to imagine equations like the ones in the text above, but with, e.g., "fact of the occurrence of an event" and "fact of the occurrence of an action" in place of "event" and "action," respectively. However exactly the putative equations are formulated, the attempt to solve them will amount to a search for differentiae and will come within the scope of these remarks.

4. In reply to his own question, Wittgenstein writes: "When I raise my arm I do not usually *try* to raise it" (*Philosophical Investigations,* §622). Whether or not it is true, the *point* of this remark is evidently to insist that the difference between the action of my raising my arm and the event of my arm's just going up cannot be explained by appeal to an inner state of *trying,* or (presumably) *willing,* or *intending*—an appeal that is more or less inevitable the minute one attempts to say "what is left over."

Davidson and Harry Frankfurt, and developed more recently by J. David Velleman, Michael Bratman, Alfred Mele, and Michael Smith.[5] What these and many other theories have in common is that they undertake to answer a version of Wittgenstein's question.[6] Insofar as they do, they must assume what the question itself assumes: namely, that there is some describable addendum in virtue of which an event is an action, or in virtue of which an action is action par excellence.

G. E. M. Anscombe rejected this assumption and with it Wittgenstein's question. It is clear, moreover, that her rejection of it was a fundamental aspect of her thinking about action, and not a small or peripheral thesis, which an otherwise sympathetic reader might casually disregard. Anscombe framed her whole account of intentional action in explicit opposition to the idea that an action is intentional in virtue of any "mere *extra feature* of events whose description would otherwise be the same."[7] The latter formulation appears to be a reference to Aristotle's definition of an accident as "something which may either belong, or not belong to some self-same thing"

---

5. Donald Davidson, *Essays on Actions and Events* (Oxford: Clarendon Press, 1980); Harry G. Frankfurt, *The Importance of What We Care About* (Cambridge: Cambridge University Press, 1988); J. David Velleman, *Practical Reflection* (Princeton: Princeton University Press, 1989) and *The Possibility of Practical Reason;* Michael Bratman, *Faces of Intention* (Cambridge: Cambridge University Press, 1999); Alfred Mele, *Springs of Action* (New York: Oxford University Press, 1992); and Michael Smith, *Ethics and the A Priori: Selected Essays on Moral Psychology and Meta-Ethics* (New York: Cambridge University Press, 2004). Other prominent examples include John Bishop, Myles Brand, Fred Dretske, Berent Enç, Carl Ginet, Alvin Goldman, Gilbert Harman, and John Searle.

6. The precise terms of the Wittgensteinian equation are different for different philosophers. Davidson's starting point is implicitly that of an event. But other philosophers begin from something rather more determinate. Some begin from the idea of "behavior"— meaning by this *anything* that a person may be said "to do" (even, for example, forgetting something)—and proceed to ask what must be added to *that* (see Kieran Setiya, *Reasons without Rationalism* (Princeton: Princeton University Press, 2007), 24n8. For most, though, the starting point is the still more determinate idea of a "bodily movement." Speaking for the field at large, Arthur Danto wrote, "An action [is] a movement of the body plus $x \ldots$ and the problem . . . is to solve in some philosophically interesting way for x." *The Transfiguration of the Commonplace: A Philosophy of Art* (Cambridge, Mass.: Harvard University Press, 1981), 5.

7. G. E. M. Anscombe, *Intention,* 2nd ed. (Cambridge, Mass.: Harvard University Press, 2000), 88; and compare 29–30, 84–89.

(*Topics,* 102b6–7).[8] So Anscombe rejected what might be called an "accidentalist" account of intentional action.

Of course, Anscombe did not deny that various things are true of an action if and only if it is intentional, so that there are, if you like, many "qualities" or "features" that all and only intentional actions bear. What she denied is only the claim that action is intentional *in virtue of bearing* the putative marks. She denied, in other words, that any such thing could provide an understanding of what it is *to be* an intentional action. Speaking of the familiar Davidsonian account, she says: "Something I do is not made into an intentional action by being caused by a belief and desire, even if the descriptions fit."[9] Anscombe is thus willing to allow, at least for the sake of argument, that the proposed descriptions "fit" their object. Her position is that, *even if they fit*—still, they do not explain.

The accidentalist account that Anscombe attributes to Davidson, and that she herself rejects, is the product of what she calls "the standard approach" in the philosophy of action. This approach has two steps. The first step is preliminary, but nevertheless crucial: it is to isolate a putative genus under which the object of inquiry falls as a species, and to suppose that the genus has already been understood—not, perhaps, that we ourselves have understood it, but merely that it is the object of some prior investigation. The second step yields the substance of the accidentalist account: it is to explain how the salient species differs from everything else of the same genus. So understood, the standard approach might be brought to bear on either of the two canonical divisions: one might take for granted the genus *event* and hunt for the differentia of *action;* or one might take for granted the genus *action* and hunt for the differentia of, say, *intentional action.*

Anscombe's opposition to the standard approach, and to the resulting accidentalist account, has never attracted much attention—not even from those philosophers, like Kieran Setiya and J. David Velleman, who adopt

8. *The Complete Works of Aristotle,* vol. 2, ed. Jonathan Barnes, trans. W. A. Pickard-Cambridge (Princeton: Princeton University Press, 1984).

9. One might question whether Davidson really held the view that Anscombe here attributes to him, and my point is not to endorse her attribution. What matters is only that Anscombe's interpretation of Davidson is the usual one, especially among philosophers who defend an accidentalist account. For Anscombe's criticism of Davidson, see "Practical Inference," reprinted in Rosalind Hursthouse, Gavin Lawrence, and Warren Quinn, eds., *Virtues and Reasons* (New York: Oxford University Press, 1995), 3.

such an approach, offer such an account, and cite Anscombe as a major influence.[10] If it is mentioned at all, it is usually dismissed as the expression of "behaviorism," which Anscombe is supposed to have inherited from Wittgenstein. This, however, is unconvincing, not only because Anscombe explicitly rejects behaviorism, but also because her denial of an "extra feature" is, on the face of it, a much more radical claim.[11] And yet, what has made it possible for philosophers to ignore the *true* source of Anscombe's opposition is in part the fact that she herself says little to explain it. Anscombe gives only one terse argument, appearing in a single dense paragraph of *Intention*, §19, where she claims to establish that "we do not add anything attaching to the action at the time it is done by describing it as intentional."[12] The argument is tremendously obscure. But even if it could be clarified, and were sound, it would not, I think, succeed in uprooting the standard accidentalist account. This is because even if her argument proved that, in fact, there is no "extra feature"—still, it would not address the most difficult question, which is how there could fail to be

---

10. See Velleman, *Practical Reflection*, and Setiya, *Reasons without Rationalism*.

11. Anscombe is called a "behaviorist," one gathers, because she openly opposes any attempt to account for intentional action by reference to mental states and other psychic phenomena. But to suppose that this rejection of psychologism explains her opposition to the standard approach is in fact to invert the order of her thought. Anscombe's claim is categorical: according to her, there is *no* feature—*none whatsoever*—in virtue of which an action is intentional. It follows as a mere trivial consequence of this claim that an action is not intentional in virtue of this or that particular feature. So, to take one instance, on a par with any other: an action is not intentional in virtue of its being related thus-and-so to the agent's "inner states." Anscombe does not deny the existence of a definitive "extra feature" because she rejects a psychological account; rather, she rejects a psychological account because she denies the existence of a definitive "extra feature." Of course, if that is true, then for the same reason that Anscombe rejects psychologism, she must also reject behaviorism. After all, it *also* follows from her categorical claim—and every bit as trivially—that an action is not intentional in virtue of its being related thus-and-so to the agent's "overt behavior." Psychologism and behaviorism involve exactly the same commitment to a definitive "extra feature," and differ over the question of *which* feature is definitive. Both are thus equally good examples of the standard two-step approach, whereby we first isolate a genus and then ask what distinguishes the relevant species from all of its congenerics. For Anscombe's view of behaviorism, see "Analytic Philosophy and the Spirituality of Man," in *Human Life, Action and Ethics: Essays by G. E. M. Anscombe,* ed. Mary Geach and Luke Gormally (Charlottesville, Va.: Imprint Academic, 2005).

12. Anscombe, *Intention,* 28.

one.[13] In the end, what maintains the standard approach in its dominant position is not the idea that there *is* an "extra feature," of the sort that Anscombe denied, so much as the idea that there *must* be one, as a matter of logical or metaphysical necessity.

One might complain on these grounds that Anscombe failed to establish a basic tenet of her theory. In any event, it is fair to say that she did not prepare one to receive it. My principal effort, here, is to make such preparations. In section 2 I will explain how there could possibly fail to be an "extra feature" in terms of which to forge the contrast between something somehow general and something more specific—between a genus, like *event,* and a species, like *action.* Doing so will require me to distinguish three different forms of generality. These three forms are associated, respectively, with the traditional ideas of an accident, a category, and an essence; and I will therefore speak of generality as being accidental, categorial, or essential. The purpose of this preliminary foray into extra-practical territory is to raise the following question: "What kind of generality is exemplified by each of the two canonical divisions drawn in the philosophy of action?"

As soon as this question is properly framed, it will have become apparent that what Anscombe called the standard approach depends upon a gross, but undefended, assumption. The assumption is that *both* of the two canonical divisions are examples of the same particular form of generality—the one I label "accidental"—this one being the only form that permits itself to be explained by reference to genus and differentia. To see this assumption *as* an assumption is already, I think, to make significant progress. If nothing else, one will have seen what it means to affirm or deny the existence of an "extra feature." And this, I think, has not always been clear.

In the latter, more speculative part of the essay, I will argue that the standard assumption is false on both counts, so that neither of the two canonical divisions is mediated by a differentia. My aim in what follows is therefore predominantly negative: it is in effect to reanimate Anscombe's claim that

13. Anscombe's argument is a classical *reductio ad absurdum:* she assumes the targeted proposition and argues that it leads to incoherence. The problem with such an argument is that it fails to address the philosophical motivation of the one whose position is under attack. The details of Anscombe's *reductio* are discussed by Rosalind Hursthouse, "Intention," in *Logic, Cause and Action,* ed. Roger Teichmann (Cambridge: Cambridge University Press, 2000), and by Candace Vogler, *Reasonably Vicious* (Cambridge, Mass.: Harvard University Press, 2002), 213–229.

the standard approach in the philosophy of action "leads us into inextricable confusions, and we must give it up."[14]

2. Three Forms of Generality

2.1 Accidental Generality

If the standard approach appears, at first blush, utterly beyond criticism, the reason is in some part simply this: every action is an event, but not every event is an action; and every intentional action is an action, but not every action is intentional. Let us say that B is a "species" of A, and that A is conversely a "genus" of B, if something's being B entails that it is A, but something's being A does not entail that it is B. Then *action* is a species of *event,* and *intentional action* of *action.*

This alone does not, in fact, support the standard approach. But it does if combined with the reflex assumption that wherever there is a contrast between a species and its genus, there must also be a differentia in terms of which to understand the contrast. The latter idea appears to be so obviously true that any claim to the contrary is apt to be met with bafflement. One is sure there must be *something* the presence of which accounts for the specificity of the species, and the absence of which explains the generality of the genus. And it is, at bottom, this idea that gives the standard approach its air of unquestionable legitimacy. Nevertheless, as we will see, the common reflex assumption is false: there is not for every difference a differentia.

Certainly, there is *one* kind of species–genus relation that *is* mediated by an "extra feature." To borrow a famous example from Aristotle, every snub nose is a nose, but not every nose is snub: so *snub nose* is a species of *nose.* And no great difficulty is posed by the equation: $nose + x = snub\ nose$. What is left over, if you subtract the fact that Socrates has a nose from the fact that he has a snub nose, is whatever it is to be concave. So here there is a definitive "extra feature." Or, to take another example, this time from Chisholm, every brother is a male, but not every male is a brother. Again, there is a straightforward solution to the equation: $male + y = brother$. What is left over, if you subtract the fact that I am a male from the fact that I am a brother, is whatever it is to be a sibling.

14. Anscombe, *Intention,* 29.

Let us consider the equation *"nose + concavity = snub nose"* in a little more detail. That which is represented by the first term of the equation—i.e., the genus—is independent from that which is represented by the other two terms. It is "independent" in the following sense: in order to explain what a nose is, one need not make reference to, much less explain, either what concavity is or what a snub nose is. Meanwhile, that which is represented by the second term of the equation—i.e., the differentia—enjoys exactly the same independence. One need not make reference to, or explain, either what a nose is or what a snub nose is, in order to explain what concavity is. By contrast, that which is represented by the third term of the equation—i.e., the species—is utterly dependent on that which is represented by the other two terms: in order to explain what a snub nose is, one must not only mention, but explain, *both* what a nose is *and* what concavity is.

Where the contrast between a species and its genus is mediated by an independent quality, or "accident," and where, consequently, a two-step approach is required to account for the species, I will call the latter an *accidental species.*

The account of an accidental species presupposes that of its genus, because the species is itself a secondary, or derivative kind of thing. Something belongs to an accidental species in virtue of belonging to the relevant genus, and not the other way around. Something is a snub nose in virtue of being *inter alia* a nose; it is not a nose in virtue of being a snub nose. And someone is a brother because he is a male, a male who happens to be a sibling; he is certainly not a male because he is a brother. Here the genus is not only logically more abstract than its species, but also metaphysically more fundamental. This is no doubt a very important form of generality. It is not, however, the only form.

2.2 *Categorial Generality*

2.2.1 THE CATEGORIAL SPECIES AND ITS GENUS. Every horse is an animal, but not every animal is a horse: so *horse* is a species of *animal*—as indeed one would expect. But to the question, "What is left over if I subtract the fact that Bucephalus is an animal from the fact that he is a horse?" no answer is forthcoming. The question assumes that Bucephalus is a horse in virtue of something additional to—and thus separable from—his animality, whereas in fact his being a horse is nothing but the determinate form that his animality takes. In that case, however, there is no solution to the equation: $animal + x = horse$. Or, to take another example, everything red is colored, but not everything colored is red: so *red* is a species of *color*. About this case, A. N. Prior writes:

> We do sometimes call "the red" and "the blue" species of "the coloured"; though we do not do so . . . because the red possesses some quality added to or conjoined with its colour, and the blue possesses some different quality added to or conjoined with its colour—some quality which, in each case, might have been given first, and "coloured" added on afterwards. The colour of what is red is its redness; and the colour of what is blue is its blueness; we can say that the red and the blue agree in being coloured, but of their difference we can only say either that their colour is different, or that one is red and the other blue.[15]

If "the color of what is red is its redness," then no version of Wittgenstein's question is legitimate, here, because no value can solve for the equation: $color + y = red$. Following W. E. Johnson and others, Prior calls *red* a "determinate" and *color* a "determinable."[16] Though I will sometimes speak this way myself, I will in general prefer the terms "categorial species" and "categorial genus," as these tend to give some indication—if only a very vague one—of the kind of specificity and generality that is at issue.[17]

15. A. N. Prior, "Determinables, Determinates, and Determinants (I)," *Mind* 58 (1949): 5–6.

16. The *locus classicus* of the determinable–determinate relation is the eleventh chapter of Johnson's *Logic,* Pt. I (Cambridge: Cambridge University Press, 1921), 173–185. Before Johnson, Brentano discussed the relation, which he attributed to Aristotle, under the name "one-sided detachability" (or "one-sided separability"); see *The Theory of Categories* (The Hague: Martinus Nijhoff, 1981), 111–116, and *Descriptive Psychology* (Hamburg: Miener Verlag, 1982), 12–19. Brentano's view is discussed by Chisholm in "Brentano on One-Sided Detachability," *Conceptus* 21 (1987): 153–154. Chisholm introduces the idea to action theory in "Adverbs and Subdeterminates," in *Actions and Events: Perspectives on the Philosophy of Donald Davidson,* ed. Ernest LePore and Brian McLaughlin (Oxford: Basil Blackwell, 1987). The idea has recently been put to work outside of action theory by Timothy Williamson, *Knowledge and Its Limits* (Oxford: Oxford University Press, 2000), 1–48.

17. A note on terminology. The relation between *nose* and *snub nose* shares something in common with the relation between *color* and *red;* and it is most natural to characterize what is common by saying that the first term in each pair is "general" and the second is "specific"; I therefore speak of a "genus" and of a "species" in both sorts of case. In order to mark that something is different in the second sort of case, I have elected to speak of a "categorial genus"

The distinction between accidental and categorial generality is revealed by the fact that no quality can account for the contrast between a categorial species and its genus—or, at any rate, no quality that is logically independent of the species. Concavity, the quality that distinguishes a snub nose from all the rest, is not a quality unique to snub noses: it belongs to many other sorts of things and has, as it were, a life of its own. But if there is a quality that distinguishes a horse from all other animals, it is a quality that nothing could possibly have except a horse. On the one hand, obviously, no other animal could have it, or else the quality would not be distinctive. On the other hand, less obviously, nothing could have it except an animal. It is true that a horse differs from an octopus in various respects, and that in many of these it also differs from an iceberg: e.g., in respect of its weight, smell, texture, volume, temperature, and flammability. But a horse also differs from an octopus in ways that it could only differ from another animal: e.g., in respect of its organs and

---

and of a "categorial species." This is preferable to speaking of a "determinable genus" and a "determinate species," first, because that could easily be construed as "general genus" and "specific species," which is clearly uninformative. A second reason for not speaking of "determinables" and "determinates"—despite the obvious attractions of maintaining continuity with the tradition—is that in the literature following Johnson these terms have become too closely associated with a certain particular array of examples. The favorites include color, shape, pitch, and pressure—all of which bring with them a "dimension of difference" by reference to which the determinates may differ *by degrees*. This narrow focus is, I think, an unfortunate limitation of the received conception of "determinability." It obscures the fact, which Brentano emphasized, that we have to do with the same phenomenon that Aristotle identified in connection with his categories—and not just the category of *quality*, where distinctions of degree are at home.

Not everything that I call a "categorial species" is a "category" in any traditional sense: *horse*, for example, is not. What makes it fitting to call *horse* a "categorial species" is the fact that, although it is not itself a category, it is a general determination of one—viz., the category of *substance*. Thus, in speaking of the contrast between a categorial genus and its species, I mean to pick out an extremely abstract phenomenon—one that is exhibited in the relation between two categories, where one is "higher" and the other "lower" (e.g., *substance* and *organism*), but a phenomenon that is *also* exhibited in the admittedly very different relation between a category and a concrete form falling under it (e.g., *organism* and *horse*). For many philosophical purposes, the important relation will be the first, which has only to do with "pure" or "formal" concepts. In fact, I think that on Anscombe's view "action" is precisely such a concept, defining a category subordinate to *event*, so that a true vindication of her positive view would require one to elucidate the inter-categorial nexus. I do not undertake that here, because the argument of this essay, which is primarily negative, does not require it, and because I think that the more abstract phenomenon is of considerable interest in its own right.

members, and in respect of its manner of nourishing itself, and of reproducing, and of moving itself from place to place. The latter are differences internal to the genus. Just as what is red and what is blue differ in respect of color, and what is a square and what is a circle differ in respect of shape, and what is over here and what is over there differ in respect of place, so, too, what is a horse and what is an octopus differ in respect of animality. And this is the respect that matters, if what we aim to understand is the nature of a horse—this is the respect in which we must reveal it as "distinct." Now given that only what is an animal can be alike or different in respect of animality, and given that whatever is indistinguishable from a horse in respect of animality is a horse—given all that, it is clear that if there is, in fact, a quality that distinguishes a horse in the salient respect, this must be a quality that nothing could possibly have except a horse. And similarly, if there is, in fact, a quality "added to or conjoined with" a thing's being colored, in virtue of which it is red, this must be a quality that only a color could possess, and only red among colors.

No such quality could ever fulfill the explanatory function of a differentia, because it is logically dependent on the *explanandum*. Since such a quality can in principle only belong to one kind of thing, an account of the quality will have to make reference to this very kind of thing: there is, by hypothesis, no other way for the intellect to grasp it. But then it will be *circular* to appeal to such a quality in an account of the kind of thing to which it belongs.

The circularity is important, for our purposes, because it shows that a philosophical account of a categorial species must be altogether different from that of an accidental species. It is necessary, as we saw in the previous section, to proceed from a prior understanding of the genus, *nose,* to a posterior understanding of the species, *snub nose,* by way of an understanding of an independent quality, which in that case was concavity. But the intellect has no similar passage from *animal* to *horse,* or from *colored* to *red.* Thus, the two-step approach, by which we first explain (or assume) the genus, and then distinguish the object of inquiry from everything else within that genus, is impossible with respect to a categorial species.

The need, here, for a different kind of account reflects a different metaphysical order. Whereas an accidental species is posterior to its genus, a categorial species is prior. Earlier we saw that something belongs to an accidental species in virtue of belonging to the relevant genus: a person is a brother, for instance, because he is *inter alia* a male. But something belongs to a categorial genus in virtue of belonging to one or another categorial species thereof. So, for instance, a surface is colored because it is red, or because it is blue; it is not red, or blue, because it is colored. And Bucephalus's being a horse does not consist in his being an animal; rather, his being an animal consists in his being a horse. The categorial species, though less abstract, is more fundamental than its genus.

These considerations show that the bare concept of a "species" is, in the words of Kit Fine, "insensitive to source."[18] If *all* that we know is that A is a genus of which B is a species, it remains to ask: "What is the source of the truth of it that, *as we know,* every B is at the same time also an A? Is it the case that something is a B because it is, among other things, an A? Or is it, perhaps, that something is an A because it is, for instance, a B? Does the species in question transpire from its genus, or the genus from its species?"

Bear in mind that nothing depends on any putative example of categorial generality. All that matters, here, is the reader's recognition of a second intelligible pattern—a pattern that could in principle receive many diverse instantiations. Arguably, *human being* is a categorial species of *rational being, water* of *liquid, four* of *number, seeing* of *knowing,* and *walking home* of *going home.* And the history of philosophy is rich with apparent examples. Take, for instance, Frege's distinction between concept and object. These, he says, are "logically simple" and cannot be given proper definitions.[19] But they surely *could* be given proper definitions, and not just Frege's "hints," if they were accidental species of a common prior genus—if, that is, we could first grasp the nature of a "logical entity," and if we could then divide the class of such things in two, distinguishing the ones with holes from the ones without.

Or take Aristotle's doctrine of the categories. It is a well-known thesis of his that no differentia mediates the contrast between *being* and, for instance, *being human,* or *being six feet tall.*[20] Thus we cannot explain what substance is, or what quantity is, by first explaining "being in general," and then pointing to an attribute of being that distinguishes one way of being from the rest. To paraphrase Prior, we can say that substance and quantity agree in being

18. Kit Fine, "Essence and Modality," *Philosophical Perspectives* 8 (1994): 9.

19. Gottlob Frege, "Concept and Object" (1952), reprinted in *The Frege Reader,* ed. Michael Beaney (Oxford: Basil Blackwell, 1997), 181–193.

20. The Aristotelian dictum that "being is not a genus" means, I think, that being is not what I have called an *"accidental* genus." See *Posterior Analytics,* 92b14; see also *Metaphysics,* B.3, 998b22.

categories, but of their difference we can only say either that their category is different, or that one is substance and the other quantity.

Consider, as a final example, the distinction we are presently drawing, the distinction between *categorial species* and *accidental species*. These latter would appear to be categorial species, not accidental species, of *species*. In that case, the super-abstract notion of "generality" from which I began is itself something that transpires from various prior concrete forms.

2.2.2 THE IRREDUCIBILITY OF CATEGORIAL GENERALITY. But is this really a second form of genus–species relation, or might it be somehow reducible to the first? One reason for suspicion is that attempts to elucidate categorial generality tend to focus on the example of color. They do so, presumably, because it is in connection with color that the existence of a second form seems to be most plausible. Faced with the question, "What distinguishes red from all other colors?" we are speechless. By contrast, we have no difficulty answering the question, "What distinguishes a snub nose from all other noses?"

But a color is in this respect quite unlike the other examples of categorial species; for often one has much to say. Sissy Jupe, in *Hard Times,* "was thrown into the greatest alarm" when asked to give the definition of a horse—much to her schoolmaster's horror: "Girl number twenty unable to define a horse! Girl number twenty possessed of no facts, in reference to one of the commonest animals!"[21] But whatever is true of a girl like her, a philosopher, far from being dumbstruck, is apt to give an answer like that of white-eyed Bitzer:

> Quadruped. Graminivorous. Forty teeth, namely twenty-four grinders, four eye-teeth, and twelve incisive. Sheds coat in the spring; in marshy countries, sheds hoofs, too. Hoofs hard, but requiring to be shod with iron. Age known by marks in mouth.[22]

What does Bitzer give, if not the definition of a horse, by reference to genus and differentia? Let us suppose that what he says is true, and that the qualities he adduces really do distinguish a horse from all other animals. In that case, it is difficult to see how the mention of these qualities is any different from the mention of concavity in connection with a snub nose. So perhaps, after all, there *is* something "left over" when we subtract the fact that Bucephalus is a

---

21. Charles Dickens, *Hard Times* (New York: Barnes & Noble, 2004), 11.
22. "Thus (and much more) Bitzer." Ibid., 12.

horse from the fact that he is animal: the metaphysical remainder is just whatever would answer to a true account of the sort provided by Bitzer.[23]

Whenever one has something to say about what differentiates the species, categorial generality threatens to collapse back into the accidental. In the face of this impending collapse, it is important to consider the logical character of *what one has to say* about how the relevant species differs from its congenerics. Recall that the original argument for the distinctiveness of categorial generality depended on the idea that the contrast between a categorial species and its genus cannot be drawn by reference to a quality that is independent of the species. If that is right, then although it may be possible to adduce a list of distinctive qualities, these qualities will be such as to logically depend on the species, in which case they cannot contribute to a non-circular account of it.

Now someone attempting to define a horse will inevitably appeal to the horse's parts and vital processes.[24] One will say, like Bitzer, that a horse has four *feet* and forty *teeth*, and that it *eats* grain and *sheds* in the spring. But such an appeal can only contribute to a real definition if something's being a "foot" or "tooth" or "eating" or "shedding" is available to thought in advance of its being that of some particular kind of animal. Such an appeal thus quietly assumes that being a "foot" is rather like being "four in number"; and this assumption appears unfounded. For just as there is no such thing as an animal in general, but only one of this or that specific kind, so, also, there is no such thing as a foot in general, but only that of, say, a horse, a clam, or a mosquito. And while it is true that each of these animals has a "foot," their feet are as different as the animals themselves, and different in exactly the same way. In other words, the genus *foot* is related to the species *equine foot, clam foot,* and *mosquito foot* exactly as the genus *animal* is related to the species

23. This is evidently the opinion of Searle, who treats the relation between being an animal and being a specific kind of animal as a paradigm case of accidental generality. See "On Determinables and Resemblance, II," in *The Aristotelian Society, Supplementary Volume XXXI* (London: Harrison and Sons, 1959), 141–158.

24. The argument of this paragraph is modeled on one by Michael Thompson, *Life and Action* (Cambridge, Mass.: Harvard University Press, 2008), chap. 2. Thompson considers the question whether *life* can be given a real definition—the question, as I would put it, whether *organism* is an accidental species of *substance*—and he argues that the answer is No. In chapters 3 and 4 of that book, Thompson gives an account of the role of a life-form in determining the content of any thought about a creature's vital parts or processes, an account that provides the material for arguing, as I do in the text above, that *horse* cannot be given a real definition, either. Reflection on Thompson's account of *life* is particularly instructive in the present context because it is explicitly modeled on Anscombe's account of *action* (see 47–48).

horse, clam, and *mosquito.* So if one tries to define a horse as a four-footed animal, the "foot" to which one appeals will have to be understood either determinably or determinately. If that to which one appeals is common to the feet of every footed creature, it will not carry enough information to adequately characterize the equine foot. But how can one specify what is distinctive about a horse's foot without appealing to—a horse?

Let us try. It is obviously insufficient to say that a horse has a *hoofed* foot, because so do many other animals; nor will it help to add that the horse's hoof is of such-and-such a size and shape, even if the horse is the only animal in existence with hooves of that description. After all, the fact that there are many kinds of animals with hoofed feet is nothing but a contingent profusion in the variety of species: the horse might have been the only one. And if the horse is, in fact, the only one with hooves of the specified size and shape, this shows nothing but the poverty of earthly fauna: another such animal might have evolved, and might still yet. But if such an animal *were* to evolve, then, just in virtue of its separate genesis, it would not be a horse and its foot would not be a horse's foot. The same goes *mutatis mutandis* for any mere chemical or physical description of any equine part or process (or any conjunction of these): it defines a categorial genus under which there could conceivably fall a part or process that does not belong to a horse.

In that case, color is not so exceptional after all. It is true that we can say much about the distinctive character of a horse, and nothing about that of redness. But what we can say about a horse does not contribute to a real definition—and so, for that purpose, may as well be nothing. The horse is like the color red in that *it does not have* such a definition. And if someone should nevertheless demand that we produce one, the best and only appropriate response is the stunned silence of girl number twenty.

2.3 Essential Generality

2.3.1 THE ESSENTIAL SPECIES AND ITS GENUS. All pure gold is gold, but not all gold is pure: so *pure gold* is a species of *gold*. And every perfect circle is a circle, but not every circle is perfect: so *perfect circle* is a species of *circle*. Nevertheless, it is pointless to ask, in either case, "what is left over" if the genus is subtracted from the species. For there is nothing extra that gold must be, over and above being gold, in order to be pure: the "purity" of pure gold is just its being gold—gold and gold alone. There is, then, no solution to the equation: *gold* + *x* = *pure gold*. And similarly, there is no solution to the equation: *circle* + *y* = *perfect circle;* for, again, there is nothing that a circle must be, over and above being a circle, in order to be perfect: the "perfection" of a perfect circle is its unimpeachable circularity. I will call a species of this third variety an *essential species.*

It came out in the previous section that the contrast between a categorial species and its genus cannot be drawn by reference to a quality that is independent of the species. The situation now is precisely the reverse: the contrast between an essential species and its genus cannot be drawn by reference to a quality that is independent of the genus.

Suppose, for example, that there was some quality that distinguished pure gold from all other gold. The only "other" gold is impure, so the imagined quality would have to distinguish pure gold from impure gold. But the difference between pure gold and impure gold is that the latter is composed, in part, of something that is not gold. So the quality would have to determine, for each part, whether it was gold or not. But if there was in fact a quality that could discriminate between what is gold and what is not, this would be the differentia of *gold,* which is the genus. Or, again, suppose there was a quality that distinguished a perfect circle from all other circles. The difference between a perfect circle and an imperfect circle is that the latter is, in some respect, not circular. So the imagined quality would have to determine, for every respect in which a shape can fail to be circular, whether it was circular or not. And if there was in fact a quality that could make the required discrimination, this quality would be the differentia of *circle,* which again is the genus.

A two-step approach is once more impossible, but this time for the opposite reason. And this reflects a third distinctive order of priority. An essential species is neither posterior to its genus, like an accidental species, nor prior to its genus, like a categorial species. If, as it seems, to be pure gold is to be gold and gold alone, then there cannot be any priority, either way, between the species *pure gold* and the genus *gold.* And if to be a perfect circle is to be in no way uncircular, then the species *perfect circle* is neither more nor less fundamental than the genus *circle.* An essential species and its genus are coeval.

2.3.2 THE IRREDUCIBILITY OF ESSENTIAL GENERALITY. But is there any such thing as essential generality? In everyday life we are happy to say that a wedding ring is gold, though we admit that it isn't *pure* gold. And similarly, we are happy to say that the ring is a circle, though we admit that it isn't a *perfect* circle. But this, it seems, is only a loose way of speaking. Strictly speaking, there is no such thing as impure gold or an imperfect circle. Even schoolchildren know that from the point of view of chemistry *all* gold is pure, and that from the point of view of geometry *every* circle is perfect. And so, from a scientific point of view, there is no logical space, and thus no distinction to be drawn, between the essential species and its genus. But if a species and its genus are the same, then, strictly, there is no species, and there is no genus to speak of.

This line of thought presents itself as an objection, but in fact it is only another way of describing what needs to be understood. There is, indeed, a striking contrast between "loose" and "strict" ways of speaking—between, on the one hand, what is good enough for ordinary talk, and, on the other hand, what rises to the need of a rational discipline. But the most striking thing about this contrast is that it only emerges in a certain sort of case. No one is of the opinion that "strictly speaking" to be a nose is to be a snub nose, or that "strictly speaking" to be an animal is to be a horse. What needs to be understood is precisely the form of generality that underwrites a contrast between "disciplined" and "undisciplined," or "rigorous" and "lax," or "scientific" and "vulgar" modes of thought and expression.

The contrast in question applies across an astonishingly wide domain of objects, so it will help to diversify our menu of examples. Arguably, the same abstract structure that we found in connection with *gold* and *circle* is also exemplified by each of the following trios.

	PRIVATIVE	ANTI-PRIVATIVE
human body	lifeless human body	living human body
human body	unhealthy human body	healthy human body
human hand	deformed human hand	undeformed human hand
human being	vicious human being	virtuous human being
doctor	incompetent doctor	competent doctor
law	unjust law	just law
contract	invalid contract	valid contract
inference	invalid inference	valid inference
calculation	incorrect calculation	correct calculation
word	meaningless word	meaningful word
judgment	false judgment	true judgment

With respect to each of the listed trios, there have been philosophers, at one time or another, who have held that the "primitive" or "original" or "fundamental" conception of what is in the left-most column is in fact a conception of what is in the right-most column; or that to explain the former is to explain the latter; or that, "strictly and philosophically speaking," *to be* the former is *to be* the latter. It is possible, of course, that all of these philosophers were wrong, and that none of the listed trios exhibits the relevant asymmetry. But it does not matter. What matters is not the purported examples themselves, but only the form they purport to exemplify, which evidently transcends the specific mode of deprivation that attaches to the privatives.

The common form exemplified here suggests that where gold is concerned, impurity is a privative condition. And we may take the claim that, strictly speaking, impure gold is not gold as marking this. Certainly there is something that seems paradoxical about the sentence, "Impure gold is not gold." But when we think of impurity as a privation, we see that it is not a contradiction.

Consider a similar charge of paradox, which has been brought against the slogan of Natural Law Theory, *"Lex iniusta non est lex"*—an unjust law is not a law.[25] The jurist John Austin dismissed this slogan as "stark nonsense": it is, he said, "an abuse of language"; and it is "not merely puerile, it is mischievous."[26] According to Austin, the natural lawyer is guilty of "confound[ing] what is with what ought to be."[27]

> The existence of law is one thing; its merit or demerit is another. Whether it be or be not is one enquiry; whether it be or be not conformable to an assumed standard, is a different enquiry.[28]

Without passing judgment on the truth or falsity of the natural law slogan, it ought to be clear that at least it is not nonsense, and that Austin's division of inquiries really is beside the point. After all, it would be obvious what to reply if someone denounced the slogan "impure gold is not gold" on the grounds that the existence of gold is one thing and its purity or impurity another. We

25. For a discussion of this slogan, see Norman Kretzmann, "LEX INIUSTA NON EST LEX: Laws on Trial in Aquinas's Court of Conscience," *American Journal of Jurisprudence* (1988): 99–121.

26. John Austin, *The Province of Jurisprudence Determined,* Lecture V (London: Weidenfeld and Nicolson, 1832), 185.

27. Ibid., 184.

28. Ibid.

would concede that the question whether some particular ring is gold—rather than, say, pyrite, or silver, or platinum—is, indeed, distinct from the question whether it is pure gold. But we would nevertheless insist that the question *what it is to be gold* and the question *what it is to be pure gold* define a single scientific inquiry.

The latter insistence does not make one guilty of confounding what gold *is* with what it *ought to be*. And the absurdity of such a charge cannot be chalked up to the fact a normative concept like "ought" has no application to chemical kinds, for normative concepts certainly do apply to the object of anatomy. Just open any anatomy textbook: every limb and organ, every bone and muscle, every cell, is shown to be exactly where it *ought* to be, doing exactly what it *ought* to do. Such a textbook does not portray defect, deformity, disability, or disease—or, if it does, they are clearly not the main event. The science of human anatomy is right to identify the question "What is the human body?" with the question "What is the healthy human body?" For, as Aristotle says, "We must look for the intentions of nature in things which retain their nature, and not in things which are corrupted" (*Politics* 1254a35–37).[29]

2.4 Comparison of the Forms

To conclude this discussion of the forms of generality, it will be useful to consider how a species of each variety relates to a contrary species, and how such a pair of contraries falls under their common genus. In the figure below, B and C are contrary species of A—"contrary" in the sense that what is A cannot be both B and C simultaneously—and the underlined terms are prior to those not underlined.

Accidental Generality	Categorial Generality	Essential Generality
$\underline{A}$	A	$\underline{A}$
B C	$\underline{B}$ $\underline{C}$	$\underline{B}$ C

With accidental generality, the genus is prior to both of its species: thus, e.g., the genus *nose* is prior to the species *snub nose* and also to the contrary species

---

29. Translated by Benjamin Jowett in *The Complete Works of Aristotle.*

aquiline nose. With categorial generality, both the species are prior to their genus: thus, e.g., being red and being blue are both prior to being colored. With essential generality, the genus is coeval with one of its species and together they are prior to the contrary species: thus, e.g., *gold* is coeval with *pure gold,* and together they are prior to *impure gold.*[30]

Having said, I hope, enough about these forms of generality, I can now formulate a thesis that I will attempt to defend in the remainder of this essay. The standard approach in the philosophy of action proceeds on the assumption that both of the two canonical divisions are instances of accidental generality. But this assumption is doubly false. The division of events into mere events and actions is an example, not of accidental, but of categorial generality. And the subsequent division of actions into the unintentional and the intentional, or the unfree and the free, or the half-hearted and the whole-hearted—in short, into the qualified and the unqualified—this division is an instance, not of accidental, but of essential generality. I will treat these points in reverse order.

3. Unqualified Forms of Action as Essential Species Thereof

3.1 Argument from the Dignity of a Philosophical Topic

The presumptive task of the philosopher of action is to answer the question, "What is action?" But the usual practice is not what one might expect: it is not, after all, to treat every genuine instance of action as equally worthy of account. Instead, philosophers tend to focus one or another species of action, presenting this as the principal object of inquiry. Thus, Anscombe inquires specifically about *intentional* action; Frankfurt about *whole-hearted* action; Velleman about *autonomous* action; and others about action that is *free,* or *purposeful,* or *conscious.* Have these philosophers each made a fetish of some particular species of action, neglecting the nature of action as such, or is the practice legitimate?

The practice does, indeed, seem legitimate, on the supposition that the relevant forms of action have an anti-privative character and are suitably arranged in a table like the one we saw before:

30. I do not claim that there are *only* three forms of generality.

	PRIVATIVE	ANTI-PRIVATIVE
action	unintentional action	intentional action
action	half-hearted action	whole-hearted action
action	un-autonomous action	autonomous action
action	forced action	free action
action	purposeless action	purposeful action
action	unconscious action	conscious action
action	involuntary action	voluntary action

Suppose that the forms of action in the final column are rightly seen as anti-privative—and thus, as picking out essential species.[31] In that case it is clear, on the one hand, why philosophers of action should focus on these topics, and, on the other hand, why such focus does not amount to neglecting the topic of action in general. An essential species is that by relation to which all other species fall under the same genus, and it is that by reference to which the genus as a whole is properly elucidated. The anatomist who seeks a general theory of the human body does not concern herself indifferently with *all* bodies—the living and the dead alike—but exclusively with the living ones, and among the living, primarily with the healthy ones. Just so, a philosopher who aims at a general theory of action does not concern herself indifferently with *all* actions—the intentional and the unintentional alike—but exclusively with the intentional ones, and among the intentional, primarily with the ones that are undeformed. This, I say, is how it will look, if the relevant forms of action are essential species thereof.

But a partisan of the standard approach is committed to rejecting this picture. So for him there is an awkward question: "What can explain the interest we have in these particular forms of action—the ones, namely, in the rightmost column of the table?" There is no mystery if the chemist takes a special interest in pure gold: her interest in pure gold is nothing apart from her interest in gold. But if she focuses instead on Peruvian gold, this will need explaining. The problem for a standard theorist is that his method commits him to thinking that *intentional action* is related to *action* as *Peruvian gold* is related to *gold*. And it is just the same for all of the other privileged forms of action. Why, then, do we privilege them? The fact that we do looks utterly mysterious.

31. There is admittedly a deep difference between the first two listed trios, a difference parallel to that between the first two trios on the list of section 2.3.2 above.

But really the problem is worse than that. In addition to being, say, whole-hearted (or not), any particular action will have an infinite number of "features." It will be done, for example, at night, in California, on the telephone, and under government surveillance. But none of these possible "features" of an action will present itself as a topic for philosophical reflection. Why not? Why, for example, has no one yet given us a theory of nocturnal action? The answer seems to be that whether an action happens to be done at night is neither here nor there as far as concerns its being an action. This suggests that nocturnal action is philosophically unmentionable precisely because it is defined by reference to an "extra feature"—that is, precisely because it is an accidental species.

Thus, the standard theorist faces a dilemma. Either (as I think) his favorite privileged form of action is *not* an accidental species, or else it is, but, precisely because it is, it lacks the dignity of a philosophical topic. So that either (as I think) it *cannot* be explained by means of the standard approach, or else it can, but, precisely because it can, it is not worth explaining.

Faced with this dilemma, a partisan of the standard approach might try to say that a certain unqualified form of action, though indeed an accidental species, is nevertheless philosophically significant, its significance deriving not directly from the nature of action, but by way of its relation to some other topic. The self-proclaimed "philosopher of action" will hereby abandon any pretense of explaining what action is; but let it be abandoned. What could be said in this vein?

Well, for example, one might try to say that the philosophical importance of intentional action is to be explained by reference to rationality. There is, after all, a close relation between rationality and intention: an action done for a reason is intentional, and intentional action is typically done for a reason. The problem with this maneuver is that it only pushes the problem back, for it raises the question of why philosophers care so much about rationality. Why not *ir*rationality? Why not whatever is shared in common by rationality and irrationality alike? Once again we seem to find a disciplinary preference for the undistorted, undiminished term. That, however, is exactly what one was trying to avoid.

Instead of appealing to rationality, one might appeal to ethics. Intentional, voluntary, free action is the principal object of moral evaluation: it is good or bad, right or wrong, virtuous or vicious. And so, one might say, it is an interest in morality that sets the agenda for the philosophy of action. But this forgets that ethics, too, is a rational discipline with its very own definite set of priorities. Its central concepts are the right and the good, not the wrong and the bad; it contains doctrines of virtue, not doctrines of vice, and it produces theories of justice, not theories of injustice.[32] But if that sort of bias is proper for ethics, then why not for the philosophy of action?

In general, a science or rational discipline privileges the "positive" over the "negative," putting order before disorder, law before lawlessness, and form before deformity. And in each particular case, the priority is explained directly by reference to the nature of the object of the discipline. But if we are going to have to say that in the end, then why not say from the very beginning that our abiding concern with intentional action, and with all of the other unqualified forms, derives directly and immediately from the fundamental question of action theory: "What is action?"

3.2 Argument from the Unity of Unqualified Forms

The foregoing argument is not, I think, conclusive, but it puts one in position to observe a certain striking unity, or mutual accord, among the unqualified forms of action. The self-same particular action may be, at once, intentional, autonomous, free, whole-hearted, voluntary, purposeful, conscious, and so on. And this is not *per accidens,* for it is perfectly clear how to extend the three-columned list. And it is clear in advance that whatever might appear in the right-most column must harmonize with everything else. Thus, the compatibility of unqualified forms is internal to the order in question.

But how is this to be explained? The anti-privative forms of a thing are always compatible in just this way: the infinite respects in which a body may fail to be deformed, or a shape irregular, or a sample impure, or a law unjust— these necessarily harmonize. But the same is not true of accidental species. Consider that *one* accidental species of nose is the snub, and *another* is the aquiline; yet a particular nose cannot be both. And, of course, a particular action cannot be both nocturnal and diurnal. For any random pair of congeneric accidental species, it will be a complete accident if they turn out to be compatible. The harmony of unqualified forms of action is totally inexplicable, except on

32. The tendency in ethics to prioritize the right and the good is criticized by John Herman Randall Jr., "The Wrong and the Bad," *Journal of Philosophy* 51 (1954): 764–775. For a compelling reply, see John Wild, "Ethics as a Rational Discipline and the Priority of the Good," *Journal of Philosophy* 51 (1954): 776–788.

the supposition that these are, in fact, essential species. In that case, however, none of them can be explained by means of the standard approach.

4. Action as a Categorial Species of Event

4.1 The Humean Circle

Earlier I observed that if one tries to explain a categorial species by reference to genus and differentia, the account is ruined by circularity. In the remainder of this essay, I will pursue the idea that *action* is a case in point.

Anscombe notes the danger of an explanatory circle where she warns against the attempt to define an action as an event that is done for (or caused by) a reason:

> Why is giving a start or gasp not an 'action', while sending for a taxi, or crossing the road, is one? The answer cannot be "Because the answer to the question 'why?' may give a *reason* in the latter cases", for the answer may 'give a reason' in the former cases too; and we cannot say "Ah, but not a reason for *acting*"; we should be going round in circles.[33]

Whether it is an "action," like sending for a taxi, or a "*mere* event," like giving a sudden start, one can ask for the "reason" "why" it "happened." On the one hand, there is the question, "Why did you give a start?" where the reason might be, "I thought I saw a face in the window." On the other hand, there is the question, "Why did you call for a taxi?" where the reason might be, "I am going to the airport." According to Anscombe, the problem with defining an action as an event that is done for (or caused by) a reason is that corresponding to the two determinate kinds of "event" are two determinate kinds of "reason," and two different senses of the question "Why?" Thus, the "reason" mentioned in the would-be account must be either a reason-for-acting or a reason-for-merely-happening. But the latter is not what one wants. And one cannot appeal to the former except by treating "acting" as something already understood, whereas as this is exactly what needs to be explained.

A version of this circle was discovered by David Hume.[34] Hume observed that we praise an action as morally good only if we think that it was done

---

33. Anscombe, *Intention*, 10.

34. Though Anscombe does not mention the Humean Circle in *Intention*, she discusses it in a series of later articles. See "On Promising and Its Justice, and Whether It Need Be Respected

from a good motive. And according to him, this presents a problem for any-one who would claim that part of what makes an action good is its having been done with regard to its goodness:

> To suppose, that the mere regard to the virtue of the action, may be the first motive, which produc'd the action, and render'd it virtuous, is to rea-son in a circle. Before we can have such a regard, the action must be really virtuous; and this virtue must be deriv'd from some virtuous motive: And consequently the virtuous motive must be different from the regard to the virtue of the action.[35]

In this passage, Hume is concerned with an agent's motive, but his deeper insight can be expressed without any reference to motivation. It is clear that in order to be motivated by the genuine goodness of her action, an agent must *know* that her action is good. And what generates the Humean Circle is really just the relation between an agent's *knowledge* that her action is good and the *fact* that it is good. According to Hume, the fact that an action is good cannot depend essentially on the knowledge that it is good, on pain of its being unintelligible what a good action is. And the argument is simple: in order to understand what a good action is, we would need to understand the agent's knowledge that her action is good; however, in order to grasp the content of this knowledge, we would need already to know what a good ac-tion is. And thus we are caught in a circle.

Hume thought he could avoid the circle that arises in connection with virtue. But according to him, there are other circles of precisely the same structure that cannot be avoided, and that cannot be explained away. Certain special things we do are, in his words, "naturally unintelligible." Examples include making a promise, signing a contract, giving a gift, and getting mar-ried. What is curious about such forms of action, and what gives rise to the Humean Circle, is that they cannot be done unknowingly.

In her own discussion of knowledge-dependent forms of action, Anscombe points out that every condition requisite for a marriage might be satisfied—the

---

in Foro Interno," and "Rules, Rights and Promises," in *Ethics, Religion and Politics* (Oxford: Basil Blackwell, 1981). See also "The Question of Linguistic Idealism," in *From Parmenides to Wittgenstein* (Oxford: Basil Blackwell, 1981).

35. David Hume, *Treatise of Human Nature,* ed. L. A. Selby-Bigge and P. H. Nidditch (Oxford: Clarendon Press, 1978), 478. This is a point that reappears in slightly different forms a number of times in his *Treatise:* see also 467, 468, 480, 526.

priest and witnesses solemnly gathered, the nuptial oaths intoned and repeated, the rings exchanged, and all the rest—but for this one thing: that one
of the parties to the would-be marriage does not know that what he is doing
is getting married. (Following Anscombe, we may imagine that he misunderstood someone's remark, "This is only a rehearsal.") Well, if he does not know
that what he is doing is getting married, then getting married is not, in fact,
what he is doing. For knowing that one is getting married is essential to getting married: it is an ineliminable constituent of the fact, whenever the fact
obtains.

It bears emphasis that getting married depends on knowledge, not merely
as an efficient cause but also for its own internal constitution. It is not as
though the agent's thought were instrumental in bringing about something
whose existence we could perfectly well understand on its own. Rather, we
seem to need to refer to the agent's thought in order to understand the substantive fact that is brought about. This means that a person's knowledge
that he is getting married is related to its object quite differently than his
vision is related to its object. It is possible to explain *what* a person sees without making reference to the fact that it is seen. By contrast, we cannot strip
away the knowledge that one is getting married and leave its object intact. If
we try to strip it away—as in the case where the groom believes it is only a
rehearsal—we find that many of the actions and circumstances that would
otherwise be named among the requisites of a marriage will simply be an-
nulled: the groom will say "I do," but he will not make a vow; he will hand a
ring to his would-be bride, but he will not give it to her; and the proceedings
will be seen, but they will not be witnessed.

It is clear that what attracted the attention of both Anscombe and Hume
was the appearance that *every* instance of getting married, or of making a
promise, is known by the relevant agent. And someone might question
whether this is unexceptionally true. (Is it really impossible to make a promise
without knowing one is doing so?) Fortunately, we can lay this doubt aside,
because counter-examples, if any exist, are simply not to the point. What
matters is not the claim that *in every case* the agent must know she is making
a promise, but only that *in the definitive case*—in the one by relation to which
every case is a case—the agent *does* know. And about the latter there can be
no doubt: a knowing promise is the essential species by relation to which any
promise is one. So let it be granted that there is such a thing as an unknowing
promise. The fact remains that its existence and intelligibility depend on that

of a knowing promise, and we are obliged to start where Hume did start, with the undiminished form.

Doing so, we find a problem of intelligibility much like the one that arose in connection with virtue. The problem is this: if it is essential to getting married that one should know that one is doing so, then we cannot understand what it is to get married unless we grasp the content of that knowledge; however, we cannot grasp the content of that knowledge unless we understand what it is to get married. It therefore seems totally unintelligible both what it is to get married and what it is to know that one is doing so.

4.2 The Humean Circle Expanded

In Hume's estimation, the problem of "natural intelligibility" had a fairly limited scope. It was limited, he thought, to actions that are associated with a human convention or practice. And Anscombe, for her part, appears to have agreed. She thought that it was necessary to expand the class of practice-dependent actions so as to include the following of a rule, and therefore also the speaking of a language.[36] But she did not defend, or even discuss, a more radical expansion of the Humean Circle, which we are now in position to contemplate. Could it be that action *as such* is "naturally unintelligible"?[37]

In considering this question, we can set aside all but one of the essential species treated above (in section 3), and we can focus on the question whether knowledge is a perfection of action. If *one* essential species of action is the action whose agent knows what she is doing, and that it is an action and not a mere event, then it belongs to the nature of action as such, as it does to that of a promise, *that the agent of it knows she is the agent of it*—so that action, too, gives rise to a Humean Circle.

Now Anscombe would be the last to deny that knowledge is a perfection of action. But even Davidson seems committed to the idea that in the fundamental case of action the agent knows exactly what she is doing, and that what she is doing is no mere event. This is implicit in his well-known discus-

---

36. Anscombe, "The Question of Linguistic Idealism."

37. The question whether action is "naturally unintelligible" is not to be confused with the question whether it is unintelligible. In its expanded form, the Humean Circle is only a special case of the circle we fall into whenever we attempt to explain a categorial species by reference to genus and differentia. The horse and the color red are "naturally unintelligible," but they are, for all that, perfectly intelligible.

sion of "deviant causal chains." Davidson finds it difficult to explain the postulated causal connection between an action and the beliefs and desires that rationalize it, for, as he writes, "Beliefs and desires that would rationalize an action if they caused it in the *right* way—through a course of practical reasoning, as we might try saying—may cause it in other ways."[38] And though he despairs of spelling out the *"right"* etiology, Davidson is nevertheless bold enough to "try saying" that it involves practical reasoning. The suggestion is apparently that if there is to be the *"right"* etiology, the agent herself must draw a connection between what she is doing and her reason for doing it. However, she cannot draw this connection if she does not know what she is doing. And if what she is doing is not an action, then, it seems, the *"right"* connection is not the right one after all.[39]

It is hard to say whether anyone would deny the claim that knowledge is a perfection of action. But if we let it stand for now as a conjecture, we find ourselves in a familiar predicament. On the one hand, we cannot understand what action is until we grasp the content of the agent's knowledge. On the other hand, we cannot grasp the content of such knowledge until we know what action is.

And this must ruin the reductive ambition of an accidentalist account. It is impossible to specify a complete set of non-circular conditions necessary for an event to be an action, if *one* of the conditions is that the agent herself should know that what she is doing is performing an action. The reason is, of course, that in specifying the crucial condition the account would have to mention the very thing it needed to explain.[40] So a partisan of the standard

38. Davidson, "Freedom to Act," in *Essays on Actions and Events*, 79.

39. It is true that, according to Davidson, a person may be doing something intentionally without knowing that he is: "A man may be making ten carbon copies as he writes, and this may be intentional; yet he may not know that he is; all he knows is that he is trying" ("Agency," in *Essays on Actions and Events*, 50). But remember, the question that concerns us is not whether everything that is intentional is done in full knowledge, but simply whether "cognizant" or "knowledgeable" action is an essential species by reference to which any action is one. And Davidson allows as much, immediately adding that, even in the case of the carbon copier, "what the agent does is known to him under *some* description" (50). So, apparently, the possibility of acting under a description that one does not know depends on something more fundamental: acting under a description that one knows perfectly well.

40. Recent attempts by Velleman and Setiya to enlist Anscombe in defense of the standard approach have turned on the idea that the agent's thought about what she is doing is self-validating or self-referential. Whether they succeed in avoiding the Humean Circle is a question

approach could say *whatever else she liked* about *whatever else she liked*—about belief-desire pairs, or bodily movements, or brain states, or what have you—but to anything else she would have to add this, that the agent, in acting, knows that she is doing precisely that: acting. And then everything else would be swept into the circle.

This would explain why the two canonical divisions are not only legitimately drawn, but rightly placed at the center of the discipline. If one essential condition of an event's being an action, and not a mere event, is that the subject of it should *know* that she is the subject of an action, and not a mere event, then the philosophical distinction between an "action" and a "mere event" is not just idle theory imposed on the world from without; the relevant distinction is drawn by the agent herself, insofar as she acts at all. In that case, the apprehension of action's distinctive character is operative in the genesis of any event that has this character. And it is only because the agent herself draws the relevant distinction that the world itself contains anything for philosophers to distinguish.[41]

I cannot consider here: it would require a paper of its own. In any event, the argument above establishes that the question of practical knowledge cannot be avoided. It is clear, moreover, that Hume himself could not have accepted any solution along the lines proposed by Setiya and Velleman. If he thought he could evade the problem just by positing a special thought, or a thought with a special causal role, justice would not have seemed to him naturally unintelligible. Hume's solution involved the appeal to an "institution" or "custom"—an extra-psychic, extra-"natural" phenomenon to which nothing corresponds in the relevant theories of action.

41. This essay is derived from my doctoral dissertation and inherits many debts, above all to my dissertation advisor, Michael Thompson; to my second reader, John McDowell; and to the other members of my committee, Stephen Engstrom, Sebastian Rödl, and Kieran Setiya. For discussion spanning many years, I am also indebted to Matthew Boyle, Matthias Haase, Ben Laurence, Douglas Lavin, and Salomé Skvirsky. Earlier versions of this essay were delivered at the University of Chicago, at a conference at Uppsala University (Sweden), and at the Auburn Philosophical Society; on each of these occasions I received challenging criticism. I am grateful, finally, to Jennifer Hornsby and Frederick Stoutland for helpful comments at various stages.

3

Actions in Their Circumstances

JENNIFER HORNSBY

Perhaps the crucial event in stimulating a new look at the concept of action was the publication of Elizabeth Anscombe's *Intention*.

Donald Davidson, "Aristotle's Action", 283

Davidson attributed to Anscombe the inspiration for his own account of action.[1] But Davidson assumed that human agency is found in a world in which the operations of causality are confined to obtainings of relations between things in the category of events or states; and this ensures that his view of the nature of agency and of actions was utterly different from Anscombe's. So I shall argue. I think that it is missed by many of those who are content to tell the story of action in Davidson's way and who suppose that the main disagreement between Anscombe and Davidson turns on a question about "reasons and causes". These people fail to grasp the distinctive character of Anscombe's account.

I

The absence from Anscombe of Davidson's assumption about causality is conspicuous in her "Causality and Determination". Anscombe's principal

1. The epigraph from "Aristotle's Action" (first published in French in 2001) can be found in Davidson's *Truth, Language and History* (Oxford: Oxford University Press, 2005). And see p. 37 of Davidson's "Intellectual Autobiography," in *The Philosophy of Donald Davidson,* ed. Lewis E. Hahn (Library of Living Philosophers, vol. XXVII; Chicago: Open Court Press, 1998), 3–70.

target there is a conception of causality exemplified by Davidson's claim about its nomological character, and her wholesale repudiation of that conception would explain her distance from Davidson on a range of questions in metaphysics. But I want to show what sets Anscombe apart from Davidson specifically on questions about the nature of human agency, so that my concern will be with the causative verbs to which Anscombe drew attention. Her list of these includes: *"scrape, push, wet, carry, eat, knock over, keep off, squash, make* (e.g., noises, paper boats), *hurt"*.[2]

In order to see why it should be right to call these verbs causatives, one needs to bring out a causal element in them. One can do so by subjecting the verbs to a sort of decompositional treatment in which an idea of *cause* makes an actual appearance. Thus:

(C) *a* is φ-ing *o* [e.g., *a* is carrying *o*, is pushing *o* to location L, . . .] ONLY IF *a* is causing something characteristic of *o*'s being φ-d [*a* is causing *o*'s being carried, *o*'s being pushed to L, . . .].

Schema (C) is surely along the right lines, even if it is not particularly illuminating. We are more familiar with formulations that use perfective aspect, saying something about what it is to *do,* or to *have done,* such-and-such. But there cannot be any objection to using the progressive as (C) does—saying something about what it is to *be doing* such-and-such. It usually *takes time* to do something; and someone who has done something that at an earlier time they hadn't done was, for at least some of the time in the interval, doing the thing. And there is a reason to start from the progressive: as Terence Parsons and many others have seen, sentences in the progressive cannot be accounted for in terms of their perfective correlates.[3] (In order to appreciate just how

---

2. In *Metaphysics and the Philosophy of Mind,* 2nd ed. (Oxford: Basil Blackwell, 1981), 137. "Causality and Determination" was first published in 1971.

There will be no need here either to define the category of causatives or to attempt any taxonomy of them. Anscombe didn't include intransitives such as "walk", "run", "speak", "sing", which, whether or not they belong on her list, we think of as action verbs inasmuch as we think that someone who walks, say, or speaks, is the source of what results from their walking or their speaking. (I've left "burn" off Anscombe's list because it belongs to a class of English causatives I speak to separately—in section II.)

3. See Parsons's *Events in the Semantics of English* (Cambridge, Mass.: MIT Press, 1990). When progressives are used (so that the aspect is imperfective), it comes naturally to speak of *processes.* For simplicity's sake, I shall take it that processes are among the events, so that some events are (as one might put it) processual. This is a terminological policy, which is not at

often (C) may be instantiated, one sometimes needs to imagine things happening in slow motion.)

If some of (C)'s instances don't ring quite true, that may be because the "cause" that (C) introduces is not equivalent to any word we ordinarily use. Indeed Anscombe's own point, when she gave her list of the verbs, was that the concepts they represent could be present in a language that contained no word for *cause* (137). The generic notion of "causing" used in (C) is something that we glean when we bring the verbs together: we understand it by recognizing the causative character that unites them. We cannot assume that we understand it by virtue of knowing what it is for one event to cause or to be causing another event.

And that cannot be how we understand it. Take a case of Ann's carrying a suitcase. When Ann is carrying the suitcase—when she is in the process of carrying it, so that her action is occurring—there seems to be no candidate for an event that her action is causing. It is true that when Ann *has* carried the suitcase, she will have caused a characteristic state of something that has been carried, which is to say that the suitcase will be in some new location. But what she has then caused is evidently not an event. And although her causing the suitcase to be somewhere else than it was is an event,[4] an event that may have effects of its own, those effects are not present while it is occurring. So long as Ann is carrying the suitcase, the only event in which the suitcase participates is its being carried. The causality here is internal to an event: Ann's carrying the suitcase *is* the event of its being carried. As Anscombe might put it herself: "Ann does what happens".[5]

---

odds, I think, with Anscombe's way of speaking, and which leaves it open whether a processual event that was ongoing is the same as the event that has occurred when it is ongoing no longer.

4. Alvarez and Hyman deny that actions are events in "Agents and Their Actions", *Philosophy* 73 (1998): 219–245. But they "concede that for most purposes, the kind of categorical refinement which is involved in either affirming or denying that actions are events is . . . otiose". Well, it has to be affirmed for the purpose of bringing Anscombe and Davidson into relation. And even though Alvarez and Hyman are disposed to say that actions are not events, they can still be right on the question that is crucial here: they do succeed, I think, in showing that agents' causings are not eliminable.

5. Anscombe introduces her formula "I *do* what *happens*" at p. 52 of *Intention*. She diagnoses the perplexity of those who found the formula "extremely paradoxical and obscure" by reference to difficulties that might be found with the idea of agents' non-observational knowledge. But if questions about such knowledge are set aside, and her formula is transposed to a

One appreciates the correctness of this identity when one thinks of oneself as witness to a person's carrying a suitcase. Or again—since it is not only "carry" that cannot be understood by understanding event causality—one may imagine seeing someone who is pushing a door, or setting a teacup down on the counter, or squashing an ant. Then Anscombe would say, gainsaying Hume, that "efficacy is plainly discoverable to the mind" (137). Efficacy is evident, not because one sees two happenings, nor yet because one sees a person and a happening that she causes, but because one sees a happening that *is* the person's causing. If you focus on the suitcase, you may see it being carried; if you focus on her, you may see her carrying. But there is only one event of carrying to be seen, and so, *mutatis mutandis,* in the other cases. In seeing this event, you see causality in operation; and that is because what you see is *her at work*—her causing this or that. (The argument here, from the visibility of efficacy, adduces the fact that causatives can be used correctly in recording what is seen. It does not say that it is *always* visible what someone is up to.)

The idea of an agent at work goes entirely missing from Davidson's story of human agency. Davidson spoke of causality as "central to the concept of agency", but he said that "it is ordinary causality between events that is relevant, and it concerns the effects . . . of actions".[6] If one wants to draw attention to what Davidson leaves out, then some of the verbs on Anscombe's list are particularly good ones to choose. For the examples we are likely to think of first, in which "carry" and "push" and "squash" have application, are like those just considered, where the event of o's being ϕ-d (being carried, or pushed, for example) cannot be pried apart from the event of a's ϕ-ing (carrying or pushing) o. We might say that in such cases the person does the thing—carry something, or, as it might be, push, or squash something—*non-mediately.*

It must be allowed that causative verbs can also describe examples of a different sort. Someone who operates a machine designed to squash tin cans relies upon doing things—pulling a lever that controls the machine,

---

third-person version, then it might be taken to record identities such as that of the carrying (which Ann "does") with the being carried (which "happens" to the suitcase).

6. Davidson, "Agency", 53. Page references to this and to six other of Davidson's essays referred to here are to the printings in *Essays on Actions and Events,* 2nd ed. (Oxford: Oxford University Press, 2001). These, with dates of original publication, are as follows: "Actions, Reasons and Causes", 1963; "Causal Relations", 1971; "The Individuation of Events", 1969; "Agency", 1971; "Freedom to Act", 1973; "Adverbs of Action", 1985; "Reply to Quine on Events", 1985.

or whatever—doings of which have effects in their turn, winding up with squashed cans. We might say that squashing then is done *mediately*. We can leave it open whether, when something is done mediately—so that the causal work involved in its happening is not all the agent's own—any further operations of causality will always be a matter of the obtaining of *event*-causal relations. The present point is only that there are examples in which we are bound to think that, insofar as a person has carried something, or squashed something, or pushed something to somewhere, the particular causal work done was the work of that person.

Given Anscombe's avowed anti-Humeanism, we can assume that she would find it obvious that we often do something non-mediately. Davidson, on the other hand, thought that everything we do (with the signal exception of *move the body,* on which more shortly) we always do mediately. If someone has brought it about that something is squashed, for example, then Davidson would say that that can only be because that person's action caused an event by virtue of whose occurrence the thing came to be squashed. "If we know that someone intentionally crushed a snail, we know that some . . . action *itself* caused a snail to be crushed", he said (my italics). And again, speaking more generally, he said: "Knowledge that an action x has a certain upshot allows us to describe the agent as the cause of that upshot, but this is merely a convenient way of redescribing x".[7] Davidson's idea was that we take people to cause things only because we take them to inherit properties that accrue to their actions by dint of the operation of event causality. But once it is accepted that causality can be internal to an action, it is evident that we need a different idea.

It might be suggested that the causative verbs that take agent as subject have two senses. The idea would be that there is a "cause" that goes with doing causal work non-mediately, and another "cause" that can behave much as Davidson would have it. The suggestion is not at all plausible, however. The fact that something may be squashed non-mediately (as when a can is trodden on) or squashed mediately (as when a machine for squashing cans is operated) does not make us think that there is an ambiguity in the verb "squash". Again, we understand what is said when we are told (say) that someone has knocked over a skittle without needing to enquire in what specific way they did it. A much more plausible idea is that a generic notion of an agent's causing something embraces both mediately causing and non-mediately causing. Using this idea, we allow for a variety of different specific ways in which an agent may be related to such things as she causes. We then take *agent* causality for granted, as Anscombe surely did. Taking it for granted, she saw no need to *speak* of agent causality: she didn't herself attempt to unearth an underlying "cause" from the causative verbs.

Some philosophers who have spoken of agents as causes have meant something very different by "cause", saying that agents cause *their actions*. Those who say this subscribe to a doctrine of agent causation: they believe that a person is sometimes a link (perhaps the first link) in a causal chain whose other links are events or states. It may be that the metaphysically repellent character of the doctrine has led to a general suspicion about the idea that there could be agent causality that is not reducible to causality of some other sort. But the notion of cause that is introduced by those who believe that agents cause their actions has nothing to do with a generic notion of causing by agents which may be seen as implicit in many verbs. One way to be clear how different the two notions are is to notice that the doctrine of agent causation makes a specific claim about the agency of human beings (or, as it may be, of beings who enjoy a peculiar kind of freedom), whereas not all the agents that cause things in the sense of the "cause" introduced in (C) are human. (It would distract from the project of contrasting Anscombe's and Davidson's views of *human* agency to speak here to the irreducibility of the notion of agent causality generally.[8])

II

In "Agency", Davidson asked, "What more have we said when we say that the agent caused the action than when we say he was the agent?" And he answered his own question, saying "The concept of *cause* seems to play no role" (52). But the right answer to the question is that if we say that the agent caused the action, we say something false, but if we say that he was the agent, we

---

8. Alvarez and Hyman speak to the general notion, and call that agent causation. For arguments that, so far from substance causality's reducing to event causality, event causality may reduce to substance causality, see E. J. Lowe, *Personal Agency* (Oxford University Press, 2008), especially 141–146 and 157–158.

may think of his action as *his* causing something or other. In answering in this way, we don't challenge the conclusion that Davidson reached at this point—that "the garden-variety of causality sheds no light on the relation between an agent and his actions". But we do challenge Davidson's assumption that light can be shed on the phenomenon of agency by making use only of that causality which, by Davidson's lights, is the garden-variety, i.e. event causality.[9]

We can see now that Davidson's wishing to reduce agent causality to event causality leads to a definite problem for his own view of actions. In order to see this, we need to look at some different causative verbs—those that behave as the verb "move" does. According to Davidson, the events that are actions are all *movements of our bodies.*

"Move" belongs to a class of English transitive verbs, which includes also, among many others, "break", "open", "close", "melt", "burn", "sink", "lower", "raise". These verbs have equiform intransitives (save that we have "rise" not "raise"), and what brings the verbs together as a class is the relation there is in each case between transitive and intransitive—a relation that starts to be uncovered using a generic "cause" such as we have already encountered, taking agent as subject. Thus it appears to be a necessary condition of agent a's moving$_{[trans]}$ (or breaking or sinking) o that a cause o's moving$_{[intrans]}$ (or breaking or sinking). Ann's moving$_{[trans]}$ of the boulder is Ann's causing the moving$_{[intrans]}$ of the boulder, Bill's breaking$_{[trans]}$ of the glass is Bill's causing the breaking$_{[intrans]}$ of the glass, and so on. The intransitives here are verbs in their own right; and when they are found in event-denoting nominals ("the breaking$_{[intrans]}$ of the glass", etc.), it becomes especially easy to suppose that there is causation between events when the transitive verbs have application.

At any rate, and predictably enough given his general outlook on the matter, Davidson took the causal element in the transitive verbs to introduce event-causation. His view was that a's V$_{[trans]}$-ing o causes o's V$_{[intrans]}$-ing. He used examples of sinking the Bismarck, breaking the window, closing the door.

---

9. I say "event causality" taking it to have been Davidson's official view that the true *relata* of "cause" are only events. But most philosophers who tell the story of action in Davidson's sort of way think that "causal phenomena consist in relations between events, states and processes", and Davidson himself, when talking about action (and not just about its explanation), often spoke of *states* as causes and of *states* as effects. For present purposes, it doesn't matter exactly what categories of item are supposed to participate in what I speak of as event-causal relations, but only that "event causality" is not a relation in which agents as such participate.

He said, for instance, that when I have closed the door, my action has caused an event of the door's closing; and it is an "error . . . to confuse what my action does cause—the closing of the door—with something utterly different—my action of closing the door" ("Agency", 56). Well, there is room for error here, no doubt. Certainly if I close the door by pressing a remote button that makes the door swing shut, then it would be a mistake to suppose that the event of the door's closing is my action—is my closing of the door. But suppose that I close a door by pushing it gradually all the way shut. In this case, my closing it does not appear to be different from the event that is its coming to be closed, its closing$_{[intrans]}$: the door's being closed—which Davidson calls a terminal state—is reached just when my action of closing it ends. We have an example of what I have called non-mediately causing. Transitive causative verbs in the particular class to which "move" belongs apparently behave much like the causatives on Anscombe's list, each one having application in cases of various different sorts. (Here there is a possible confusion different from the one that Davidson warned against. "The door's being closed", "the teacup's being moved", "the glass's being broken" can all be used to denote what Davidson calls a terminal state. But these phrases can also be used to denote an event that may visibly be ongoing even as someone is closing the door, or moving the teacup or breaking the glass. Such events are left out of account if *denotata* of the two sorts are confused and the phrases taken always to have application to terminal states.)

Davidson found himself forced to dispense with the causal element that he held to be generally present in the verb "move" when it came to talking about bodily movements—"move an arm", say. Even here, Davidson allowed a *seeming* causal character. He acknowledged that "if we ask what makes a particular case of an arm going up a case of an arm being raised, a natural answer is that the agent *made* his arm go up". And he went on to explain that, despite the naturalness of speaking even here about what the agent makes happen, there is nevertheless a reason not to distinguish one's raising one's arm from one's arm's rising. If one's causing what happens were always an event causally prior to what happens, then in order to cause something to happen, one would need to cause causing-what-happens to happen, and in order to cause *that*, one would need to cause causing-what-happens-to-happen to happen, and so on, regressively. So Davidson thought that when we trace the chain of events an agent can be said to cause upstream, and we reach the agent's body—we reach an arm's rising, say—we then reach the action itself. At this point, we have a description of an action that makes no allusion to effects, he concluded. According to Davidson, a person's closing the door is always an event that causes the door's closing, but a person's moving her body just *is* her body's moving. He thought that in this special and particular case, "raises $_{[trans]}$ o" does not imply "causes o's rising$_{[intrans]}$", and "moves$_{[trans]}$ o" does not imply "causes o's moving$_{[intrans]}$".[10]

We saw that it would be implausible to say that "push", "carry", "squash", etc., are ambiguous. Nor of course would Davidson have said that. But with this account of "moves the body", he surely commits himself to something even more implausible. Given that we must avoid an absurdly regressive account, we have to consent to a *special* sense that "move" takes on when it occurs in "move the body". And we shall need special senses also for "raise", "lower", "bend", "clench", "close", and "open", but *only* for the cases where their grammatical objects denote body parts—"raise one's arm", "lower one's head", "bend one's knees", "clench one's fist", "close one's eyes", "open one's mouth".[11]

In truth, however, there is no call for Davidson's ad hoc measures, and no need to deny that there is a genuine causal element in "making it happen that one's arm is up". For raising one's arm (in the usual case) is surely a matter of non-mediately causing. And causative transitives such as "move" and "raise" are accounted for with a schema along the same lines as (C). Thus:

$$(T) \ a \text{ is } \phi_{[trans]}\text{-ing } o \text{ ONLY IF } a \text{ is causing } o\text{'s } \phi_{[intrans]}\text{-ing.}$$

Casting this in the perfect tense, without the progressive, gives: a has $\phi_{[trans]}$-d o only if a has caused o's $\phi_{[intrans]}$-ing. For example: Ann has moved her teacup only if Ann has caused her teacup's moving. What we have seen is that there is no valid transition from "a has caused so-and-so" to "the event of a's $\phi_{[trans]}$-ing o has caused so-and-so". For example: there is no valid transition from *Ann* has caused her teacup's moving to *the event* of Ann's moving her teacup has caused its moving. It is this transition that Davidson found he had to

---

10. People have questioned whether Davidson committed himself to this in "Agency". But he is unequivocal in "Problems in the Explanation of Action", where he gives the regress argument, and says "Some arm risings are deeds" (102).

11. Actually, he will need a special sense only to deal with the usual case, in which an agent moves a part of her body *directly,* as we find ourselves saying. Davidson has an example in which he raises his paralysed left arm *in*directly—by using his right arm to pull on the rope of a pulley system. I bracket such examples here. But evidently it is possible to account for them: they are cases of someone's moving a part of his body mediately.

subject to some special exceptions. But if he were not determined to treat a person's causing something, or making something happen, as always a matter of the obtaining of an event-causal relation, then he would have no need for any exceptions. There would be no premise for his regress argument.

So a person's raising her arm (when she raises it) is indeed the same as her arm's rising (then), as Davidson said. But this is not a special case, as Davidson thought.[12] Raising an arm is not a special case, because an identity of the sort in question obtains whenever something is done non-mediately. When the example is raising one's arm, the identity obtains because a person who is raising her arm is causing what she has caused when she stops raising it, namely her arm's being up. This was Aristotle's account.[13] Anscombe surely took it quite for granted. It must be doubtful whether Davidson ever contemplated it.

III

We can now start to see that Davidson and Anscombe are poles apart on the matter of the individuation of events in general and of actions in particular.

When Davidson claimed that "we never do more than move our bodies; the rest is up to nature", he meant to contrast the contribution that *we* make when we act with any contribution that nature makes: *our* contributions are our bodies' movements.[14] Consider now his example of a queen who poured poison

12. Although it is not a special case, it can still be that a person stands to parts of her body in a special relation: see further note 25 below.

13. See Ursula Coope, "Aristotle on Action", *Proceedings of the Aristotelian Society Supplementary* 81 (2007): 109–138. I owe to Coope my understanding of an Aristotelian treatment.

In *Actions* (London: Routledge, 1980), I rejected the special, ad hoc account that Davidson gives of moving the body (rightly, as it still seems to me) but followed Davidson's general line on causative verbs and event-causation (wrongly, as I hope is clear). The conclusion I reached was that even when a person's action is described as her moving her body, it is still described as a cause. Plenty of people have found that conclusion unbelievable. I owe to Helen Steward an understanding of the real force of the objections to it: see her "Do Actions Occur Inside the Body?" *Mind & Society* 2 (2000): 107–125.

14. We can assume that Davidson did not really mean to deny that moving one's body is the only thing one ever does, although, taken literally, Davidson's sentence surely does deny this, despite his own protestations to the contrary in "Note added in 1979". There he acknowledged at least that we *move* things other than our bodies ("Agency", 59n20).

In order for "we never do more than move our bodies" to be construed as Davidson intended, the things we do have to be equated with the events that are actions. Such an equation leads to mistakes of two different sorts. (1) The correct thought that doing something may be causing something gets translated into the thought that a person who acts relates to her *action*

into a king's ear. Davidson would say that the queen's contribution is her hand's movements, and the poison's arriving in the king's ear is "up to nature". And he contrives to describe the particular example as if this were so: when he writes "The queen moved her hand thus causing the vial to empty into the king's ear", he makes it sound as if the queen's hand's movement caused an event in which the vial played its own part.[15] According to Davidson, then, the action is characterized relationally—by allusion to something other than itself—when it is said to be a pouring of poison; only when it is described as a moving of her hand is the action itself, just as such, described. But Anscombe would say that, given the circumstances, nothing extrinsic to the action is introduced when it is described as a pouring of poison. The queen's causing poison to be in the king's ear is correctly conceived as something in which the vial containing the poison, the poison, and the queen are all participants.

It makes a significant difference to take Anscombe's view of how actions are correctly conceived. What someone may be non-mediately doing as they move their body depends upon what their body is in contact with; and anything one's body may be in contact with is a particular thing, having its particular weight, shape, etc., and belonging among other objects to which it stands in particular relations. So the character of an action depends hugely upon the particularities of the circumstances. A person's using her arms and hands in a certain way may in some circumstances be her pouring poison into someone's ear, in other circumstances her introducing some benign stuff into a filter. A person's moving her fingers in a certain way may in some circumstances be her kneading the dough, in other circumstances her massaging someone's back. In such examples we find two actions between which Davidson would find no inherent difference, because (a) he would say that the events are of different kinds only insofar as they relate differently to other events, and (b) the bodily movements are of the same kind *ex hypothesi*. But as far as Anscombe is concerned, and surely entirely plausibly, the actions in each pair are inherently different.

Notice that the *identities* endorsed by both Anscombe and Davidson are not affected by this. For instance, both would hold that, when circumstances actually are a certain way, the queen's moving her hand *is* the queen's pouring

---

as its cause, so that the doctrine of agent causation (mentioned at the end of §1) comes to be espoused. (2) See the next note.

15. Davidson, "Agency", 58. Here we have an example of a second sort of faulty inference, which results from equating the things people do with their actions: it is made to appear that *a*'s action is said to have caused *e* wherever *a* is said to have done something which caused *e*.

poison into the king's ear, and the person's moving her fingers *is* her kneading the dough. The fact that they can agree about such things has helped to sustain the false impression that they share a view about the individuation of actions. The use of the label "the Anscombe-Davidson view" has probably helped more than anything else to ensure that the impression survives.[16]

Although Anscombe herself may have given the impression that she shared a view with Davidson (see the Appendix below), she made it plain nevertheless that she and Davidson are actually not on the same page on questions about what is singled out when an event is singled out. Anscombe said that she and Davidson "part company . . . when it comes to his theory of event-identity". And she "maintain[ed] that the demand for a criterion of identity of particular occurrences *just as such* is not a reasonable one".[17] Here she signals a very basic difference of outlook toward the domain of events. In Davidson's view, events constitute a neutral, unconceptualized category. He thought of the domain as, so to speak, standing ready—ready for us to pick out this or that item belonging in it. That is how he could seek a criterion for things in the entire domain, "for occurrences *just as such*"—as if the intrinsic nature of any event were a matter simply of its being an event, and independent of the nature of any other things. It is true that Davidson changed his mind about what a correct criterion would be;[18] but he always sought to provide the sort of criterion that might be given from a high level of abstraction, without using any of the concepts that are actually used in singling out events. In Anscombe's view, by contrast, the specific concepts brought to bear when it is said that there was an event of such-and-such sort may be determinative of the nature of what it is that is picked out.

The full import of this for Anscombe's conception of *actions* emerges in a place where she is plainly criticizing Davidson. When she charges him with "a failure of percipience", she conjectures that the failure is owed to his taking what she calls "the standard approach".[19] Those who take that approach "first

---

16. "The Anscombe-Davidson view/thesis" has come to be a textbook epithet. So far as I know, it was first used by Goldman, in "The Individuation of Action", *Journal of Philosophy* 68 (1971): 761–774.

17. "Under a Description" (originally published 1979), in *Metaphysics and the Philosophy of Mind,* 2nd ed. (Oxford: Basil Blackwell, 1981), 217.

18. For the change of mind, see first "The Individuation of Events", then "Reply to Quine on Events". And see further the Appendix below.

19. "Practical Inference", in *Human Life, Action, and Ethics,* ed. M. Geach and L. Gormally (St. Andrews Studies in Philosophy and Public Affairs, vol. IV; Exeter: Imprint Aca-

distinguish between 'action' and what merely happens, and then specify that [they] are talking about 'actions.'" Anscombe's own view is that we must treat actions as a class in order to talk about them, and that it is not possible to define the class by saying how actions differ from mere happenings.[20] This rules out giving a general criterion for the individuation of events, with actions simply among them. For treating the broad category of events as a fundamental kind would ensure that questions about identities in respect of actions were secondary to questions about identities in respect of events. But in Anscombe's view, a general principle for individuating events of just any sort cannot serve as a principle for individuating *actions*. Actions must be treated as individuals in their own right.

Anscombe comes close to registering this idea of actions as individuals in their own right when she says:

> Suppose we take a countable concept of an action or event like, say, administering poison. Such an event will split up into a lot of sub-events or sub-actions; there might even be a gap in the process, which yet counts as one administration of poison—the administration being interrupted, say, by a fit of coughing on the part of the administerer. However we are willing to count the whole episode as just *one* time that the person administered poison, one administration. ("Under a Description", 216)

This passage well illustrates Anscombe's general outlook on events. What unifies the sub-events in the example—what holds them together, so to speak—shows up only insofar as "administering poison" has application. The whole event is not something one could latch onto by first descrying smaller events to be treated as its parts; for there is seen to be *one* administration of poison only when the concept of administering poison is in play.[21] This makes a general point about what is involved in an event's individuation. Still, the example is of an action, and Anscombe's idea of the unity of *an action* is on display. The allusion to a possible coughing fit in the middle of an administering of poi-

---

demic, 2005), III. (The essay was originally published in 1989 as "Von Wright on Practical Inference".)

20. See "Action and Generality", Anton Ford's essay in this volume.

21. In "Physicalism, Events and Part-Whole Relations", in *Actions and Events,* ed. E. LePore and B. McLaughlin (Oxford: Basil Blackwell, 1986), 444–458, I argued that those who give theories of events at a high level of abstraction require a mereological conception of them, a conception I criticized. I treated Davidson as a target, but didn't see that I was taking Anscombe's side.

son reminds us that, where actions are in question, *intention* does the work of unification. Although the coughing fit would prevent the person from continuing to make the movements needed in order to administer the poison, she would revert to making such movements when she stopped coughing. And that is because she was making such movements *in order* that the poison should be administered. Thus does the process count as a single action at completion, and thus would it count so even if there were such a gap.[22]

IV

Actions being individuals in their own right, an account of them should treat them as such. In Anscombe's treatment, an action's various properties (to which its various descriptions are owed) do not have their source in the workings of event-causality, but in the means/end structure of pieces of practical reasoning. This began to emerge in the example of administering poison. More can be learned from a passage in *Intention* in which Anscombe spoke of her man who pumped poisoned water.[23]

> Moving his arm up and down with his fingers round the pump handle [A] *is,* in these circumstances, operating the pump [B]; and, in these circumstances, it *is* replenishing the house water-supply [C] . . . and, in these circumstances, it *is* poisoning the household [D]. . . . So there is one action with four descriptions, each <u>dependent on wider circumstances,</u> and each related to the next as description of means to end. . . . If D is given as the answer to the question, "Why?" about A, [then] B and C can make an appearance in <u>answer to the question, "How?"</u>. When terms are related in this fashion, they constitute a series of means, the last term of which is, just by being given as the last, <u>so far treated as an end.</u> (*Intention,* 46–47)

Let me expand on three things here, signalled with the underlining I have introduced, which highlight Anscombe's differences from Davidson. (Other

---

22. Given the usual, broad understanding of the progressive, "He was administering poison" would have been true throughout the process even if there had been a gap. So the gap here, like the "hiccups" or "glitches", which Haddock speaks about at section 8 of his essay in this volume, would not count against the truth of a statement recording what the agent is doing.

23. Julia Annas noticed how un-Davidsonian this passage is: see her "Davidson and Anscombe on 'The Same Action'", *Mind* 85 (1976): 251–257.

essays in the present volume bring out some of the details, and more of the merits, of Anscombe's view.)

(1) The man's operating the pump is the same as his moving his arm up and down because the *circumstances* are ones in which the man's fingers are around the pump handle. These are circumstances which the man himself has put in place and which obtain before the man's action of pumping the water could play the role of cause. Evidently the man could not play *his* role unless these are actually the circumstances, and are *known* to him to be.

(2) Anscombe's treatment of agency turns around a certain *Why?*-question, which can be asked of rational agents about something they are doing, whose answers give their reason for doing it (see *Intention*, §§5–17). This *Why?*-question goes hand in hand with a certain *How?*-question: answers to both provide links between things intentionally done. Consider:

> "WHY are you operating the pump?"; "[My reason is that] I'm replenishing the water-supply".
>
> "How do you replenish the water-supply"; "By [means of] operating the pump".

Here two descriptions of an action are linked because the agent's doing one thing (replenishing the supply) rationally explains his doing another (operating the pump), *and equally because* doing the other is *how* he does the one (he replenishes the supply by operating the pump). Thus the means/end structure, which shows up in series of descriptions linked by "by", is a sort of front-to-back reflection of the structure of reasons. Davidson would, of course, agree that different descriptions of a single action can be linked in a "by"-chain, and he accepted that circumstances have some role to play in understanding identities.[24] But insofar as he took "by"-chains to reflect the workings of event-causality, Davidson was unable to see the structure of reasons as present in actions themselves. In order to see them so, one has to appreciate that agents make use of their knowledge of means–end relations in acting, and that they exercise capacities, some of which their knowledge provides them with, so as to bring things about. The pumper, for instance, has the capacity to move his arms up and down, and, knowing that he can replenish the water

---

24. Davidson allows a role to circumstances when he speaks of "context": for his understanding of "context", see the Appendix below. My present concern is with cases where Davidson would attribute redescribability not to context, but to the kicking in of "nature".

supply by moving his arms with his fingers around the pump handle, he has the capacity also to replenish the water supply.[25]

(3) When Anscombe mentions something's being "so far treated as an end", her thought is that replenishing the water supply stands to operating the pump as end to means, even though replenishing the water supply is a means in its turn and not the agent's final end. Here there is what one might think of as a simple action: an agent now does something by now doing some other thing. But "so far treated as an end" can remind us of *compound* actions—actions having actions as components—in which the agent does something by *first* doing this thing, and *next* that thing, and *later* some third thing. Perhaps she makes an omelette by getting out the eggs, taking each in turn and lifting it and breaking it against the bowl, mixing, finding the frying pan, etc., etc. So long as she is looking for the frying pan, finding it is "*so far* treated as an end". But *only* so far: it is in order to make an omelette that she is finding the pan, and for that, further actions are needed.

Where actions are compound, their components constitute the whole by virtue of the intention that unites them. The answer to the question why she is doing what she is now doing (whisking eggs, say) can at any point be that she is doing the whole thing (making an omelette, say). There is then a sort of structure in "by"-chains that makes no appearance in Davidson's account. It would obviously be wrong to think that when an agent achieves her end by doing a series of things, the component actions must be related to one another causally. If we want to introduce causality in saying why the several components belong in something correctly considered to be one whole action, then we can advert to the fact that the agent uses knowledge of what things *she* needs to bring about in order that her end be reached (that an omelette be made, say).

V

This takes us back to questions about individuation.

For the sake of vividness, I started from an example in which the object that an agent affected by acting in some way was in contact with her body

---

25. The fact that capacities to move our bodies require no knowledge of circumstances may explain why bodily movements have seemed to need to be given a prominent place in an account of agency. *Moving the body* is something that can be done *directly:* cf. note 11 above. The point against Davidson here has been that something may be done *directly,* even while other things are also *non-mediately* done—which other things depending upon the circumstances as these are known to the agent.

throughout her acting on it. I said that we find something non-mediately done in these examples, and I used them to show that the spatial extent of an action is wrongly conceived in Davidson's picture. Examples of different sorts are needed to show that Davidson's treatment of actions as event-causes also gets their temporal extents wrong. I shall suggest a couple. But I find that we don't always have firm intuitions about when an event of someone's doing something is/was ongoing, and I shan't try to state any principles that deal with every case. (The idea of a thing's being done non-mediately is surely vague, and it can remain vague. And I don't rule it out that we should need another idea if we were to be in a position to take a definite view of all possible examples.)

The first thing to notice is that a person may start or stop acting on an object before or after she makes contact with it. When someone treads on an ant, for instance, her foot is moving before it touches the ant. But we don't distinguish two parts of the treading, according as the foot has already, or has not yet, touched the ant. Treading on an ant is non-mediately done, even though, from an observer's point of view, the ant is not patently involved throughout the event of its being trodden on.

Now consider a case where the agent is not patently involved throughout doing some particular thing. Suppose that Bill closes a door by pushing it some way and hard enough to close it. Inasmuch as Bill's purpose is achieved by communicating his own efficacy to the door, his closing it will be taken at least to encompass its closing. We might well treat this as another example of non-mediate closing, thinking that, even though the door acquires a momentum of its own, the causal work involved in its closing is Bill's work. But even someone who insists that the door itself does causal work, and who thinks that this shows that the bit of the door's closing$_{[intrans]}$ which takes place after Bill's hand has left the door is not Bill's work, will not think, as Davidson would, that the closing$_{[trans]}$ caused the closing$_{[intrans]}$. (Presumably in their view Bill's closing$_{[trans]}$ the door is a proper part of the door's closing$_{[intrans]}$.)

A different example shows the relevance of an agent's intentions to individuation.[26] Suppose that you have just clicked on the "print" icon on your computer screen so as to print your document, whose pages take a full twenty

---

26. The example is taken from David Mackie, who used it to good effect in "The Individuation of Actions", *Philosophical Quarterly* 47 (1997): 48–54. But Mackie treated it as a counter-example to "the [*sic*] view defended by Anscombe, Davidson and Hornsby".

seconds to emerge from the printer. You are now printing your document. So the movement you made in order to set the printer to work cannot be the same as your printing the document, which is taking place while your body is at rest. The explanation of why the event of your printing the document should be ongoing when you are not patently active is that the printer remains somewhat under your control, and your intention to print the document survives long enough for you to be able to deal with paper jams or the like. Your action of printing comes to an end only when your intended end is reached and you have a printed document.

Anscombe spoke of "the time of the completion of an action" as "the time by which the agent has completed his activity in the matter". Well, we have just seen there can be activity in a matter which is not *bodily* activity. It is one thing for an action concept to require for its satisfaction an active, bodily being, and another thing for an agent's instantiating the concept at any time to require that her body then be moving. In Davidson's treatment, it can seem that getting anything done requires unremitting bodily activity. This ought to strike us as wrong for a wide range of things we do that very evidently require thought as well as motion—speaking, say, or doing the crossword, or pruning the roses. We see that it must be wrong when we realize that an answer to the question whether someone is intentionally doing something now is determined by what intentions they are now executing. Admittedly, Davidson hoped to secure the claim that actions are bodily movements by "interpret[ing] 'bodily movement' generously". "The generosity must be open-handed enough", he said, "to encompass such 'movements' as standing fast, and mental acts like deciding and computing" ("Agency", 49). But this will not give Davidson the identities he wants. His idea was that an action is someone's intentionally doing something; and it is not as if at any moment at which the body of someone who is, say, pruning the roses happens to be stationary, they must intend then to stand fast or to decide or compute—although their staying still or "deciding or computing" may be part of the ongoing process of their pruning the roses.

Although Anscombe clearly has a different view from Davidson of what it is for actions to be ongoing, sometimes she can seem to have shared Davidson's view about when actions end. When she speaks of "the consummation of an action under descriptions . . . after the agent has completed his part", she appears to echo Davidson, who had said, about his queen who killed a king, that "after she has moved her hand in such a way as to cause the king's

death . . . [no] deed remains for her to do or complete". Well, the agreement
on this is explained by the fact that Anscombe thought that actions are *sometimes* described in terms of consequences to which they lead.[27] For instance,
she would say, about her man who pumped poisoned water, that his action
came to fall under the description "poisoning" only when there had been
enough ingestion of the poison he transmitted. By Anscombe's lights, there
are examples like this because one can sometimes do what one intends to do
by relying on one's actions having effects of their own. Still, triggering a
chain of events is just *one* sort of way in which an agent may cause something: it corresponds to just one sort of way in which an agent's means and
ends may be related. And even when an agent acts in such a way, there is no
call to think about things as Davidson always does—no need to say that our
"knowledge that the man's operating the pump results in the inhabitants being poisoned allows us to describe the man as the cause of their being poisoned, but this is merely a convenient way of redescribing the event of the
man's operating the pump".

Davidson pointed out that an agent "may be dead when the consequence
of his deed" brings the deed under some particular description ("Adverbs of
Action", 300). The point is often used in an argument—known sometimes as
"the no further effort argument"—which says that the temporal boundaries
of actions must be narrowly drawn, given that no one acts at a time at which
they might already have died—at a time at which no further effort of theirs
is called for. A version of this argument shows, for instance, that the man's
operating the pump did not take as long as it took for the inhabitants to be
poisoned. But Anscombe could not use such an argument to reach the general
conclusion that Davidson wanted to reach by using it. The argument has
force only where so-called consequences are genuinely distinct events in terms
of which actions come to be described. And the argument cannot lend support to a Davidsonian picture of actions as *mere* movements of the body. (It
can be allowed that if you dropped dead immediately after you used a bit of
your body to set the printer in motion, then "You are printing the document"
would be false while the printer did its work. It would then be false because
death extinguishes intentions as well as the makings of movements.)

27. See her discussion of an example of killing by shooting in "Under a Description", 213–
216. For the echo of Davidson, see his "Agency", 58, and her "Under a Description", 216, and
see further the Appendix below.

It is no wonder that in Anscombe's view both the spatial and temporal extents of actions fail to coincide with those of bodily movements. In seeing that agents cause things by deploying the means they have of doing so, she had a quite different idea from Davidson's of what it is to act. In order to see the full scope of the difference, one has to think about what I called compound actions. In Anscombe's treatment, when there is a compound action, the series of means the agent takes are united by reference to the agent's end, not by summing the several, separately conceived components of the action (still less to summing such bodily movements as those components might involve). But the examples of simple actions may be enough to show that Anscombe's conception of actions is radically different from Davidson's, and to show something of the liberating effect it has to discard Davidson's idea that circumscribing actions is a matter of circumscribing such bodily movements as have certain causes and effects.[28]

VI

Davidson spoke of actions as "sandwiched between cause and effect" ("Problems", 108). "Sandwiched" is apt for his view, because Davidson thought the antecedents of actions, not only their consequents, can be characterized in terms suitable for showing them to stand to actions in event-causal relations. In this, Davidson is followed by almost everyone in contemporary philosophy of mind and action. But when it is allowed that event-causality does not rule the day, the usual account of actions as caused by mental states and events is surely put in doubt.

Still, one particular argument that Davidson gave, whose conclusion he put by saying that "rationalization is a species of causal explanation", need not be in doubt. *That* argument, about *one* sort of action-*explanation*, is not affected by anything I have said here in taking Anscombe's side.[29] And if one

---

28. In Part 2 of his *Life and Action* (Cambridge, Mass.: Harvard University Press, 2008), Michael Thompson vividly brings out the Anscombian conception, treating what I call compound actions. In thinking about examples, one needs to realize that what an agent can be said to be intentionally doing at any time depends upon how much can then be taken for granted and how much is a "matter of course". Anscombe gives examples that illustrate this: *Intention*, 39–40.

29. In "Anomalousness in Action" (in Hahn, ed., *The Philosophy of Donald Davidson*, 623–636), I distinguished the claim that "rationalization is a species of causal explanation" from a

wants to allow that our actions are located in the causal world at large, then one seems bound to accept the argument, and to allow that a causal explanation is given of why a person did something when it is said (e.g.) that she did it because she thought such-and-such. Anscombe, for her part, appears to reject that conclusion. But that may be because she rejected the conception of causal explanation of which Davidson made use, and because answers to her *Why?*-question encompass far more than Davidson's "rationalizations". Still, whatever exactly Anscombe's own view may have been, many have thought that a disagreement over "reasons and causes" is what principally separates Davidson from Anscombe. And those who have found themselves on Davidson's side over this have felt free to think that the agenda in philosophy of action might as well be set by Davidson, on whom, as he says, Anscombe had her influence. It may then have seemed unnecessary to attend to *Intention;* or, inasmuch as it is allowed that *Intention* contains important claims that are absent from Davidson's work, it may have seemed that those claims need to be incorporated somehow into a story of action of the sort that Davidson told.

My concern here has been to demonstrate Anscombe's opposition to the events-based story of agency, which so many have followed Davidson in telling. It is this story that we must reject. We must give *agents* the central place in a story, and allow that agents have powers to affect things and that what they bring about intentionally is shaped by their reasoning.[30]

Appendix

People who think that any deep difference of opinion between Anscombe and Davidson in the philosophy of action stems from a disagreement about actions' antecedents—about "reasons and causes"—make the assumption that the two philosophers see eye to eye on questions about the nature of actions themselves. I have argued against their assumption, and blamed its being made (1) on failure to take account of what Anscombe has to say about

---

different claim that Davidson also makes in his "Actions, Reasons and Causes"—that "reasons are causes", and maintained that his argument establishes only the former.

30. I have several people to thank. Jason Bridges was a most helpful commentator at the Chicago conference, where I gave a talk on which this essay has been based. Matthew Chrisman, David Hunter, and Eric Marcus also helped with comments on the conference paper. Conversations with Anton Ford have been very illuminating, and Fred Stoutland gave me useful detailed comments on a draft of the present essay.

causality, (2) on the widespread use of the label "the Anscombe-Davidson view", (3) on noticing Anscombe's and Davidson's agreement (strictly limited as actually it proves to be) about "the consummation of an action under descriptions". But the assumption has sources also in Anscombe's and Davidson's own writings.

I think that neither Anscombe nor Davidson was fully aware of the distance that there was between them. More specifically, I think that for Anscombe the idea that causality might be of the single kind event-causality was so far from credibility that she was unable to countenance Davidson's view of agency, and that this led to her failing to see problems with his formulations. Meanwhile, Davidson took his own account to be rooted in an idea of actions he had gotten from Anscombe (see p. 37 of his "Intellectual Autobiography", cited at note 1), and thus encouraged the impression that he was more in agreement with Anscombe than he actually was.

In "Under a Description", Anscombe is mainly concerned to counter opposition that she had met to the idea of actions as redescribable, so that much of what she says there is directed against accounts to which she and Davidson are both opposed. One should expect points of agreement to be at the fore there, then. But in two places Anscombe makes it seem as if she were more in agreement with Davidson than she actually is. (1) She says "As Davidson has put it, all that he (or I) meant by speaking of many different descriptions of one action is, e.g., that the executioner of Charles I, having taken his head off, did not have to add any further performances . . . to make his act one of killing" (211). Given the restricted nature of the particular example, it might be a stretch to see Anscombe as wanting to convey that she would agree with Davidson on all questions about actions' identities. But her "as Davidson put it", along with "all that he meant", may have given that impression. (2) She says "the consummation of an action under [a particular description] is left to circumstance or, as Davidson puts it, to nature" (216, my italics again). Here she makes it seem as if her "circumstances" and Davidson's "nature" (i.e., the working of event causality) had much the same role to play in an account. It is as if she failed to appreciate the extent to which Davidson's account of agency was informed by a conception of causality to which she was totally opposed.

Davidson did not think that it was solely the workings of "nature" that "allow us to redescribe actions in ways which we cannot redescribe other events". He said that "the redescription of an action afforded by a reason may place the action in a wider social, economic, linguistic, or evaluative context" ("Actions, Reasons and Causes", 8). Davidson would have agreed, then (to take an example more or less at random), that when Jane sticks to her diet by eating only salad for lunch, we can appeal to circumstances—to his "context"—to account for Jane's eating only salad's being Jane's sticking to her diet. What Davidson failed to see was that the redescription of an action afforded by a reason places the action in *all* of the particularities of the agent's circumstances as the agent takes them to be. It may be that Anscombe failed to see that he failed to see that.

Davidson's lack of understanding of his distance from Anscombe shows up in two places. (1) When he retold the example of Anscombe's man who operated a pump, he changed things and had the man "pouring the contents of a bucket into a reservoir" ("Intellectual Autobiography", 37). Davidson's conception of actions, as event-causes of what agents cause, lends itself to thinking of actions as if they were never in progress but were always over-and-done-with; and in changing the example, he moved to one in which that way of thinking comes slightly more easily. Presumably, Davidson didn't realize that he had changed the example, still less that he had changed it away from one that more straightforwardly illustrates Anscombe's account. (2) When Davidson talked about individuation at large, he appeared to be unable to get his mind around an Anscombian view of the matter. In his "Reply to Quine on Events", he apparently settled for a spatiotemporal principle of individuation for events in general. However, Davidson went on to say: "Perhaps it is obvious that individuating items in a grand category like events or objects is quite different from individuating kinds within those categories, such as desks or people; I had not fully appreciated this" (310). Well, one who does appreciate it will doubt whether there could be any principled account of the individuation of things in "a grand category". Evidently, Davidson never took the point that Anscombe made when she said that "the demand for a criterion of identity of particular occurrences just as such is not a reasonable one" ("Under a Description", 217).

4

Anscombe on Bodily Self-Knowledge

JOHN MCDOWELL

I

As everyone knows, G. E. M. Anscombe argues in *Intention*[1] that intentional actions are known by their agent without observation.

But she introduces the class of things known without observation by mentioning a different sub-class of it: the position of one's limbs, when that is known in a way in which "a man usually knows the position of his limbs" (13).

This comes up while she is engaged in her well-known project of singling out intentional actions as goings-on that admit the question "Why?" understood in a particular way.

If the applicability of the question is to explain the very idea of acting intentionally, there are certain ground rules on what she may do to identify the relevant sense of the question. She may not exploit concepts one could understand only if one already understood the concept of acting intentionally. For instance, she is not allowed to explain the question as a request for someone's reason for doing something.

---

1. Oxford: Blackwell, 1957; 2nd ed., Cambridge, Mass.: Harvard University Press, 2000.

Her procedure is to isolate the relevant sense of the question by eliminating cases in which it does *not* have application. First she notes that it "is refused application by the answer: 'I was not aware I was doing that'" (11). Next she turns to excluding a certain class of involuntary bodily movements, exemplified by "the odd sort of jerk or jump that one's whole body sometimes gives when one is falling asleep" and "tics, reflex kicks from the knee, the lift of the arm from one's side after one has leaned heavily with it up against a wall" (13). Anscombe takes her ground rules to preclude using the term "involuntary" to specify this class of movements. And it is to define the class without violating that prohibition that she introduces the idea of things known without observation. Using that idea, she can specify these movements as "movements of the body, in a purely physical description, which are known without observation, and where there is no such thing as a *cause* known without observation" (15).[2]

En route to that specification, Anscombe devotes a paragraph to the example with which she introduces the idea of things known without observation, the position of one's limbs when that is known in the relevant way. Next—before she goes on to define that class of involuntary movements in a way that conforms to her ground rules—she exploits the idea of things known without observation in a preview of her doctrine that knowledge of one's own intentional actions is not observational (14):

> Now the class of things known without observation is of general interest to our enquiry because the class of intentional actions is a sub-class of it. I have already said that 'I was not aware I was doing that' is a rejection of the question 'Why?' whose sense we are trying to get at; here I can further say 'I knew I was doing that, but only because I observed it' would also be a rejection of it. E.g. if one noticed that one operated the traffic lights in crossing a road.

In a wide-scale view of what Anscombe is doing in this region of her text, this remark is perfectly in place. She has excluded cases in which one is doing things without knowing it, and she is working toward excluding that class of involuntary movements without violating her ground rules. Here she adds

---

2. This specification actually exploits a new sub-class of bodily things known without observation; she introduced the idea in connection with the *position* of one's limbs, and here she applies it also to certain bodily *movements*.

another class of cases in which the question "Why?" in the relevant sense is denied application: cases where it is only by observation that one knows what one is doing. So the remark contributes to her project of isolating the relevant sense of the question by eliminating cases in which it does not apply.

But her task in the immediate context is to define that class of involuntary movements without describing them as involuntary. That is the immediate purpose for which she introduced the idea of things known without observation (13):

> What is required is to describe this class [the class of involuntary movements she has put in place by means of some examples] without using any notions like 'intended' or 'willed' or 'voluntary' and 'involuntary'. This can be done as follows: we first point out a particular class of things which are true of a man: the class of things which he *knows without observation.*

And in this immediate context, her preview of the doctrine about knowledge of one's own intentional actions has the character of a digression. After the digression, she reverts to the immediate task (14):

> But the class of things known without observation is also of special interest in this part of our enquiry, because it makes it possible to describe the particular class of 'involuntary actions' which I have so far indicated just by giving a few examples [i.e., the class exemplified by reflex kicks, etc.]: . . . our task is to mark off this class without begging the questions we are trying to answer [i.e., in particular, without using the concept of the involuntary].

And she proceeds to exploit the idea of knowledge without observation in constructing the specification of that class that I have already quoted.

If one does not appreciate the way these pages are organized, one can be led to misconstrue Anscombe's aim when she cites the position of one's limbs as her first example of things known without observation. Kieran Setiya, for instance, notes that Anscombe compares knowledge of what one is intentionally doing with the relevant kind of knowledge of the position of one's limbs. And of course that is right: she says both are without observation. But Setiya goes on to complain that Anscombe's "explanation" of knowledge of what one is intentionally doing

> is not particularly helpful. For it is not at all obvious how we know the position of our own limbs, or how Anscombe thinks we do. . . . Matters

are further confused by Anscombe's insistence that knowledge of position is speculative or receptive in a way that knowledge of intentional action is not. How does this contrast fit together with her explicit comparison?[3]

And this presupposes a promise of illumination from the comparison that is not in Anscombe's text. (That is not all that is wrong with what Setiya says here; I shall come back to this.) All the comparison amounts to is that knowledge of what one is intentionally doing is like the relevant kind of knowledge of limb position in being without observation. There is no suggestion that an account of the relevant kind of knowledge of limb position is supposed to constitute an *explanation* of the character of knowledge of what one is intentionally doing.

Though his complaint misfires, Setiya is right that it is not clear what account Anscombe wants to give of the relevant kind of knowledge of the position of one's limbs. I am going to try to tease this out, for its own sake at first, though a connection with agency will emerge in due course.

II

Anscombe grants that "it may be because one has sensations" that one has the knowledge of limb position she is concerned with (*Intention*, 49). But she says "that does not mean that one knows [the position of one's limbs] by identifying the sensations one has" (ibid.). The concession is that sensations may be *causally* necessary for this knowledge, and her point is that it would not follow that sensations are *epistemologically* relevant to it.[4]

But there are two different possible interpretations for the thought that sensations have a place in the epistemology of this knowledge. I think Anscombe wants to reject both of them. But her remarks on the topic do not

---

3. "Practical Knowledge", *Ethics* 118 (April 2008): 388–409, at 392–393.

4. The concession is that sensations *may* be causally necessary for the kind of knowledge in question. In a later essay she notes, in effect, that the causal necessity of sensations might be queried on the basis of "the anaesthetic boy cited in James's *Principles*, II, pp. 489–90": "On Sensations of Position", in *Collected Philosophical Papers*, vol. 2: *Metaphysics and the Philosophy of Mind* (Oxford: Blackwell, 1981), 71. She need not settle the question; her interest is in the denial of epistemological relevance, not the possible causal relevance of sensations. But, tempted by the idea of a possible causal relevance of sensations (or perhaps we should say "of sensation"), we might wonder if "the anaesthetic boy" knew the position of his limbs in the way she has said that "a man" usually does.

make the necessary distinction. In fact her treatment, at least in *Intention*, focuses on the wrong version of the thought for a denial of it to be relevant to her thesis that this knowledge is not observational.

On one interpretation of the thought, this knowledge is *inferential*, grounded on independently describable characteristics of certain sensations. This version of Anscombe's target is suggested by the formulation I have just quoted, where she says her concession of a possible relevance for sensations does not imply that one knows the position of one's limbs "by identifying the sensations one has". There is the same suggestion when she says, in the same context, "it is not as if [a man] were going by a tingle in his knee, which is the sign that it is bent and not straight". And similarly in "On Sensations of Position", where she writes (72):

> The idea that it is by sensation that I judge my bodily position is usually the idea that it is by other sensations, not just the 'sensation' of sitting cross-legged, say, that I judge that I am sitting cross-legged, i.e. by a pressure here, a tension there, a tingle in this other place; such sensations are supposed to be sensations of being in that bodily position because, perhaps, they have been found to go with that.

Anscombe has no difficulty arguing that this inferential picture does not give a satisfactory account of the knowledge she is concerned with. But her thesis was supposed to be that this knowledge is *without observation*. And surely observational knowledge is not inferentially grounded on independently describable characteristics of sensations. To reject the inferential picture is not to establish that the relevant kind of knowledge of limb position is not observational.

This leads Edward Harcourt, who finds nothing in Anscombe's argument against an epistemological relevance for sensations except her rejection of the inferential picture, to "suspect . . . that the term 'without observation' wasn't the best way of expressing what Anscombe really meant".[5] I am going to pursue Harcourt's reading of Anscombe a bit, because it will help bring into view the other of the two ways one might attribute an epistemological significance to sensations in an account of knowledge of limb position. Anscombe is certainly unclear about this. But if we take it that she means to reject this

5. "Wittgenstein and Bodily Self-Knowledge", *Philosophy and Phenomenological Research* 72 (2008): 299–333; the quotation is from 306–307.

second picture as well as the inferential picture, that will enable us to make sense, as Harcourt cannot, of her thesis that this knowledge is not observational.

III

Harcourt cites this from Anscombe (*Intention*, 13–14):

> a man usually knows the position of his limbs without observation. . . . Without prompting, we *can say* [how our limbs are disposed]. I say however that we *know* it and not merely *can say* it, because there is a possibility of being right or wrong.

And he says:

> Although we find the unhelpful "without observation" terminology here too, the passage reveals that what Anscombe means by the claim that we know the position and movement of our limbs "without observation" is that *all there is* (normally) to knowing the position and movement of one's limbs is that we can say where they are, together with the possibility of error; otherwise put, that knowledge of posture and movement reduces, in the normal case, to the exercise of a fallible disposition to judge these things.[6]

He supports this with another passage from Anscombe ("On Sensations of Position", 73):

> If only my leg had been bent, there would very likely have been just that fact and my knowledge of it, i.e. my capacity to describe my position straight off: no question of any appearance of the position to me, of any sensations which give me the position.

Here too, he takes her to be claiming that knowing limb position in the relevant way reduces to the exercise of a fallible disposition to judge limb position. And in this passage he finds "an identification of the claim that knowledge of posture is not inferred from 'separable' sensations (no 'sensations which give me the position') with what sounds like the claim that it is not perceptual (no 'appearance of the position to me')".[7]

6. Ibid., 307.
7. Ibid.

As Harcourt reads her, Anscombe thinks that by establishing that the relevant kind of knowledge is not inferentially based on sensations, she can show that it is nothing but the exercise of a fallible disposition to judge. That means she has no good ground for rejecting the option of supposing that the knowledge is perceptual. Harcourt writes:

> Perceptual experience is belief-independent: I can have a perceptual experience as of things' being a certain way without being disposed to believe or therefore to judge that they are that way. So my having the perceptual experience as of their being that way—to use Anscombe's phrase, my being subject to an appearance as of their being that way—cannot reduce to the disposition to judge that they are. "No appearance of the position to me" and "no sensations which give me the position" are thus very different ideas, and the reductive claim [i.e., the claim that this kind of knowledge reduces to the exercise of a fallible disposition to judge] is as yet far from proved [i.e., it is not established by the rejection of the inferential picture].[8]

As Harcourt sees things, Anscombe's arguments leave the idea that the knowledge in question is perceptual still a live option.

In fact he thinks this knowledge *must* be perceptual. He thinks this follows from the fact that there can be illusions of limb position that are belief-independent.[9] Since such illusions do not involve believing that things are as they appear to be, they cannot be faulty actualizations of a disposition to judge the position of one's limbs. Harcourt thinks they can only be perceptual appearances of the position of one's limbs, defective instances of a kind of experience whose non-defective instances yield perceptual knowledge of the position of one's limbs.

IV

But this starts from an unpersuasive reading of Anscombe.

When Anscombe speaks of what "we can say" and of "my capacity to describe my position straight off", we should not take her to be putting forward what Harcourt calls "the reductive claim"—the claim that a case of the kind

---

8. Ibid., 308.

9. See ibid., 300 (where he is anticipating an argument he gives at 314–315): "the possibility of belief-independent illusions of posture and movement makes a perceptual account of our standard knowledge of these things mandatory".

of knowledge in question is nothing but an exercise of a fallible *disposition* to *judge* one's limb position. What she is claiming is that a case of this kind of knowledge is nothing but an exercise of a fallible *capacity* to *know* the position of one's limbs. ("Nothing but", as in Harcourt's reading, serves to emphasize that there is no epistemological role for sensations.)

It is true that Anscombe glosses knowledge of the kind she is concerned with as an ability to *say* how things are. This makes it natural that when she considers cases in which the capacity for this knowledge misfires, she focuses on cases in which one would say something false, cases in which one believes something false. Thus she writes ("On Sensations of Position", 73–74):

> The difference between the two situations [one in which I know that my leg is bent and one in which it merely seems to be] may lie only in this, that in one case my leg is bent and I know it, and in the other it is not bent but—off my own bat—I believe that it is.

She is not alert here to the possibility of a belief-independent reading of locutions like "To me it is as if my leg is bent". But that does not imply that she is *identifying* being under the illusion that one's leg is bent with being disposed to judge that it is bent. Suppose one found oneself regularly subject to the illusion in certain circumstances. One surely would not go on believing one's leg was bent when it seemed to be bent in such circumstances. So it is wrong to think that being subject to the illusion *consists* in being disposed to judge that things are as they seem. This is perfectly compatible with the point Anscombe is making in the passage I have quoted. What she says is that the difference between the two situations *may* be only that in one there is knowledge of limb position and in the other a false belief about it; not that whenever the relevant capacity for knowledge misfires there is a false belief.

The most obvious way for a fallible capacity for knowledge to misfire, as we acknowledge it can when we acknowledge its fallibility, is for things to seem to the possessor of the capacity to be otherwise than they are.[10] The subject in such a misfire *may* be disposed to judge that things are the way they seem, and that is how it is in the kind of case Anscombe focuses on. But we should not *identify* being subject to such a seeming with being disposed to judge that things are the way they seem. We should resist that identification in connec-

---

10. Things can be as they seem in cases in which the relevant kind of knowledge is not available, and such seemings are misfires, too. But I shall ignore this.

tion with any fallible capacities for knowledge, not just perceptual capacities. It is Harcourt's own thought that the identification would be wrong in the case of the kind of fallible capacity for knowledge that a perceptual capacity is. And what Anscombe's words point to, in the case of the capacity to know the position of one's limbs in the relevant way, is a different kind of fallible capacity to know things, a capacity that is not perceptual. As I have acknowledged, she is not alert to the possibility of belief-independent seemings. But if it arose for her, she would be at liberty to hold that an identification of having things seem to one to be otherwise than they are, in a defective exercise of a capacity for knowledge, with a disposition to judge that they are that way would be just as wrong with this capacity as it would be with capacities that are perceptual.

This undermines Harcourt's attempt to make out that the capacity to know the position of one's limbs in the relevant way *must* be perceptual, on the ground that its deliverances are belief-independent. Belief-independence does indeed distinguish deliverances of perceptual capacities from the alternative he thinks he finds in Anscombe: namely, exercises of fallible dispositions to make judgments on certain topics. But she is talking about capacities to know, not dispositions to judge. And it is open to her, and us, to suppose that the capacity to know the position of one's limbs in the relevant way issues in belief-independent seemings but is not perceptual. The seemings are not appearances in the sense that figures in her claim that in the relevant kind of awareness of the position of a limb there is no appearance of the limb's position to the subject.

On this account, only some capacities for non-inferential knowledge are perceptual. What marks out perceptual capacities is not belief-independence in their deliverances, but the fact that the knowledge they issue in, though not inferentially grounded on the character of independently describable sensations, is epistemologically mediated in a certain way by sensations—something that, according to Anscombe, is not so with the relevant kind of knowledge of the position of one's limbs.

V

How, then, is perceptual knowledge mediated by sensations without being inferentially grounded in them?

We can find an answer in Anscombe's essay "Substance",[11] where she reflects on the idea that a substance can be defined as the sum of its appear-

11. "Substance", in *Collected Philosophical Papers,* vol. 2, 38–43.

ances. Something's *appearances* are its sensible properties in a restricted sense: "the secondary qualities, together with their qualifications of size, shape and mutual arrangement" (39). These properties are sensible in a sense in which not just any property that something can be, for instance, seen to have is thereby shown to be sensible: "To receive impressions of secondary qualities, you merely have to let the appropriate sense-organ be affected; that is why one can always imagine that the quality is a *mere* sense-content" (ibid.). Of course it can look as if something is, say, malleable, and something can be seen to be malleable. But malleability is not a sensible property in the restricted sense. The fact that something can look malleable, or be seen to be malleable, "does not mean that 'malleability' is itself a word for an appearance—for a way things strike the senses" (40).

Consider a capacity for knowledge that *is* perceptual, for instance, the capacity to know the colors of things by looking at them. Suppose I know, in an exercise of such a capacity, that something I see is red.[12] In that case there is an appearance of its color to me. And it is simply another way of expressing the same thought to say that there is a sensation (a visual sensation, of course) that gives me the thing's color. I am given the thing's color—to echo Anscombe—by merely having the appropriate sense-organ affected in the way it is. (Of course it is only against a certain background that having the sense-organ affected in the right way gives me the thing's color. I need to have the concept of colors as properties of things, which presupposes a great deal of background knowledge. And the affecting of the sense-organ needs to happen in a good light for determining the colors of things by looking.)

In a remark I cited (in section III) about knowledge of limb position, Anscombe implicitly equates "no question of an appearance of the position to me" with "[no question] of any sensations which give me the position". I quoted Harcourt reading that equation as a conflation. As he reads her, Anscombe reveals here that she thinks her rejection of the inferential picture (which he finds in her saying there are no sensations that give one the position) entitles her to deny that the relevant kind of knowledge is perceptual (which she expresses by saying there is no appearance of the position to one). But if I say that in an experience in which I see something to be red there is a sensation that gives me the color, I am not pointing to an inferential basis for the knowledge of the thing's color that is made available to me by the experience. There is no conflation in that passage from Anscombe. It is a single-minded

12. Strictly, perhaps, that its facing surface is red.

rejection of the second of the two conceptions of an epistemological relevance for sensations that I said we need to distinguish, a conception according to which sensation matters to the relevant kind of knowledge of limb position in the way sensation matters to knowledge that is perceptual.

Sensible properties in Anscombe's restricted sense are secondary qualities "together with their qualifications of size, shape and mutual arrangement". Bringing the "qualifications" into the picture, we can say that a visual impression of red is an impression of, for instance, an expanse of red with a certain shape, size, and orientation, at a certain angle to the direction in which one is looking. That exemplifies how sensations that give one the secondary qualities of things mediate perceptual awareness of the spatial properties of the things.

Now if the position of a limb were present to one in a perceptual appearance, on Anscombe's conception of perceptual appearances, it would have to be by way of sensations giving one secondary qualities in the volume of space occupied by the limb, or on its surface. That would be a counterpart to how the spatial properties of a colored surface are present to one by way of visual sensations that give one its color.

But if one takes "proprioception" or "kinaesthesis" to name a mode of perceptual sensing, what are its associated secondary qualities? Admittedly, they would not need to be homogeneously sensed through the space or over the surface. This would parallel the fact that visual sensing is typically not homogeneous in an impression of an expanse of color, even if the impression enables one to perceive a surface as uniformly colored.[13] But even if we look for qualities that are not homogeneously sensed through a space or over its surface, we find no secondary qualities associated with this supposed mode of perceptual sensing. The presence to one of the position of a limb, when one knows it in the relevant way, has no sensuously qualitative character. And it comes to the same thing to say that the position of a limb is not given to one by sensations, or that there is no perceptual appearance to one of the position of the limb. (I shall consider a possible objection to this claim in section VIII.)

VI

Harcourt accepts this phenomenological point. He puts it in terms of the "introspective elusiveness" of the "sensations" of limb position that figure in

---

13. See Anscombe's discussion of "the visual object": "Substance", 41–43.

Anscombe's discussion as "inseparable": the "sensation" of one's leg being bent and the like. One might put the point like this: there are no sensations—affections of relevant sense-organs—that constitute those "sensations".

Harcourt does not credit this point to Anscombe; as I said, the only argument he finds in her against an epistemological significance for sensations, in connection with the relevant kind of knowledge of limb position, is her attack on the inferential picture. But he finds a consideration in this area operative, though inconclusively, in Wittgenstein, as a ground for denying that this knowledge is perceptual.

Harcourt thinks one can acknowledge the phenomenological point and still maintain that this knowledge is perceptual. He thinks the point leaves it still possible to maintain that those introspectively elusive inseparable "sensations" of limb position are perceptual experiences.

But he contrives to make out that this is possible only by working with a disputable construal of the phenomenological point. As he understands it, the point is that there is no "non-representational sensuous vehicle" (320) for content that would be specified by saying what position someone "feels" a limb to be in, in one of those inseparable "sensations" of limb position. He takes secondary qualities to be "the properties of a non-representational vehicle of representational content" (321); so, as he sees things, to say there are no secondary qualities in the relevant kind of awareness of limb position is just a way of denying that there is an intrinsically propertied vehicle for the content of such awareness. But as he points out, according to "a widespread alternative view" there is anyway no intrinsically propertied vehicle for the content of experiences whose perceptual character no one would dispute, for instance visual experiences. As he puts it, "perception can be 'transparent'" (322). So construed, the introspective elusiveness of "sensations" of limb position does not establish that they are not perceptual experiences of limb position.

But this passes Anscombe by. (And I doubt that it has much to do with Wittgenstein either.) Perceptual sensations, as they figure in the conception of perceptual experience that I elicited from Anscombe's "Substance", are not elements in "a non-representational vehicle of representational content", items in consciousness with characteristics specifiable independently of what experience purports to disclose about the perceiver's environment. On the contrary, there is no way to describe the character of a perceptual sensation except by giving the secondary quality (with its "qualifications") that the sensation is an impression of. And secondary qualities are not intrinsic properties of vehicles for content that consists in how things appear to be in perceptual experience. On the contrary, they are elements in that content, elements in how things appear to be in perceptual experience. So Anscombe's view of perceptual experience, on which it embodies sensations that give one the secondary qualities of things (with their "qualifications"), is consistent with the idea that perception is transparent in Harcourt's sense. And now the phenomenological point, the absence of secondary qualities, still seems to afford an argument that the capacity to know limb position in the relevant way is not perceptual.

Harcourt mentions a claim of Michael Ayers that there is no perception of spatial properties without perception of secondary qualities, which do not include spatial properties themselves.[14] Ayers himself does not use this claim to argue that the capacity to know limb position in the relevant way is not perceptual. He thinks secondary qualities are present in the relevant sort of awareness of limb position, though so inconspicuously that it is easy to miss them.

But what if someone, insisting on the phenomenological point that Ayers rejects, did use the claim that perception of spatial properties always involves perception of secondary qualities to argue that the relevant kind of awareness of limb position is not perceptual? Harcourt says that if "secondary" just means "perceptible", that would simply beg the question: "whether spatial properties alone are perceptible—in the form of the spatial properties of our bodies—is just what is at issue" (321). This is the context in which he declares that "secondary qualities" is best interpreted to mean non-representational properties of a vehicle for how things appear to be in perceptual experience. But secondary qualities, in Ayers's claim, are surely not properties of a supposed vehicle for perceptual content. Secondary qualities are elements in that content. They are some of the properties objects appear to have, and are sometimes perceived to have, in perceptual experience: those one receives impressions of by merely letting the appropriate sense-organ be affected, as Anscombe puts it. And the plausibility of Ayers's claim, understood that way, affords a non-question-begging argument that the capacity to know limb position in the relevant way is not perceptual—that is, if we dissent from Ayers's own view that there are indeed secondary qualities associated with the capacity. We can find this argument adumbrated in Anscombe's claim that

---

14. "Wittgenstein and Bodily Self-Knowledge", 321, citing Ayers, *Locke: Epistemology and Ontology* (London: Routledge), 183.

when I know the position of one of my limbs in the relevant way, there is no appearance to me of the position of the limb.

VII

To reject the idea that knowledge of limb position of the relevant kind is perceptual, we do not need to rely on merely finding intuitive plausibility in the claim, explicit in Ayers and implicit in Anscombe, that there is no perceptual awareness of spatial properties of things without sensing of secondary qualities. The claim is not just intuitive; it is underwritten by the immediately *receptive* character of perceptual knowledge.

In receptive knowledge, the knower is affected by what is known. The idea of a sense is the idea of a potential for being affected by objects in a way that is suitable for coming to have perceptual knowledge of them. Perceptual knowledge, in the narrowest sense, is receptive knowledge that one has just by having one's senses affected by objects (against a suitable background, as before: see section V). The very idea of such knowledge brings with it the idea of appearances in the sense Anscombe explains: properties of the things known that are sensible in her restricted sense, so that the concept of such a property is the concept of a way things strike the senses, the concept of a way one senses something as being just by letting it affect a sense (against a suitable background).

We can bring this point into relief by noting that it applies only to immediately receptive knowledge, receptive knowledge not grounded in inference. Consider the chicken-sexers of philosophical folklore. They know, surely receptively, whether chicks are male or female, though there is no difference in the appearances the chicks present to them, the ways the chicks strike their senses. But this knowledge is inferential—not in that it is reached by inference, but in that it owes its epistemic credentials to the goodness of inferences from inclinations to say things about the sex of chicks, mediated by an entitlement to suppose that those inclinations correlate reliably with the sex of chicks that are being inspected. The credentials of perceptual knowledge are not like that. Perceptual knowledge owes its status as knowledge to the fact that what is known is present to the knower by virtue of affecting her senses. So it is not a mere contingency that perceptual knowledge is by way of appearances in Anscombe's sense.

And now we can say this: the absence of any such thing, in the relevant kind of knowledge of the position of one's limbs, reflects the fact that this knowledge is *not* receptive, not knowledge that depends on being affected by what is known.

Here I have come to the other thing I said was wrong with Setiya's complaint about Anscombe's comparison. Setiya speaks of Anscombe's insistence that knowledge of the position of one's limbs, even the kind she says is not observational, is speculative or receptive. Others besides Setiya, expressing the kind of puzzlement he expresses about the comparison, have claimed that this knowledge is receptive.[15] But I do not believe Anscombe says that herself, and I believe she would be wrong if she did. No doubt this knowledge is not "the cause of what it understands", as Anscombe, following Aquinas, says practical knowledge is (*Intention,* 87). But it does not follow that it is speculative, "derived from the objects known" (ibid.), if that means that "the facts, reality, are prior, and dictate what is to be said, if it is knowledge" (*Intention,* 57), as is the case with receptive knowledge.

In receptive knowledge, what is known is other than the knower; or if that is not so, it is known *as other*.[16] That is exactly not so with this knowledge of limb position. This knowledge is *self*-knowledge; what is known is the self-conscious bodily being who is the knower.

The self-awareness of a self-consciously competent bodily agent includes a familiarity with the possibilities for bodily acting that come with having the kind of body she has: for instance, a familiarity with the different movements that are feasible at different joints. And self-knowledge as a bodily agent is not just a matter of knowing which bodily movements are *in general* within one's powers, for instance that the kind of joint a knee is allows a leg to be bent so as to take the foot to the rear but not to the front or the side. Self-knowledge as a bodily agent extends also, in normal waking life, to knowing which *specific* movements of those general kinds are possibilities for one *here and now*. If one of one's legs is, say, not bent at the knee, straightening it is not one of one's present options, and self-knowledge as a bodily agent includes knowing that. Knowing the position of the parts of one's body that one can move at will is part of one's self-knowledge as a bodily agent. It is not

15. See, e.g., Richard Moran, "Anscombe on 'Practical Knowledge'", in John Hyman and Helen Steward, eds., *Agency and Action* (Cambridge: Cambridge University Press, 2004), 48.

16. See Sebastian Rödl on Aristotle's claim that the art of healing is a principle of change in something other, or in oneself as other: *Self-Consciousness* (Cambridge, Mass.: Harvard University Press, 2007), 8.

knowledge of something other than oneself, or knowledge of oneself as other; it is not receptive, and that is why it is not perceptual or observational.

It should not seem surprising that the division of knowledge into practical and speculative or receptive is not exhaustive. Consider knowledge of one's own sensations. This knowledge is not practical, not "the cause of what it understands". But it is not receptive either. Feeling a sensation is not a reality separate from knowing that one feels it, a reality that makes itself known by affecting the subject. There is affection of the senses in feeling the sensation, but there is not an extra affection in being aware that one feels it.

I have said that knowledge of the position of one's limbs is knowledge of oneself as a bodily agent. Such knowledge cannot be simply separate from practical knowledge. It can be had only by a bodily agent, who is as such a subject of practical knowledge. That may make it tempting to say this knowledge just is practical knowledge.

It is true that sometimes to have one's limbs in a certain position is to be holding them in that position, or to be passing through a stage in the execution of a bodily movement, either of which would be an object of practical knowledge. But having one's limbs arranged in a certain way is not in general a case of activity. And if that is right, knowledge of limb position is not just a species of practical knowledge.

But even if the relevant kind of knowledge of limb position is not just a species of practical knowledge, it is, as I have described it, essentially had by a bodily agent. Its non-observational character is intelligible only as part of a picture of the kind of knowledge that is characteristic of a bodily agent. That means there is something misleading about the way Anscombe introduces this knowledge, as if it could be clearly and intelligibly in view as non-observational before we even consider agency and practical knowledge. Perhaps this belongs with the fact that impresses Harcourt, that her explicit case for holding that this knowledge is not observational is mainly an irrelevant attack on the inferential picture; I had to bring in the later essay "Substance", where she does not discuss knowledge of limb position, to construct an Anscombean case against the view that this knowledge is perceptual. This region of Anscombe's presentation is not very well thought out, at least in *Intention*. What I have been offering is less a reading of her treatment of knowledge of limb position than a charitable reconstruction of what might underlie her thinking on the topic.

VIII

I may have seemed too quick in saying, in section V, that there are no second-ary qualities associated with the relevant kind of knowledge of the position of one's limbs.[17] Suppose someone said there *are* such secondary qualities: they are qualities given by sensations of the sort Anscombe exemplifies by "a pres-sure here, a tension there, a tingle in this other place" ("On Sensations of Position", 72: I quoted the passage more fully in section II). When Anscombe mentions such sensations, she is arguing against the inferential picture. But suppose someone tried to conceive them, not as bases for inferential knowl-edge of limb position, but as playing a role analogous to the role of sensations of color in color perception: as sensations that give one secondary qualities—tingliness, say—belonging to the relevant parts of one's body. That would be to construe tingliness and the like as suitable to be appearances, in Ans-combe's sense, of the relevant parts of one's body. Would this be a way to hold on to the idea that the knowledge we are concerned with is perceptual?

These putative secondary qualities would be at best gappy, not pervasive. One does not feel pressures, tensions, tingles, and the like everywhere in a limb in which one "has sensation", as we naturally say. But perhaps that need not be a problem. Perhaps it is only a contingency that the qualities we are given by visual sensations, say, are given in a way that is spatially continuous. So far as that goes, perhaps perceptual knowledge of the position of one's limbs, from within, could be acquired by means of appearances that are spatially gappy.

But there is a deeper disanalogy between tingles and the like and, for in-stance, visual sensations. These bodily sensations are themselves located (they are, as Anscombe says, "here . . . there . . . in this other place"), as opposed to locating items—instances of secondary qualities—that might be conceived as given by them. In contrast, perceptual sensations are not located (except unspe-cifically, where their subject is), and they locate the instances of secondary qualities that they give. When, in a visual sensation, an instance of a visual secondary quality is given with its "qualifications of size, shape, and mutual arrangement with other data", the sensation places its object with respect to the perceiver, for instance at such-and-such an angle to her direction of vision.

---

17. Bare assertion was dialectically permissible at that point, because the claim is accepted by Harcourt, whose position was my target then. But it is reasonable to require more than an ad hominem case for the premise of the argument I have suggested against the idea that this knowledge is perceptual.

This opens into the most crucial disanalogy. Even if, against what I have just been urging, someone insisted on separating these bodily sensations from things they are of, instances of secondary qualities, which they are taken to locate, this spatial locating of the supposed objects ("here . . . there . . . in this other place")—which, on a proper understanding, is the spatial located-ness of the sensations themselves—is not on a par with the location of the objects of visual sensations. It is not that one knows where a felt tingle, say, is, independently of knowing how one's body is disposed in space, so that an aggregation of such knowledge of the location of objects of sensations—or, better, of the sensations themselves—might enable one to know how one's body is disposed in space. That gets things backwards. One locates these sensations in space only by locating them in one's body. Spatially organized awareness of one's bodily self is a presupposition for the capacity to locate bodily sensations, not something enabled by that capacity.

As I said, it is natural to talk of "having sensation" in a limb. I think this idiom is best understood not as registering that one is actually feeling tingles and the like in the limb, but to acknowledge that one is susceptible to the "sensations", so called, of its position that figure in Anscombe's discussion as "inseparable". (Perhaps the capacity to feel tingles and the like in the limb is causally necessary for this.) To say one has sensation in a limb, so under-stood, is just to say the limb is within the scope of one's self-consciousness as the bodily agent one is. That can be worth remarking on, because limbs can drop out of the scope of that self-consciousness, for instance, with paralysis or anaesthesia.

IX

One final remark. It may seem mysterious how some spatial arrangement of matter could be known otherwise than receptively. But it is not just any ma-terial thing whose layout is known in the kind of knowledge we are consider-ing. It is oneself as a bodily agent, characterized at a time by specific possi-bilities of moving the parts of oneself that one can move at will. No doubt someone else could know how the matter that constitutes one is disposed in space without even viewing one as an agent. And the agentive knowledge we are considering would put its possessor in a position to know truths that would match that knowledge in content. If this agent-neutral content were the whole of what a bodily agent knows about the spatial organization of her material self, it would perhaps be mysterious how the knowledge could be anything but receptive. But this agent-neutral knowledge of the layout of the relevant matter is at the subject's disposal, at least insofar as it is available to her by virtue of her having the kind of knowledge of limb position that is our topic, only derivatively from her self-knowledge as a bodily agent. And it should not seem mysterious how self-knowledge as a bodily agent can be otherwise than receptive. It is not receptive just because it is *self*-knowledge.

The objection I am considering might be expressed like this: "Surely the relevant reality, the spatial arrangement of the relevant matter, is the way it is independently of the subject's knowledge of it, so the knowledge must be speculative". But that is wrong. If we think away the subject's self-consciousness, we think away the reality she knows in the relevant way, which is herself as bodily agent. It is irrelevant that we do not think away the spatial arrangement of the matter she is composed of.[18]

18. Thanks to Matthias Haase for his thoughtful comments at the Chicago meeting, from which I have profited less, no doubt, than I should have.

5

"The Knowledge That a Man Has of His Intentional Actions"

ADRIAN HADDOCK

The question does not normally arise whether a man's proceedings are intentional; hence it is often 'odd' to call them so. E.g. if I saw a man, who was walking along the pavement, turn towards the roadway, look up and down, and then walk across the road when it was safe for him to do so, it would not be usual for me to say that he crossed the road intentionally. But it would be wrong to infer from this that we ought not to give such an action as a typical example of intentional action.

G. E. M. Anscombe, *Intention*, 29

Even sympathetic readers of G. E. M. Anscombe's *Intention* express puzzlement as to why, and as to what she means when, she says that "the knowledge that a man has of his intentional actions" is not merely knowledge "without observation" (14) but *"practical knowledge"* (57).[1] The aim of this essay is to do something to dissolve this puzzlement by offering an account of what she means when she says these things, and a description of the reasoning that leads her to say them.

---

1. Richard Moran is one such reader, Rosalind Hursthouse is another. See Moran, "Anscombe on 'Practical Knowledge'", in *Agency and Actions,* ed. John Hyman and Helen Steward (Cambridge: Cambridge University Press, 2004), and Hursthouse, "Intention", in *Logic, Cause, and Action,* ed. Roger Teichmann (Cambridge: Cambridge University Press, 2000).

The reference in the epigraph, and all unattributed references in what follows are to G. E. M. Anscombe, *Intention,* 2nd ed. (Cambridge, Mass.: Harvard University Press, 2000).

I

Anscombe tells us (14) that "the class of things known without observation is of general interest to our enquiry because the class of intentional actions is a sub-class of it". It is a mark of intentional actions that they are known without observation by their agents. But what is knowledge without observation?

In a recent essay, Hanna Pickard[2] claims that the mark of knowledge *with* observation is that it is acquired by inference from (what Anscombe calls) "separately describable sensations" (13). The sensations are said to be separately describable because the objects of the knowledge said to be acquired by inference from them are distinct from the objects of the sensations; e.g., there is knowledge of the position of one's leg acquired by inference from sensations of tingling in the knee (13); knowledge of the position of a man acquired by inference from sensations of an apparent man (49–50); etc. Pickard's claim makes it look as if what Anscombe means when she insists that "the knowledge that a man has of his intentional actions" is knowledge without observation is simply that, however this knowledge is acquired, it is not acquired by inference from such sensations.

But Anscombe says that "where we can speak of separately describable sensations, having which is in some sense our criterion for saying something, then we can speak of observing" (13). She does not say that where we can speak of observing then we can speak of separately describable sensations, having which is our criterion. Moreover, her reason for insisting that "the knowledge that a man has of his intentional actions" is not knowledge with observation is independent of whether this knowledge is inferentially acquired. Consider the following passage (51):

> Say I go over to the window and open it. Someone who hears me moving calls out: What are you doing making that noise? I reply 'Opening the window'. I have called such a statement knowledge all along; and precisely because in such a case what I say is true—I do open the window; and that means that the window is getting opened by the movements of the body out of whose mouth those words come. But I don't say the words like this: 'Let me see, what is this body bringing about? Ah yes! the opening of the

2. Hanna Pickard, "Knowledge of Action without Observation", *Proceedings of the Aristotelian Society* 104 (2004): 205–230.

window'. Or even like this[:] 'Let me see, what are my movements bringing about? The opening of the window'.

Saying the words in these last two ways would imply that the knowledge I have of what I am doing is knowledge with observation, for two related reasons: first, it would imply that in order to know what I am doing I need to look to see what my movements are bringing about; secondly, it would imply that in order to be doing what I am doing I do not need to look to see what my movements are bringing about—that I am opening the window *before* I draw on the observational powers required for knowing what I am doing, i.e., before I look to see what my movements are bringing about. Looking to see this is needed to supply me with an assurance that I am doing what I say I am doing; it is not needed to enable me to *be* doing what I say I am.

This suggests the following general account: to possess knowledge with observation of what I say I am doing it is not enough that I am doing it. I also require the operation of a perceptual faculty, so as to acquire an observational reason for my statement as to what I am doing, which shows or suggests that I am actually doing it, i.e., a reason that concerns not just what I perceive, but what I perceive in virtue of the operation of the very perceptual faculty through which this reason is acquired. More generally still: to possess knowledge with observation, the actuality of its object is not enough; I also require an observational reason, acquired through the operation of a perceptual faculty, which shows or suggests that its object is indeed actual. Whether or not the operation of this faculty can only yield separately describable sensations, if, in addition to the actuality of its object, possession of the knowledge requires that its possessor acquires an observational reason through this operation, then the knowledge will count as knowledge with observation, by Anscombe's lights.

We can now advance the following general account of knowledge *without* observation: its possession does not require, in addition to the actuality of its object, that its possessor acquires—through the operation of a perceptual faculty, on his part—an observational reason that shows or suggests that its object is indeed actual. This does not say that its possession does not require anything in addition to the actuality of its object, as if this actuality were to suffice all by itself for its possession. It merely says that its possession does not require, in addition to this actuality, that its possessor acquires such a reason through the operation of his perceptual faculty. This is consistent with there being a species of knowledge without observation whose possession, by a suitably placed subject, is a simple consequence of the actuality of its object; as we shall see, practical knowledge belongs to this species.[3] But here we have the idea of the genus, consistent with but distinct from the idea of this species.

II

What exactly does Anscombe think is wrong with the idea that "the knowledge that a man has of his intentional actions" is knowledge with observation?

The only indication she gives in *Intention* as to what she thinks is wrong with this idea is her claim—implicit in the foregoing passage—that if this knowledge was with observation then we would "say the words" in a way that, in fact, we do not say them. But perhaps we can hazard the following suggestion, based on something else she says in *Intention,* and on one of her other writings: she thinks that this knowledge consists in "unmediated conceptions"[4] of its objects, and for this reason cannot be observational.

She tells us (50–51) that "By the knowledge that a man has of his intentional actions I mean the knowledge that one denies having if when asked e.g. 'Why are you ringing that bell?' one replies 'Good heavens! I didn't know *I* was ringing it!'" This reply can seem to show "a lapse of self-consciousness"[5] on the part of the agent: I am ringing the bell; I have the idea—indeed, I know—that *someone* is ringing the bell; but I do not know that *I* am doing so. (I might have asked: "Who is ringing the bell?") My behaviour seems relevantly similar to that of William James's character "Baldy", who on falling out onto the road from a moving carriage asks, "Who fell out?" On being told that Baldy fell out he says, "Did Baldy fall out? Poor Baldy!"—but as

---

3. It is also consistent with there being a species of knowledge without observation whose possession requires, in addition to the actuality of its object, that its possessor acquires, through something other than the operation of a perceptual faculty, a non-observational reason which, e.g., shows that it is actual. Perhaps Christopher Peacocke's account of knowledge of action as acquired through the operation of a (putatively) non-perceptual faculty of "action-awareness" understands this knowledge as belonging to this species; see Peacocke, "Mental Action and Self-Awareness (II): Epistemology", in *Mental Actions,* ed. Lucy O'Brien and Matthew Soteriou (Oxford: Oxford University Press, 2009).

4. G. E. M. Anscombe, "The First Person", in *Mind and Language: Wolfson College Lectures, 1974,* ed. Samuel Guttenplan (Oxford: Oxford University Press, 1975), reprinted in *Self-Knowledge,* ed. Quassim Cassam (Oxford: Oxford University Press, 1994), 156. Page references are to the reprinted edition.

5. Ibid., 159.

Anscombe notes, the fact that he uses "Baldy" and not "I"/"me" is not the important thing; "his behaviour already showed the lapse of self-consciousness", in the fact that "he had just fallen out of the carriage, he was conscious, and he . . . knew that someone had [fallen out of the carriage], but [he] wondered who!"[6] His knowledge of what is happening—of falling out of the carriage—does not consist in an unmediated conception of what is happening, precisely because there is a gap between his knowledge that someone had fallen out and his knowledge as to who had done so. It seems there must be such a gap when the person in question is someone other than oneself.[7] But if I exhibit self-consciousness with respect to my behaviour, falling out of the carriage, then there is no such gap: it is not possible that I am falling out of the carriage; am conscious; know that someone is falling out; but do not know that I am falling out. Similarly, it seems, if I exhibit self-consciousness with respect to my intentional action, ringing the bell, then there is no such gap: it is not possible that I am ringing the bell; am conscious; know that someone is ringing the bell; but do not know that I am.

However, if "the knowledge that a man has of his intentional actions" is knowledge with observation, then there must be such a gap, precisely because the required operation of his perceptual faculty might be in some way impeded. Consider: I am opening the window, and I know that someone is opening the window, because I can see someone's hands pushing the window open; but because my vision of my own hands is occluded, I cannot see whether these hands are my hands, and so cannot see whether my movements are bringing about the opening of the window; and so, even though I know that someone is opening the window, I do not know that I am. If it is so much as possible that I am opening the window, and know that someone is opening the window, but—because of occlusion in the operation of my perceptual faculties—fail to know who (and so fail to know that I am) then I fail to exhibit self-consciousness with respect to my intentional action, opening the window. The knowledge that I have of my intentional action will consist in a mediated conception of its object. And that "the knowledge that a man has of his intentional actions" consists in mediated conceptions of its objects is, I think, precisely what Anscombe denies.

---

6. Ibid.

7. "Other" is the operative word here. See Sebastian Rödl, *Self-Consciousness* (Cambridge, Mass.: Harvard University Press, 2007), especially chapters 1 and 6.

The problem is that it can look as if, e.g., opening the window can only be known with observation. Behaviour of the sort that shows a lapse of self-consciousness with respect to falling out of the carriage seems to be possible with respect to opening the window: if asked "Why are you opening that window?" I might say, "I didn't know *I* was opening it". But if knowledge of opening the window can only be observational, it would surely be wrong to suppose that *this* sort of behaviour shows a lapse of self-consciousness: surely it can only do that if opening the window is a possible object of knowledge without observation; if knowledge of opening the window can only be observational, then it seems the only relevant thing that this sort of behaviour can show is occlusion in the required operation of the perceptual faculties—not a lapse of self-consciousness, merely a lack of observational knowledge. Part of Anscombe's ambition, in insisting that "the knowledge that a man has of his intentional actions" is knowledge without observation, is—we might say—to enable a lapse of self-consciousness to be shown by this sort of behaviour.

III

However, it can be very hard to see how opening the window could possibly be known without observation, because it is—it is natural to say—a certain sort of intervention in the public world; or, as Anscombe says, a case of "what takes place" (51), or "what happens"—and it seems that "what happens must be given by observation" (53). Included amongst "what happens" are many things that we are strongly inclined to think of as intentional actions, such as opening the window; indeed, anything of the form "making such-and-such movements with such-and-such a result" (51). So, if what happens cannot be known without observation, then these things cannot be known without observation. And if they cannot be known without observation, then they cannot be intentional actions, because—as we saw in section I—it is a mark of intentional actions that they *are* known without observation.

The difficulty, then, is that it looks as if intentional actions—the objects of "the knowledge that a man has of his intentional actions"—must be distinct from what happens, or what takes place—the objects of "knowledge with observation of what takes place". Anscombe expresses this difficulty in the form of a question (51):

> Now if there are two *ways* of knowing here, one of which I call knowledge of one's intentional action and the other of which I call knowledge by observation of what takes place, then must there not be two *objects* of knowledge?

The question seems to merit a positive answer. But it only seems to do so once two assumptions are made, i.e., first, that a mark of the objects of "the knowledge that a man has of his intentional actions" is that they are known without observation; and, second, that the objects of knowledge by observation of what takes place cannot be known without observation. Her aim is to show us how we can abandon the second of these assumptions—and thereby answer the question in the negative, and thereby hold on to the first assumption—by getting us to see that what takes place *can*, sometimes, be known without observation, and so can count as an intentional action.

Sympathetic commentators have found Anscombe's question puzzling. Richard Moran thinks that "it is not clear just what sort of difficulty"[8] it expresses: "the position and movement of one's limbs has already been mentioned [earlier in *Intention*] as something that can be known in two different ways, without this raising issues of two *objects* of knowledge".[9] Moran is puzzled because he sees Anscombe as thinking—most mysteriously—that there is a perfectly general difficulty about one thing being known in two different ways. But for the very reason given by Moran, this cannot be what Anscombe thinks. Her thought is that there is a specific difficulty pertaining to the two specific forms of knowledge she mentions: "knowledge of one's intentional action", and "knowledge by observation of what takes place"— where the objects of these two "knowledges" have the properties I have outlined, i.e., where it is a mark of the objects of the former that they are known without observation, but where the objects of the latter cannot be known without observation. Moran can see no difficulty here because he reads the question as equivalent to "Now if there are two ways of knowing then must there not be two objects of knowledge?" That effectively elides the heart of the question—the very thing which makes it apt.

But even though he slides over her way of expressing the difficulty, Moran appreciates part of the difficulty that concerns her, i.e., that it looks as if, in many cases, "the knowledge that a man has of his intentional actions" *must* be by observation. As Moran sees it, her response to this difficulty is to insist that "various kinds of observation-based knowledge *are* presumed in the context of ordinary intentional action".[10] She insists that observational knowledge of "what is the case, and [of] what can happen—say Z—if one does

8. Moran, "Anscombe on 'Practical Knowledge'", 50n3.
9. Ibid.
10. Ibid., 49.

certain things, say ABC" (50)—e.g., of the fact that there is a window over *there,* and of the fact that this window will open if I do *this* and *this*[11]—can enable one to "have the intention of doing Z in doing ABC", and can thereby enable doing Z (in doing ABC) to be one's intentional action. (There is no general requirement that one must know such things—let alone know them by observation—in order to do ABC with the intention of doing Z; perhaps "an opinion held without any foundation at all" (50) will be enough, in at least some cases.) And, perhaps more centrally, she claims (53) that, further to this role for "knowledge or opinion about [what she calls] the matter in which we perform intentional actions", observation and observational knowledge can function as an aid in doing, and in knowing, what we are doing.

> Isn't the role of all our observation-knowledge in knowing what we are do-ing like the role of the eyes in producing successful writing? That is to say, once given that we have knowledge or opinion about the matter in which we perform intentional actions, our observation is merely an aid, as the eyes are an aid in writing.

However, Moran thinks this response generates a difficulty of its own.

IV

The difficulty, as Moran sees it, is that Anscombe now faces the following charge: "given the admitted dependence of [a man's] action on empirical ob-servations and assumptions"—e.g., as reflected in the talk of an "aid"—"all the real epistemological work involved in knowing what he is doing is carried by his observational knowledge".[12] In other words, if "the knowledge that a man has of his intentional actions" depends on his observational knowledge, in such a way as to make it intelligible how he can have knowledge of, e.g., opening the window, how can this knowledge be knowledge *without* obser-vation? Insisting on this dependency, in the way required to make sense of this possibility, seems to obviate the non-observational character of this knowledge. E.g., "we might agree . . . that if we add to my [non-observational] knowledge of my immediate bodily movement the empirical 'knowledge . . .

---

11. Here you might imagine me indulging in a bit of dumb show, in which I display the kind of movements needed for opening a window—a sash window, perhaps.

12. Moran, "Anscombe on 'Practical Knowledge'", 53.

concerning what is the case . . . and what can happen . . . if one does certain things' then I may indeed be credited with the knowledge . . . that I am ringing the bell".[13] But, according to Moran, this would be just "a two-factor approach to the knowledge of what [I am] doing [which restricts] its non-observational content to the confines of [my] body, and then [adds] to it the empirical knowledge of [my] surroundings and the impact of [my] body upon them"[14]—not a picture of my knowledge of ringing the bell as itself knowledge without observation.

To avoid this charge, Anscombe needs to do something that she does not do in *Intention,* or elsewhere: supply "an account of how the agent's [knowledge of what he is doing] goes beyond his observational knowledge".[15] Moran takes up the challenge, with the example of a man who is walking up Fifth Avenue, but suddenly ceases to know what he is doing, and so ceases walking.[16] His capacities for observational knowledge are unaffected by this change. But they do not enable the man to recover knowledge of the sort he has lost, because although "he sees Fifth Avenue, and he sees it from a particular perspective which indicates what direction has was heading in . . . he does not see his goal . . . he sees *everything* around him . . . the strangers' faces [and so on; but] nothing in these details enables him to discern a destination, a point to his being right here facing in this direction".[17] The man comes to be in this unfortunate predicament because he loses knowledge of his intention, and no amount of observation will enable him to acquire *this* knowledge. "And in this way", Moran suggests, "we can begin to see how [his knowledge of what he is doing] *could not* be observational, could not be perceptually derived from the world".[18]

But merely showing us that because observation alone does not suffice for knowledge of intention it does not suffice for knowledge of what one is doing does not show us how knowledge of what one is doing can be non-observational, given its dependency on knowledge with observation. E.g., it does not show us that knowledge of what one is doing does not factor into observational and

13. Ibid., 49. I have reintroduced the necessary ellipses into the embedded quotation from Anscombe, 50.

14. Ibid., 46.

15. Ibid., 53.

16. The example is David Velleman's; see his *Practical Reflection* (Princeton, N.J.: Princeton University Press, 1989).

17. Moran, "Anscombe on 'Practical Knowledge'", 57.

18. Ibid.

non-observational components, in just the way Moran criticizes. Indeed, for all that Moran's account has to say, it seems that the man could arrive at knowledge of walking down Fifth Avenue by adding to his non-observational knowledge of his immediate bodily movements, and his observational knowledge concerning the effects of these movements, non-observational knowledge of his intention (plus, presumably, non-observational knowledge of causation between his intention—or something suitably related to his intention—and his bodily movements).[19] This would not be a two-factor, but a three-factor or a four-factor approach to knowledge of what he is doing, which restricts its non-observational content to "the confines of [his] body", in the sense of his intention and his bodily movements, "and then [adds to it] empirical knowledge of [his] surroundings and the impact of his body upon them".[20] If the two-factor approach does not constitute a picture of knowledge of what one is doing as itself knowledge without observation, it is hard to see why this approach should do so.

An approach of this shape would be unacceptable, by Anscombe's lights, if it made the man's possession of the knowledge turn on his acquisition of an observational reason that shows or suggests that he is walking up Fifth Avenue. And it seems this is what it does; otherwise what does its talk of "adding" come to? Merely knowing, without observation, that he is walking, and that he intends to walk up Fifth Avenue, will not supply him with a reason showing that he is walking *up Fifth Avenue;* the point of also requiring "empirical knowledge of his surroundings"—acquired through the operation of his perceptual faculties—is precisely to plug this gap. This ensures that his knowledge of walking up Fifth Avenue is knowledge with observation, and so not "the knowledge that a man has of his intentional actions". The only knowledge the man has which is so much as a candidate for *this* title is his non-observational knowledge of his intention and his bodily movements: "what [he] knows as intentional action is only the intention, [and] the bodily movement. . . . But that [as Anscombe says] is a mad account" (51–52), for it entails that only the intention, and the bodily movement, can so much as

19. For the relevant ideas of something suitably related to an intention, and of non-observational knowledge of causation, see Donald Davidson, "Actions, Reasons, and Causes", *Journal of Philosophy* 60 (1963): 685–700, reprinted in his *Essays on Actions and Events* (Oxford: Oxford University Press, 2001). And compare the idea of non-observational knowledge of causation, which Anscombe develops on 15–16.

20. Moran, "Anscombe on 'Practical Knowledge'", 46.

count as intentional actions. Things such as opening the window, and walking up Fifth Avenue, cannot so count.

Anscombe produced her formula "I *do* what *happens*" (52) precisely to reject
this upshot. What I do, the objects of "the knowledge that a man has of his
intentional actions", need not be distinct from what happens, e.g., from opening the window. So, what I *do* can include opening the window, walking up
Fifth Avenue, etc. And so, what happens can itself be known without observation, at least sometimes, i.e., when there is no distinction between what I do
and what happens. Of course, we are not yet in a position to see how this *can*
be true: that is her difficulty, and ours. Seeing how she tries to solve this difficulty will shed light on the idea of observation serving as an aid to knowing,
and thereby enable us to see why—if she succeeds—she does not face Moran's charge, and so does not need to supply "an account of how the agent's
[knowledge of what he is doing] goes beyond his observational knowledge".

V

What is her attempted solution to this difficulty?

Her attempted solution begins with what can seem a puzzling change of
tack: the drawing of a parallel between statements as to what one is doing,
and orders.[21]

The point of this change of tack is to address one reason for thinking that
such things as opening the window cannot be known without observation.
We might think that a statement expresses knowledge, on the part of the
subject who makes the statement, only if the subject has a suitable reason for
the statement—a reason that justifies the statement. And we might think
that, in the case of statements about what happens, e.g., opening the window,
a suitable reason for the statement must be an observational reason. The upshot—if this is right—is that statements about what happens that express
knowledge must express knowledge with observation.

Why must a suitable reason for a statement about what happens be an
observational reason?

---

21. I have been aided here by Stanley Cavell's highly illuminating discussion of "rule-
statement complementarities" in his "Must We Mean What We Say?" *Inquiry* 1 (1958): 172–
212, reprinted in his *Must We Mean What We Say? A Book of Essays* (Cambridge: Cambridge
University Press, 1969).

Here is a suggestion: because of the *kind* of statements which statements about what happens are. They are *reports,* and reports can only be justified by observational reasons. The parallel Anscombe draws with orders is supposed to show us that these statements are not reports, when there is no distinction between what I do and what happens—as well as to say something positive about the kind of statements they are.

What she says harkens back to her famous example of someone moving his arm up and down with his hand around a pump handle, thereby operating the pump, thereby replenishing the house water supply, and thereby poisoning the household. Reports on the man's behaviour, such as these, are vulnerable to the failure to obtain of certain matters of fact. As Anscombe would put it, the contradictory of the report "He is replenishing the house water supply" is the further report "He is not, because (e.g.) the water is running out of a hole in the pipe". Reports contrast with orders, in that an order's contradictory is not a report but an opposing order; the contradictory of "Clench your teeth!" is "Do not clench your teeth!" Put rather grandly: contradictories must be of the same *logical* order. However, orders are still vulnerable to reports, when the latter state matters of fact, e.g., if true, "He has no teeth" undermines this order by disenabling its execution—in the face of the fact that the man has no teeth, the order "falls to the ground" (57).

Contrast statements in the first person as to what one is doing, e.g., "I'm replenishing the house water supply". Their contradictory is not the report "You are not, because (e.g.) the water is running out of the pipe", but (55) " 'Oh, no, you aren't' said by someone who thereupon sets out, e.g., to make a hole in a pipe with a pick-axe". Anticipating the results of the sequel, we can say that their contradictory is not a report but an opposing expression of practical knowledge—or, as Anscombe at one point puts it (61), an opposing action "in a verbalised form". And, as with orders, these statements too can be undermined by—i.e., they too can fall to the ground in the face of—matters of fact such as that reported in the report given above. Perhaps it is too strong to say this about all statements in the first person as to what one is doing; but it suffices for present purposes to say that the logical order of some such statements is not that of reports, in view of the nature of their contradictories.

There is at least this much of a parallel between orders, and some statements in the first person as to what one is doing: unlike reports, both have *two* distinct dimensions of vulnerability—to matters of fact, and to distinctively practical episodes (to opposing orders, and to opposing actions "in a verbalised form" [61], respectively).

The parallel holds the promise of enabling us to see that, and why, my statement is not a report; it bears empirical content, but its way of doing so is no different from the way orders do so, and orders are not justified by observational reasons. Orders are justified by reasons of a radically different order: not observational, but *practical* reasons; just so for at least some statements as to what one is doing.

The statement "I am opening the window" (or just "Opening the window", said in reply to the earlier question) no more reports on the state of the window than the order "Clench your teeth!" reports on the state of your mouth. It *presupposes* that there is a window, just as the order presupposes that your mouth houses teeth. But because this fact can hardly show that the order is made or justified on grounds of observation, it can hardly show that this statement is justified on the same grounds. "The reasons justifying an order are not ones suggesting what is probable, or likely to happen, but, e.g., ones suggesting what it would be good to make happen with a view to an objective, or with a view to a sound objective" (4)—they are practical reasons; just so for the reasons justifying at least some statements as to what one is doing.

So, an order has a practical and indeed an ethical vulnerability: it, and the person who issues it, can be impugned on the grounds that the order is not the best way of securing the end—as well as on non-instrumental grounds. It also has a non-practical vulnerability, in view of its empirical presuppositions: it, and the person who issues it, can be impugned if it falls to the ground—e.g., for not looking to see whether the person to whom the order is given has any teeth. But it does not follow that the observational reasons that the person who issues the order can be impugned for not acquiring belong to the order's justification. And yet: observation of such matters on the part of the person who issues the order can certainly help, to ensure that the order that is issued is stable and effective—i.e., that it will not fall to the ground, or (a different, related case) totter and then fall on account of being out of tune with the given capacities of the one ordered. In other words, observation can *aid* the order, and the one who issues it, in this way.

These points carry across to statements as to what one is doing. Observational reasons for whether or not there is, or will soon be, a hole in the pipe can also help, to ensure that my statement as to what I am doing does not fall to the ground, or perhaps, totter and then fall, on account of a now-shaking and soon-to-burst pipe. The reasons justifying the statement remain practical, not observational, in nature. But, to ensure a stable and effective statement, it can help to look to see, and if I do not it may be legitimate to criticize me for not doing so. (Whether it *is* legitimate depends on what it is reasonable to expect me to be able to do, in the given case.)

It is worth noting that the fact that the person ordered does not do what the order says does not necessarily impugn the order; it might point to a ground for impugning the order, which may be observational (e.g., the failure of an empirical presupposition), or practical (e.g., the existence of a more effective way of bringing about the objective, the recognition of which on the part of the one ordered led him to disobey the order); but it may be that criticism is only legitimately directed at the person ordered for disobeying a perfectly good order, or for what Anscombe calls a mistake of performance ("If the order is given 'Left turn!' and the man turns right, there can be clear signs that this was not an act of disobedience [but a case of] obeying an order wrong" (57)). So, it may be that the order, and the person who issues the order, are not impugned, e.g., it may be that "the mistake is not one of judgment but one of performance" (57)—that it is the performance, and not an observational judgment aiding the order, nor a judgment as to practical effectiveness, nor the order itself, which is to be impugned. Similarly, failure on the part of the person who makes the statement to do what the statement says does not necessarily impugn the statement; it might point to an observational or practical ground for impugning the statement; but it may be that criticism is only legitimately directed at the person for what he *does*, or fails to do, because he has, e.g., changed his mind, or himself made a mistake of performance. ("As when I say to myself 'Now I press Button A'—pressing Button B—a thing which can certainly happen" (57), especially if, like me, you are rather accident prone.)

The parallel seems to be getting us somewhere. The fact that statements as to what one is doing bear empirical content makes us tempted to see them as reports. But their parallel with orders suggests that just as this temptation should be resisted in the case of orders, it should be resisted in this case as well—and the way in which we can resist it sheds further light on the idea of observation serving merely as an aid.

However, Anscombe asks (55), "is there not a point at which the parallelism ceases: namely, just where we begin to speak of knowledge?"

VI

It can seem that a reason that justifies a statement which expresses *knowledge* cannot be a reason of the practical sort proper to orders. The reasons justifying an order suggest why so ordering someone is good to do, in the light of a certain objective. But the reasons justifying a statement expressing knowledge must show or suggest that one is doing what the statement says one is. The reasons must be theoretical, not practical, in character. And there is a seemingly unbridgeable chasm separating these: reasons showing why something is good to do with a view to a certain objective cannot amount to reasons showing that one is doing this thing.

It can seem as if the parallel with orders gets us nowhere. Perhaps certain statements as to what I am doing can be justified by practical reasons. But if these statements express knowledge, then they must be justified by theoretical reasons. And if there is no distinction between what I am doing and what is happening, what can these theoretical reasons be, if not observational reasons?

However (57):

Can it be that there is something that modern philosophy has blankly misunderstood: namely what ancient and medieval philosophers meant by *practical knowledge?* Certainly in modern philosophy we have an incorrigibly contemplative conception of knowledge.

The contemplative conception says that objects are prior to our knowledge of them: possessing knowledge requires more than the actuality of its objects. We are tempted by this conception when the relevant objects are cases of what happens. So, on being told "I *do* what *happens*", and given the assumption that a mark of what I do (in the relevant sense) is that it is known without observation, the mind can start to boggle: it can seem that to have knowledge of what I do I need reasons acquired through a source which is at once non-observational (because the knowledge is of what I do), and observational (because "I *do* what *happens*")—not a seeing eye, and yet a seeing eye ("a very queer and special sort of seeing eye in the middle of the acting" (57)).

To think that we enjoy practical knowledge requires that we abandon this conception, by thinking of "the knowledge that a man has of his intentional actions" as a simple consequence of the actuality of its objects: not as something distinct from, but as an aspect of, his intentional actions themselves. To conceive of a species of knowledge in that way is to conceive of the species of knowledge non-contemplatively. But the notion of practical knowledge is not simply the notion of non-contemplative knowledge, i.e., of knowledge which is a simple consequence of the actuality of its objects, and which for this reason is properly described as being (87) "'the cause of what it understands', unlike 'speculative' [or contemplative] knowledge which 'is derived from the objects known'". "The notion of 'practical knowledge' can only be understood if we first understand 'practical reasoning'" (57). And this is not true of the notion of non-speculative knowledge as such.

The remark that I have just cited can appear rather gnomic. But if the suggestion is that practical knowledge is a kind of knowledge, the possession of which requires not observational but practical reasons, it is at least plausible to think that for grasping the notion of this kind of knowledge, grasping the notion of practical reasoning might be of some help. And I think this is indeed the suggestion.

Two points about this suggestion are worth noting. First, it is intended not to supplant, but to supplement—or, better, to unfold further—the point of the parallel between statements as to what one is doing and orders; i.e., that these statements are not justified by observational reasons, but justified by practical reasons. Immediately after raising the question that I mentioned at the end of section V, Anscombe considers her famous case of the "man going round a town with a shopping list in his hand" (56), the point of which is further to cement the parallel. And the point of introducing the notion of practical knowledge is precisely to show how statements that exhibit this parallel, and that consequently are not justified observationally but practically, are nevertheless capable of expressing knowledge.

Secondly, there is an important difference in the kinds of role that theoretical and practical reasons are required to play in the respective cases of theoretical and practical knowledge. In the case of speculative knowledge, the role of the reasons is to build a bridge between the subjects and the objects of the knowledge, and thereby to explain why the subject possesses the knowledge, and so why his statement expresses the knowledge. But in the case of practical knowledge, there is no such bridge to build; the role of the reasons is to explain the actuality of its objects, and—given that practical knowledge is an aspect, and so a consequence of the actuality, of these objects—*thereby* to explain why the subject possesses, and so why his statement expresses, the knowledge in question.

VII

How, then, are we to understand "practical reasoning"?

Practical reasoning involves something wanted, and at the heart of the idea of practical reasoning is the idea of calculating what to do to attain something wanted. E.g., I want: to put the good men in; but I know: the ruling bad men are in that house. So, I calculate: to put the good men in, I'll poison the inhabitants of the house; to do that, I'll replenish the house water supply; to do that, I'll operate the pump; and to do that, I'll move my hand, currently wrapped around the pump handle, up and down. This is artificial for a number of reasons. "It has an absurd appearance when practical reasonings . . . are set out in full" (79). Moreover, this looks to be reasoning that someone could engage in from his armchair, without making any "movement towards" (68) the thing wanted (putting the good men in). But wanting—or at least, the kind of wanting presupposed to practical knowledge—involves movement toward the thing wanted: it involves doing things in order to attain this thing. Practical reasoning—which also involves this movement—is of interest because it describes not "actual mental processes" (that "would in general be quite absurd"), but "an order which is there whenever actions are done with intentions" (80).

This order is exhibited by what one is doing, and is properly represented as a series of answers to a series of "Why?" questions, addressed to an agent who is in a position to answer them (correctly, of course), e.g., "Why are you moving your hands?" "I am operating the pump"; "Why are you doing that?" "I am replenishing the water supply"; "Why?" "I am poisoning the inhabitants"; "Why?" "To put the good men in". Each of these answers displays a certain sense of the "Why?" question to have application to each of the things I am doing. The first three answers display the first thing I am doing (moving my hands) as how I am doing the second thing (operating the pump); the second thing as how I am doing the third thing (replenishing the supply); and so on; and the final answer in turn displays not just the fourth thing but—when this answer is taken together with the earlier answers, in accordance with the order that they collectively reveal—each of the four things as so many steps on the way toward the objective it expresses. Taken together, the answers, by revealing this order to be exhibited by the things I am doing, display each of them as good to do "with a view to [this] objective", and thereby display them as my intentional actions.[22]

It is because I am in a position to answer instances of the "Why?" question with correct answers of the right sort that the things I am doing are my intentional actions. Otherwise put: it is because I have practical reasons that explain why I am doing each of the things I am doing that these things are my intentional actions.[23] Consequently, because the knowledge that a man has of his intentional actions is an aspect of the actuality of its objects (his intentional actions), we can say that it is because I am in this position that I enjoy this knowledge—what we can now call *"practical knowledge"*, precisely because its possession is explained by its possessor's being in a position suitably to answer instances of the "Why?" question, and thereby display what they are doing as good to do, given their objective, i.e., precisely because its possession is explained by its possessor's possession of practical reasons.

Having practical reasons which justify a statement as to what one is doing is a matter of having practical reasons that explain why one is doing what the statement says one is doing. Here the reasons as it were pass right through the statements, to emerge as reasons that explain the actions which the state-

---

22. The agent's ability to answer these questions correctly will turn on whether the view he takes as to *how* to do the various things he says he is doing is based in fact; here is one place where knowledge, or at least correct opinion, as to "what can happen—say Z—if one does certain things, say ABC", can matter. E.g., an agent who answers the question "Why are you replenishing the water supply?" with "I am converting the inhabitants to Catholicism" is unlikely to be answering correctly—although those who think there can be such things as religious-conversion-drugs might want to dispute this.

23. The relevant sense of the question "Why?" is not refused application by the answer "For no particular reason". But nor is it thereby granted application. Anscombe's claim that practical reasoning describes "an order which is there *whenever* actions are done with intentions" (my emphasis) suggests that even though what I am doing can be an intentional action even if the answer to the "Why?" question in its case is "For no particular reason", this is so only if in the course of doing this thing I am doing other things that exhibit the order of practical reasoning. (Compare Michael Thompson, "Naïve Action Theory", in his *Life and Action: Elementary Structures of Practice and Practical Thought* (Cambridge, Mass.: Harvard University Press, 1998), 106–112.) So long as we bear firmly in mind the (so to say) recessive nature of this particular answer, I think we can treat it as giving a practical reason of a—necessarily exceptional—sort.

ments concern; or, to employ and extend Anscombe's metaphor: statements of this sort are actions "in a verbalised form", in part because the practical reasons that justify these statements are practical reasons that explain the actions that—"in a verbalised form"—these statements are. These reasons thereby explain why the objects that these statements concern are intentional actions. And because practical knowledge is but an aspect of intentional actions, they thereby explain why these statements express practical knowledge.

Finally, let me note that it would be wrong to saddle Anscombe with the view that the statements which express practical knowledge are not justified by theoretical reasons. Statements' expression of practical knowledge is not explained by their justification by theoretical reasons, but by their justification by practical reasons. But that is consistent with the thought that a statement which expresses practical knowledge is justified by a theoretical reason, i.e., by a theoretical reason supplied by the very practical knowledge which the statement expresses, and constituted by the very fact which constitutes the content of this practical knowledge; e.g., if the statement "I am opening the window" expresses practical knowledge, then it is justified by a theoretical reason constituted by the fact that I am opening the window. (This reason is not an observational reason, so there is no opening here for the charge that this will prevent practical knowledge from being non-observational in character.)

VIII

We are left with a picture in which "the knowledge that a man has of his intentional actions" does not require observational reasons. The statements that express this knowledge are justified not by observational but by practical reasons (because the statements are not reports, but more akin to orders). And they express this knowledge because they are so justified (because practical reasons explain the actuality of their objects, and the knowledge in question is a simple consequence of this actuality). Knowledge whose expression is explained in this way is practical knowledge. Practical knowledge depends on observational knowledge, just as Moran highlights. As Anscombe puts it, possession of observational knowledge can enable one to do ABC with the intention of doing Z, and it can aid one in the process of doing Z itself; as we saw in section V, it can help to ensure a stable and effective statement—or, as we might equally say, again exploiting Anscombe's metaphor, a stable and effective action. But, in this picture, there is no danger that this dependency will usurp the non-observational character of practical knowledge—precisely because its associated statements do not require observational reasons for their justification.

However, it might be hard to see how there can be knowledge of "what takes place" that is a simple consequence of the actuality of its object. Knowledge of what takes place is fallible. And we might think that the possession of fallible knowledge surely requires, in addition to the actuality of its objects, some sort of theoretical reason—other than the fact that constitutes the content of the knowledge—precisely so as to do something to assure its possessor that the possibility of falsehood is not an actuality; e.g., it is possible that, even though I say I am opening the window, I am not opening the window because the window is not getting opened; so, surely I need some sort of theoretical reason—other than this fact—which does something to rule out this possibility, if I am to know what I am doing.

Anscombe clearly grants the fallibility of knowledge of what happens, even when "I *do* what *happens*". E.g., as we saw in section V, she mentions a mistake in my performance which serves to falsify my statement as to what I am doing ("As when I say to myself 'Now I press button A'—pressing button B—a thing which can certainly happen"). Her point in mentioning this is to help expose the vulnerabilities to which certain statements of this sort are subject, so as to clarify—and to defend—the parallel between these statements and orders. But one potential danger of this strategy is to make these statements look more vulnerable than, in fact, they are, by making it look as if mistakes in doing what these statements say one is doing always serve to falsify the statements. More generally, the potential danger is to make it look as if the falsification of statements of this sort is a more straightforward matter than, in fact, it is. Getting us to see that, and how, this is not so straightforward is, I think, Anscombe's way of freeing us from—or, at least, starting to pry us apart from—the line of thought just sketched, which begins with the fact of fallibility and ends with the claim that there cannot be practical knowledge of what happens.

I want to end by suggesting that getting us to see this is at least part of the point of the following notorious remarks (82).[24]

---

24. These remarks have troubled her sympathetic commentators. See Hursthouse, "Intention"; Moran, "Anscombe on 'Practical Knowledge'"; and Judith Jarvis's review of *Intention* in *Journal of Philosophy* 56 (1959): 31–41.

I wrote 'I am a fool' on the blackboard with my eyes shut. Now when I said what I wrote, ought I to have said: this is what I am writing, if my intention is getting executed; instead of simply: this is what I am writing?

Orders however can be disobeyed, and intentions fail to get executed. That intention for example would not have been executed if something had gone wrong with the chalk or the surface, so that the words did not appear. And my knowledge would have been the same even if this had happened. If then my knowledge is independent of what actually happens, how can it be knowledge of what does happen? Someone might say that it was a funny sort of knowledge that was still knowledge even though what it was knowledge of was not the case! On the other hand Theophrastus' remark holds good: 'the mistake is in the performance, not in the judgment'.

There is agreement that the answer to the first question she raises here is "No". However, opinions diverge as to how we are to make sense of the ensuing remarks.

Is Anscombe committing herself to the "non-factivity" of practical knowledge, i.e., to the claim that practical knowledge can still be knowledge, even if what it is knowledge of is not the case?[25] That would seem to conflict with her earlier claim, in the passage cited in section I, that "I have called such a statement [i.e., 'Opening the window] knowledge all along; and precisely because in such a case what I say is true" (51). And it sits uneasily with the suggestion that "non-factive" knowledge would be "a funny sort of knowledge"—a suggestion which, contrary to what a cursory reading might suggest, her remark beginning "On the other hand" is not intended to reject; this last remark rather rejects a claim implicit in the previous sentences, i.e., that *if* "my knowledge would have been the same even if this had happened" *then* "my knowledge is independent of what actually happens". (This should become clear in what follows, if it is not already.)

When she says "And my knowledge would have been the same even if this had happened", is she speaking in the voice of an interlocutor, who is making a claim which the succeeding remarks, said in her own voice, are designed to reject? This is a very difficult reading to make work. Presumably the interlocutor starts speaking with "Orders however can", or with "That intention for example"; for unless Anscombe is being unconscionably obscure, the interlocutor can

---

25. Jarvis is troubled to think that Anscombe is hereby committing herself to this claim; see Jarvis's review of *Intention*.

hardly start speaking with "And".[26] But if the rest of the passage, from "If then my knowledge" onwards, is in Anscombe's own voice, what exactly is the re-mark beginning "On the other hand" supposed to be rejecting? Surely not the "funny sort of knowledge" suggestion, because the point of this reading is that it is an alternative to the "non-factivity" reading. And surely not the claim that I think it rejects either, because that claim, on this reading, is precisely a claim made by *Anscombe*, rather than by her supposed interlocutor; also, rejecting this claim rather casts doubt on the point of this reading. There seems to be nothing for it but to force the whole paragraph, apart from the remark begin-ning "On the other hand", into the mouth of the interlocutor—and thereby render the dialectical structure of the passage utterly obscure.

Let me end by suggesting a different, and I think far less strained, reading.

Imagine that I am writing "I am a fool" on the blackboard with my eyes shut, and I get as far as the second "a" when my bit of chalk crumbles to dust. That is annoying, but hardly serious; I just pick up a new bit of chalk from the desk and finish the job. It is a way of acknowledging the so-called broad-ness of the progressive[27]—a phenomenon to which Anscombe explicitly draws our attention[28]—to acknowledge that I am still writing "I am a fool" on the blackboard when I am picking up the new bit of chalk. In actual fact, this does not happen—all goes swimmingly. But even if this had happened, I would still have been writing "I am a fool" on the blackboard at this time—even though my intention to write "I am a fool" on the blackboard would not have been executed by this time—and I would still have known I was doing

26. Thanks to Jen Hornsby for this point.

27. See Thompson, "Naïve Action Theory". According to Thompson, "the intuition that in 'I am doing A,' in particular, we have essentially to do with something real, particular and individual, in the shape of *an act of doing A,* as we don't in, say, 'I intend to do A,' . . . is . . . a mistake . . . arising from a failure to perceive the distance between imperfective and perfective employments of event- or process-descriptions" (137), e.g., between "I am writing" and "I wrote", e.g., "I am a fool" on the blackboard. We might say that it is because we are not deal-ing with such a "real, particular, and individual" thing in "I am doing A" that falsifying state-ments of this form is not as straightforward a matter as we may be apt to assume.

28. She offers, as examples (40), " 'I am seeing my dentist' [and] 'He is demonstrating in Trafalgar Square' (either might be said when someone is at the moment, e.g., travelling in a train)". This builds on her discussion, on the previous page, of the so-called openness of the progressive ("a man can *be doing* something which he nevertheless does not *do,* if it is some process or enterprise which it takes time to complete and of which therefore, if it is cut short at any time, we may say that he *was doing* it, but *did not do* it" [39]).

so, i.e., "my knowledge would have been the same, even if this had happened". (And, of course, to acknowledge this is not to deny that my knowledge is of what is happening, i.e., of writing "I am a fool" on the blackboard; Anscombe is right to reject the claim that if "my knowledge would have been the same even if this had happened" then "my knowledge is independent of what actually happens".)

Contrary to what we might have assumed, therefore, mistakes of performance do not always serve to deprive one of practical knowledge. They may rather constitute what we might call "hiccups" or "glitches"—mistakes of performance that do not falsify statements as to what one is doing, and thereby allow for the possibility of one's practical knowledge remaining the same, in spite of one's mistake.

Anscombe certainly thinks it is possible to falsify statements purporting to express practical knowledge; this comes out in her example of pushing button B. But the moral of her discussion of writing "I am a fool" is that falsifying statements of this sort is not as straightforward as we might assume—e.g., if we take the pushing button B example as our paradigm of a mistake of performance, or if we concentrate on cases where our statements fall to the ground, at the expense of a focus on hiccups. Not all mistakes of performance are hiccups; but some are—and that is a useful reminder, given the assumption that none are which we might be tempted to make.[29]

29. Maria Alvarez, Olav Gjelsvik, Jen Hornsby, David Hunter, Colin Johnston, Richard Moran, Alan Millar, Fred Stoutland, Peter Sullivan, Jonathan Way, and Hong Yu Wong each gave me very helpful comments; many thanks to them all. And special thanks to Jen, for her help and encouragement throughout the process of writing this essay. Thanks also to Wolfram Gobsch and Matthias Haase, for some very illuminating conversations about *Intention,* from which the impetus for writing this essay sprang.

6

Knowledge of Intention

KIERAN SETIYA

Readers of Anscombe's *Intention* tend to fall into two opposing groups. On the one hand, there are those for whom her book begins with exaggerated claims about knowledge of intentional action, according to which we know "without observation" whatever we are doing intentionally and the demand for reasons is "refused application by the answer: 'I was not aware I was doing that.'"[1] Rejecting these claims outright, the sceptic finds *Intention* fundamentally unsound.[2] On the other hand, there are those for whom "being incompatible with Anscombe is a little like being incompatible with the facts."[3]

I belong with the relative minority who find some truth in Anscombe's premises, while disputing her conclusions.[4] The present essay is, however, less

---

1. G. E. M. Anscombe, *Intention,* 2nd ed. (Cambridge, Mass., 2000), 11.

2. This is the attitude of Michael Bratman and Michael Smith, among others.

3. I owe this turn of phrase to John Gibbons, "Seeing What You're Doing," *Oxford Studies in Epistemology* 3 (2010): 63–85 at 74. Recent Anscombians include Candace Vogler, *Reasonably Vicious* (Cambridge, Mass., 2002); Richard Moran, "Anscombe on 'Practical Knowledge,'" in *Agency and Action,* ed. J. Hyman and H. Steward (Cambridge, 2004), 43–68; and Michael Thompson, *Life and Action* (Cambridge, Mass., 2008), part two.

4. Kieran Setiya, *Reasons without Rationalism* (Princeton, N.J., 2007), part one. See also J. D. Velleman, *Practical Reflection* (Princeton, N.J., 1989).

concerned with Anscombe's arguments than with claims she does not argue for. It is addressed to those who insist that we must have prior evidence for beliefs about what we are actually doing, as opposed to beliefs about our intentions or other mental states. Is there any way to demonstrate, on independent grounds, that intentional action is subject to what Anscombe called "knowledge without observation"? Is there any way to bring sceptics to the place from which *Intention* departs? In what follows, I argue that there is.

My argument turns on the possibility of self-knowledge, and on a picture of "transparency" that is both familiar and obscure.[5] In section 1, I explain what I take the premise about knowledge of action to be, how it diverges from the letter but not the spirit of Anscombe's formulation, and what is involved in the alternative picture I mean to argue against. In section 2, I explain and motivate the notion of transparency in connection with belief. In section 3, it is applied to knowledge of intention and Anscombe's premise is vindicated.

1. Knowledge of Action by Inference?

Intentional action is that "to which a certain sense of the question 'Why?' is given application; the sense is of course that in which the answer, if positive, gives a reason for acting."[6] Thus, what we do for reasons, we do intentionally.[7]

Anscombe makes a second claim about intentional action, that what we do intentionally, we do knowingly.[8] If I do not realize that I am speaking out loud as I type, this is not an intentional action, nor can it be something I am doing for a reason. This is not to say that one must consciously attend to whatever one is doing intentionally. It can be said of me as I sleep that I am writing a paper on *Intention,* and that I know I am, just as I know who my parents are and where I was born. But for Anscombe, as for Stuart Hampshire, "doing something . . . intentionally . . . entails knowing what one is doing."[9]

---

5. Appeals to transparency in recent work derive from Roy Edgley, *Reason in Theory and Practice* (London, 1969), 90; Gareth Evans, *The Varieties of Reference* (Oxford, 1982), 224–228; Fred Dretske, "Introspection," *Proceedings of the Aristotelian Society* 94 (1994): 263–278; and Richard Moran, *Authority and Estrangement* (Princeton, N.J. 2001), 60–64.

6. Anscombe, *Intention,* 9.

7. The converse is less clear; but the dispute about acting intentionally "for no particular reason" will not be relevant here.

8. Anscombe, *Intention,* 11.

9. S. Hampshire, *Thought and Action* (Notre Dame, Ind., 1959), 102.

Although I will defend the idea that we have "knowledge in intention" of what we are doing, and that such knowledge is epistemically distinctive, such claims must be significantly qualified. Imagine that I have recently been paralyzed, unable to move my arm or hand. As it lies under the sheets, I cannot see or feel its movements. In a moment of irrational optimism, I believe that I am cured. Now, as it happens, my belief is true: I am able to clench my fist. But when I do so intentionally, although I believe that I am clenching my fist, my belief does not amount to knowledge.[10] Other cases exhibit a failure not only of knowledge but belief. Suppose that, as I recover from paralysis, my hopes are modest. I think that I might be able to clench my fist, without being sure. When I try to do so, I succeed: I clench my fist intentionally. Still, I need not believe that I am clenching my fist. If there is a connection between doing ϕ intentionally and knowledge or belief that one is doing ϕ, it cannot be as simple as Anscombe takes it to be.

Elsewhere, I have argued that such examples force us to weaken Anscombe's picture, not dismiss it altogether. We can attribute the problems to a simplification: that of ignoring partial belief. A complete epistemology must deal not only with knowledge but with the justification of confidence, which comes by degree. Likewise, the doctrine that connects intentional action with belief must be qualified to allow for doubt.[11] Perhaps the truth is this: when one is doing ϕ intentionally one is more confident that one is doing it than one would otherwise be; one has a higher degree of belief. At any rate, this condition is met in the case of cautious optimism. Although I cannot see or feel my fist, I am more confident that I am clenching it than I was before I began.

No doubt there is more to say about these suggestions; the topic of partial belief is taken up again in section 3. But saying it here would do little to convince the sceptic. There is a profound division among action theorists, be-

---

10. Anscombe might resist the assumption, implicit in this paragraph, that knowledge of what one is doing intentionally involves *belief*. Thus, when "a man is *simply* not doing what he [intends to be doing]"—as in a failure to execute a basic action—"the mistake is not one of judgement but of performance" (Anscombe, *Intention*, 57). On the more natural view, his mistake is one of judgement *and* performance. When I intend to be pushing button A and I am actually pushing B, there is a mistake in what I do—but also a mistake in what I believe about myself. For a similar response to Anscombe, see Moran, "Anscombe on 'Practical Knowledge,'" 60–61.

11. As in D. F. Pears, "Intention and Belief," in *Essays on Davidson: Actions and Events*, ed. B. Vermazen and M. B. Hintikka (Oxford, 1985), 75–88; and Kieran Setiya, "Practical Knowledge," *Ethics* 118 (2008): 388–409, and "Practical Knowledge Revisited," *Ethics* 120 (2009): 128–137.

tween those for whom the principle that we know what are doing intentionally is a pivotal guide to the nature of intentional action and those for whom
it is not. For the former, examples of paralysis are clues to the proper statement of this connection, calling for refinement, not wholesale rejection. For
the latter, such attachment to Anscombe is merely stubborn.

My hope is that we can make progress in this dispute by considering a side
of Anscombe's doctrine that I have so far suppressed: the idea that one's intentional actions are known "without observation."[12] Anscombe means to
exclude not only perception by the five external senses but proprioception
and inference. Her final view appears in the following passage:

> [The topic] of an intention may be matter on which there is knowledge or
> opinion based on observation, inference, hearsay, superstition or anything
> that knowledge or opinion ever are based on; or again matter on which an
> opinion is held without any foundation at all. When knowledge or opin-
> ion are present concerning what is the case, and what can happen—say
> Z—if one does certain things, say ABC, then it is possible to have the in-
> tention of doing Z in doing ABC; and if the case is one of knowledge or if
> the opinion is correct, the doing or causing Z is an intentional action, and
> it is not by observation that one knows one is doing Z; or in so far as one is
> observing, inferring etc. that Z is actually taking place, one's knowledge is
> not the knowledge that a man has of his intentional actions.[13]

Anscombe does not deny that knowledge of what one is doing intentionally
typically depends on empirical or other knowledge of the world. In the example of paralysis, I cannot know that I am clenching my fist in doing so
intentionally unless I know that I have recovered. But even when I have that
knowledge, I do not know that I am clenching my fist on the basis of *sufficient prior evidence*. Likewise, in the well-known vignette from *Intention,* one
cannot know that one is pumping water into the house unless one knows that
the equipment is working properly; but when all goes well, one's knowledge
of what one is doing is not perceptual or inferential. It is the possibility of
knowing what one is doing without sufficient prior evidence that is denied by
Anscombe's critics.[14] What matters here is that we can address this possibility

---

12. Anscombe, *Intention,* 13–15.

13. Ibid., 50.

14. See Keith Donnellan, "Knowing What I Am Doing," *Journal of Philosophy* 60 (1963):
401–409; H. P. Grice, "Intention and Uncertainty," *Proceedings of the British Academy* 57
(1971): 263–279; Rae Langton, "Intention as Faith," in *Agency and Action,* ed. J. Hyman and

without worrying about its prevalence and thus without engaging, for the most part, with examples like those above. Our questions can be framed in terms of agents' capacities and by reflection on the following claim:

> *Anscombe's Principle:* If *A* has the capacity to act for reasons, she has the capacity to know what she is doing without observation or inference—in that her knowledge does not rest on sufficient prior evidence.

Since the capacities at issue here are general, this claim is consistent with cases in which the first is exercised but the second is not, and with the performance of particular intentional actions one is incapable of knowing without observation or inference, as perhaps when I clench my fist while recovering from paralysis.

My purpose is not to explain Anscombe's Principle, or to examine doubts that have been raised against it—as when Grice complains of "licensed wishful thinking" or Langton of unwarranted "leaps of faith."[15] Those are matters I have taken up elsewhere.[16] Instead, I will argue directly that the principle is true. My argument will not appeal to further doctrines of *Intention,* about the meaning of the question "Why?" or the nature of the practical syllogism, which tend to presuppose this principle. Nor do I aim to give reasons that Anscombe would herself endorse. The plan is rather to rely on grounds acceptable to those who deny Anscombe's Principle and thus to give a novel argument on its behalf.

Begin with the following point: even those who reject non-observational, non-inferential knowledge of intentional action should concede that we often know what we are doing not solely on the basis of perceptual evidence. Imagine, for instance, that my hand is anaesthetized and held behind my back. I can still know that I am clenching my fist when I decide to do so. The basis of my knowledge is not observational. The same is true in perfectly ordinary cases. This comes out as soon as we shift our focus from brief movements of the body to projects that take considerable time.[17] If I decide to build a shed and start by taking out my tools, the perceptually available evidence for what

---

H. Steward (Cambridge, 2004), 243–258; and Sarah Paul, "How We Know What We're Doing," *Philosophers' Imprint* 9 (2009): 1–23.

15. Grice, "Intention and Uncertainty"; Langton, "Intention as Faith."

16. In Setiya, "Practical Knowledge" and "Practical Knowledge Revisited."

17. For a similar argument, see Falvey on the "broadness" of the progressive: Kevin Falvey, "Knowledge in Intention," *Philosophical Studies* 99 (2000): 21–44, 25–27.

I am doing is extremely thin. Imagine someone watching and trying to guess. Unlike that observer, I know perfectly well that I am building a shed, not mending the cupboard. The upshot is that even if we reject Anscombe's Principle, we should accept its weaker implication:

> *Non-Perceptual Knowledge:* If *A* has the capacity to act for reasons, she has the capacity to know what she is doing without observation—in that her knowledge does not rest on sufficient perceptual evidence.

Again, this is a claim about general capacities. It allows for intentional actions that cannot be known without observation and need not get entangled with paralysis and the like. What is more, it suggests a diagnosis of Anscombe's allure. She is right to say that knowledge of what one is doing intentionally is, or can be, knowledge without observation in a modest sense: knowledge that is not perceptual. We do not have to wait and see what we are doing intentionally. Anscombe's mistake is to move from this fact to the more radical doctrine that knowledge of intentional action is knowledge without observation *or inference*. This is what the sceptic resists, noting that our evidence may outstrip what perception provides. Knowledge of what one is doing intentionally may rest on sufficient prior evidence, after all.

It remains to say what this evidence could be if it is not derived from proprioception and the outer senses. According to the sceptic, a capacity for non-perceptual knowledge of action is contained in the capacity to act for reasons—but it is a capacity for knowledge by inference. What is it that we make the inference from? In the ordinary case, *not* from our own past behaviour. We have a kind of access to what we are doing intentionally that is distinctively first-personal. Nor do we predict what we are doing from general knowledge of our own beliefs and desires. For the sceptic, the capacity for non-perceptual knowledge of action that flows from the capacity to act for reasons depends on having special access to our own intentions.[18] First-person knowledge of what I am doing intentionally rests on an inference from premises of the following form:

---

18. This picture originates in Donnellan's critical response to Anscombe in "Knowing What I Am Doing." It was taken up by Grice in "Intention and Uncertainty" (where he distinguished unhelpfully between "willing" and intending), and has been developed most carefully by Paul in "How We Know What We're Doing."

I. I have the intention of doing ɸ.

II. I have the ability to ɸ in the simple conditional sense: if I were to have the intention of doing ɸ, I would be doing it.

The first premise is a matter of self-knowledge, not self-observation. It ascribes the intention of acting in a certain way without assuming that I am acting as I intend. I could have the intention of clenching my fist while being entirely paralyzed, or the intention of pumping water into the house when there is a hole in the pipe. The second premise is broadly empirical, though it need not rest on perception of what is presently going on.[19] Conditionals like (II) may be learned from past experience. On this inferential model, I can ordinarily say what I am doing intentionally without observation because I know what I intend to be doing, and I know that I have the ability to do it. The inference is ready to hand.

It is this model that affords the most intractable opposition to Anscombe's view and is the principal target of the arguments to come. One objection I note only to set aside. It contends that there is no fundamental contrast between intending and doing, so that knowledge of intention already amounts to knowledge of an action in progress, though perhaps at a very early stage. There is no need to make an inference from one to the other. If we can know that we intend without sufficient prior evidence, we thereby know what we are doing. This view can be refined and made more subtle.[20] But I ignore it here, for two reasons. First, although I have focused mainly on intentional action, there is a corresponding doctrine for prospective intention:

If *A* has the capacity to plan for the future, she has the capacity to know what she is *going* to do without observation or inference—in that her knowledge does not rest on sufficient prior evidence.

It is not at all clear how the metaphysics of intending as doing would help us to resist an inferential picture of such prospective knowledge or provide an

19. See Grice, "Intention and Uncertainty," 276; Velleman, *Practical Reflection,* 20; and Paul, "How We Know What We're Doing," §V.

20. As in Thompson, *Life and Action,* part two, and Richard Moran and Martin J. Stone, "Anscombe on Expression of Intention: An Exegesis" (this volume), sections 2 and 3. For an earlier view in much the same spirit, see George Wilson, *The Intentionality of Human Action* (Stanford, Calif., 1989), 222–230, and for the relevance of this metaphysics to the epistemology of action, see Falvey, "Knowledge in Intention," 25–26, 28–29.

adequate alternative. Even if it suffices for action, intending to φ does not entail that I am going to φ.[21] Second, I think the metaphysics in question is false. At any rate, my ambition is to say what is wrong with the inferential model without disputing the picture of intention as a mental state distinct from and causally responsible for its own execution.[22]

We can do this by reflecting on the nature of self-knowledge. The problem with the inferential model is that it gets things backwards in assuming a capacity to know what we intend that does not rest on a prior capacity to know what we are doing. In a sense to be explained, knowledge of intention is transparent to knowledge of action; it is by knowing what we are doing, or what we are going to do, that we know what we intend. This formula is deliberately reminiscent of a more familiar claim: that knowledge of belief is transparent to the world. In the following section, I defend the transparency of belief, laying the groundwork for a defence of Anscombe in section 3. It transpires that the cases are parallel. Our capacity for self-knowledge of belief exploits a prior capacity to know the world by forming beliefs about it. Likewise, our capacity to know what we intend exploits a prior capacity to know what we are doing by forming intentions. As I will argue, we must have non-observational, non-inferential knowledge of intentional action in order to have such knowledge of intention as a mental state.

2. Transparent Beliefs

Our text is a justly influential passage from *The Varieties of Reference:*

> In making a self-ascription of belief, one's eyes are, so to speak, or occasionally literally, directed outward—upon the world. If someone asks me "Do you think there is going to be a third world war?", I must attend, in answering

---

21. A related point is made in Setiya, "Practical Knowledge," 400n39.

22. Compare Anscombe, *Intention*, 95: "The relation of *being done in execution of a certain intention,* or *being done intentionally,* is [not] a causal relation between act and intention." Anscombe's arguments are criticized in Setiya, *Reasons without Rationalism*, 56–59. Rosalind Hursthouse objects that "on the causalist view, an agent's knowledge-of-his-present-or-future-intentional-action *must* be speculative knowledge of action-caused-by-certain-mental-items." ("Intention," in *Logic, Cause and Action,* ed. R. Teichmann [Cambridge, 2000], 83–105, 105.) But she gives no argument for this, and Anscombe (*Intention*, 15–16) explicitly denies it. Why must knowledge of mental causation be "speculative" or based on evidence, anymore than knowledge of what one is doing?

him, to precisely the same outward phenomena as I would attend to if I were answering the question "Will there be a third world war?" I get myself in a position to answer the question whether I believe that *p* by putting into operation whatever procedure I have for answering the question whether *p*.[23]

Many philosophers find insight in the claim that our beliefs are transparent to the world.[24] But what exactly does this slogan mean? And what problem about self-knowledge does it help to solve?

Let's begin with the second question. Although I sometimes come to believe that I believe that *p* on the basis of inference, as from my own past or present behaviour or in the course of therapy, this is typically not the case. If Ryle meant otherwise when he wrote that the "sorts of things I can find out about myself are the same as the sorts of things that I can find out about other people, and the methods of finding them out are much the same," he was mistaken.[25] I often know what I believe without having behavioural evidence for the self-ascription of a kind that would justify the attribution of that belief to someone else.[26] Nor does my belief that I believe that *p* typically rest on *appearances* of belief: its seeming to me that I believe that *p*. It is not that there are no such appearances—we are familiar with feelings of conviction and doubt—but that I often know what I believe without experiencing them. Knowledge of one's own beliefs is often *groundless,* in that it does not rest on quasi-perceptual appearances of belief or on inference from evidence of other kinds.[27]

This might be thought enough to generate a puzzle: How is groundless self-knowledge so much as possible? But the force of this challenge is unclear. As John McDowell writes, when a philosopher wonders how something is

23. Evans, *The Varieties of Reference,* 225.

24. Along with the authors cited in note 5, see André Gallois, *The World Without, the Mind Within* (Cambridge, 1996); Alex Byrne, "Introspection," *Philosophical Topics* 33 (2005): 79–104; and Matthew Boyle, "Two Kinds of Self-Knowledge," *Philosophy and Phenomenological Research* 78 (2009): 133–164.

25. G. Ryle, *The Concept of Mind* (London, 1949), 149.

26. This point is decisively made in Paul Boghossian, "Content and Self-Knowledge," *Philosophical Topics* 17 (1989): 5–26, 7–8.

27. The wording in the text leaves room for Christopher Peacocke's view that self-knowledge of conscious belief is supported by evidence from which it is not inferred. (C. Peacocke, "Conscious Attitudes, Attention, and Self-Knowledge," in *Knowing Our Own Minds,* ed. C. Wright, B. C. Smith, and C. McDonald [Oxford, 1998], 63–98, 71–72, 82–83.) As we will see, appeal to such evidence does not address the most pressing question about self-knowledge.

possible, "one's first move . . . should be to ask: why exactly does it look to you, and why should it look to me, as if such-and-such a thing (e.g., baseless authority about oneself) is *not* possible?"[28] What principle threatens the possibility of groundless self-knowledge? It would beg the question to assume that knowledge always rests on inference or on quasi-perceptual evidence. Of course, we can ask in general terms when a belief is justified and when it counts as knowledge. But that these questions can be raised is hardly evidence of some sceptical problem for groundless knowledge of belief.

A better question—one that points us in the direction of transparency—is how it can be *rational* to form beliefs about one's own beliefs not on the basis of perception or inference. This is not a demand for proof or refutation but for further specification. By what rational means are such beliefs acquired? What rational capacity operates in their formation? The paradigm capacities of epistemic reason, perception and inference, are apparently ruled out. Is there some further power at work?

In framing things this way, we do not beg the question against reliabilism in the epistemology of self-knowledge. Here I am thinking of Armstrong and Mellor, among others.[29] "How do I know so much about my own beliefs?" asks Mellor.[30]

> My answers of course will be causal not conceptual. . . . When I perceive other people's beliefs (and wants), part at least of the mechanism is that of my outer senses. . . . Not so with assent. . . . But some perceptual mechanism there must be. Assent does not occur by magic, nor is it an accident that it generally reveals what I believe. So we must have an "inner sense" . . . which I take the liberty of calling "insight". And just as neurophysiology must account for the workings of the eye and ear, so it must account for the workings of insight.[31]

Although I am sceptical of reliabilism, there is nothing so far to prevent its advocates from treating insight as a rational capacity distinct from perception and inference, a rational source for groundless knowledge of belief.

---

28. John McDowell, "Response to Crispin Wright," in *Knowing Our Own Minds,* 47–62, 57–58.

29. David Armstrong, *A Materialist Theory of Mind* (London, 1968), chapter 15; D. H. Mellor, "Conscious Belief," *Proceedings of the Aristotelian Society* 78 (1977–1978): 87–101.

30. Mellor, "Conscious Belief," 97.

31. Ibid., 97–98.

The problem is rather one of psychological extravagance.[32] In an important series of essays, Sydney Shoemaker has urged the impossibility of "self-blindness" as an objection to what he calls the "broad perceptual model" of self-knowledge. As he defines the term, a "self-blind creature would be one which has the conception of the various mental states, and can entertain the thought that it has this or that belief, desire, intention, etc., but which is unable to become aware of the truth of such a thought except in a third-person way."[33] Shoemaker argues that an epistemically rational creature could not be self-blind, but that she could lack insight, understood as a contingently realized causal mechanism for the detection of beliefs. In that respect, the capacity for groundless self-knowledge is unlike our perceptual capacities, each of which is a contingent supplement to epistemic rationality.[34] For our purposes, the key insight of this argument is that self-blindness is impossible. If one is capable of reasoning, and has the concept of belief, one has first-person access to one's own beliefs. Although Shoemaker gives reasons for this premise that others reject, I think both sides of that dispute mistake the dialectical situation.[35] The impossibility of self-blindness is not a doctrine to be argued for, but a datum in the study of self-knowledge to be taken for granted and explained. More carefully, the following principle is true:

> *Cognitive Self-Knowledge:* If *A* has the capacity for inference and can ascribe beliefs to others, she has the capacity for groundless knowledge of her own beliefs.

We hoped to specify the rational capacity responsible for such knowledge. This principle dramatically constrains our answer. The only capacities to which we can appeal are those required for making inferences and for the attribution of beliefs to other people. The problem for Armstrong and Mellor's

---

32. For the use of this term in this context, see Byrne, "Introspection," 92, to which I am indebted throughout this section.

33. Sydney Shoemaker, "On Knowing One's Own Mind," in *The First-Person Perspective and Other Essays* (Cambridge, 1996), 25–49, 30–31.

34. Here I paraphrase the argument of Shoemaker, "On Knowing One's Own Mind," which is repeated in "Self-Knowledge and 'Inner Sense'" (in Shoemaker, *The First-Person Perspective and Other Essays*). Related considerations appear in Burge, "Our Entitlement to Self-Knowledge," *Proceedings of the Aristotelian Society* 96 (1996): 91–116.

35. Shoemaker, "On Knowing One's Own Mind," and "Self-Knowledge and 'Inner Sense,'" 235–241; Amy Kind, "Shoemaker, Self-Blindness and Moore's Paradox," *Philosophical Quarterly* 53 (2003): 39–48, 44–45; Byrne, "Introspection," 88–92.

reliabilism is that it conceives of insight as something distinct from these, a further mechanism that may be absent while they are present. According to Cognitive Self-Knowledge, there must be some other way to know what we believe.

With this much in place, we can begin to generalize. There is, it turns out, an argument behind the question how we have groundless knowledge of belief. Such knowledge must derive from the exercise of a rational capacity. What is it? In answering this question, we have to respect the conditional above. Assuming that the concept of belief does not bring with it a new capacity of epistemic reason, the capacity for groundless knowledge of one's own beliefs must be contained in the capacity for inference. But to say that this knowledge is groundless is in part to say that it is *not* inferential! What source can it possibly have?

Perhaps ironically, the emerging paradox is not addressed by Shoemaker in his critique of the broad perceptual model. Although he objects to a version of reliabilism on which first-person knowledge of belief rests on insight as a causal mechanism, Shoemaker's position involves no fundamental break with the reliabilist approach. He holds it as a necessary truth that first-order beliefs are typically accompanied by second-order beliefs in rational subjects. Still, such beliefs "count as knowledge, not because of the quantity or quality of the evidence on which they are based (for they are based on no evidence), but because of the reliability of the mechanism by which they are produced."[36] Shoemaker declines to specify the nature of this mechanism, except to say that it is "constitutive" of belief.[37] Insisting that self-knowledge draws on capacities

---

36. Shoemaker, "Self-Knowledge and 'Inner Sense,'" 222.

37. Shoemaker, "On Knowing One's Own Mind," 34, and "Self-Knowledge and 'Inner Sense,'" 242–244. The persisting reliabilism of these passages is criticized by Peacocke, "Conscious Attitudes, Attention, and Self-Knowledge," 77, 83, 93–94, and M. G. F. Martin, "An Eye Directed Outward," in *Knowing Our Own Minds,* 99–121, 106: "If we are told simply of a general constraint—that on the whole one must have correct higher-order beliefs to have lower-order beliefs—this tells us nothing about the relation between any particular higher-order belief and its subject-matter, the corresponding lower-order belief." Similar concerns apply to Burge, "Our Entitlement to Self-Knowledge." Peacocke's own view is that conscious judgements give us evidence for self-ascriptions of belief (Peacocke, "Conscious Attitudes, Attention, and Self-Knowledge," 71–72, 82–83). Insofar as these self-ascriptions are not *inferred* from such evidence, however, this no more answers our question than does Shoemaker. By what rational capacity do we form beliefs about our own beliefs and how is this power contained in the capacity for inference?

involved in being rational, he does not tell us how these capacities work or what they are.

This is a sin of omission; but it is difficult to see how the gap could be filled. On the face of it, the capacity for inference cannot be responsible for groundless and so non-inferential knowledge. (As we will see, this appearance is deceptive; but it is initially compelling.) That leaves only one way to account for our conditional. Self-knowledge must derive from a further rational capacity, one that is similar to insight except that its possession by subjects capable of inference is not contingent. This necessity must be explained, in turn, by the fact that inference exploits and relies upon self-knowledge. On this proposal, making an inference from p to q requires the belief that one believes that p, acquired by a capacity distinct from both perception and inference.[38] That is why self-blindness is impossible, and why the conditional above is true. Call this strategy for explaining Cognitive Self-Knowledge the Presupposition Approach.

The difficulty for this approach is that, while some sorts of epistemic self-management rely on self-knowledge, as when I notice a contradiction in my beliefs or reason hypothetically (distinguishing what I believe from what I merely suppose), the bare capacity to form one belief on the basis of others does not.[39] In its simplest form, inference is wholly world-directed, moving from premise to conclusion without self-ascription. There are puddles on the sidewalk, so it must have rained. In reasoning thus, I am sensitive to my own beliefs, but I need not ascribe them to myself. That there are puddles on the sidewalk is strong evidence that it rained; it is redundant to mention my *belief* about the puddles. Something similar holds for other rational capacities. In forming beliefs on the basis of perception, I must be sensitive to how things appear, but I can learn that there is a hand in front of me without drawing on beliefs about my own perceptual state.

A more abstract argument supports this view. The claim that inference relies upon self-knowledge is an instance of a more general claim:

38. Here, as elsewhere, I will be careless about the distinction between schematic letters and propositional variables.

39. The role of self-knowledge in critical thinking is emphasized by Shoemaker, "On Knowing One's Own Mind," 28–29, 33–34, and Burge, "Our Entitlement to Self-Knowledge," 98–100, but they seem to allow the possibility of inference without it. Compare Boghossian, "Content and Self-Knowledge," 9, who attributes the contrary view, I think implausibly, to epistemic internalists.

Presupposition: Rational capacities rely on beliefs about our mental states, not just the realization of those states.

But if Presupposition were true, groundless self-knowledge would be impossible. Making an inference from p to q would require not only the belief that p but the belief that I believe that p. This belief, in turn, must be acquired by a distinctive rational capacity, a capacity to form the belief that I believe that p when I do in fact believe that p.[40] According to Presupposition, however, the exercise of this capacity in that circumstance depends on the belief that the circumstance obtains: that is, on the belief that I believe that p. Self-knowledge is always already presupposed. This problem would not arise if the capacity in question did not appeal to prior self-knowledge. But if one capacity is exempt from this requirement, why not others? In particular, why can't inference also draw on the belief that p without second-order belief? If it can, the Presupposition Approach must fail. We cannot account for the impossibility of self-blindness by noting that inference requires self-knowledge acquired by other means, for that is not the case.

How, then, to make sense of Cognitive Self-Knowledge? If A has the capacity for inference and can ascribe beliefs to others, she has the capacity for groundless knowledge of her own beliefs. Since inference does not presuppose such knowledge, but the capacity for inference entails it, the latter capacity must be the *source* of groundless knowledge. But groundless knowledge is not inferential. It is this paradox that transparency helps us to solve. The solution has two steps. The first is to recognize inference as a species of *epistemic rule-following:* the application to evidential rules of a more general capacity to form beliefs on the basis of other beliefs. ("Rule-following" could mislead if it suggests intentional action: the deliberate use of rules that one articulates to oneself.[41] I doubt that we can form beliefs intentionally,[42] and we need not do so in gaining knowledge by inference.)

---

40. There is no implication here of temporal priority. Even if I form the belief that I believe that p as I form the belief that p itself, we can ask for the rational capacity involved. Nor can we simply cite the capacities for perceptual judgement or inference responsible for the first-order belief, since they are capacities to know that p on the basis of apparent evidence that p, and I come to believe that I believe that p without apparent evidence. We need to explain *how* the capacities in question can be used in this way—as the transparency account purports to do.

41. See, for instance, Shoemaker, "Self-Intimation and Second Order Belief," *Erkenntnis* 71 (2009): 33–51, 36, responding to Byrne, "Introspection."

42. Kieran Setiya, "Believing at Will," *Midwest Studies in Philosophy* 32 (2008): 35–52.

The second step is to formulate a *rule of transparency for belief* inspired by Evans: "whenever you are in a position to assert that *p*, you are *ipso facto* in a position to assert 'I believe that *p*'."[43] This way of putting things gives the misleading impression that I first ask what I am in a position to assert, then make an inference from my answer: "I am in a position to assert that *p*; so I believe that *p*." On a more attractive view, I draw directly on the state in virtue of which I am in a position to assert that *p*. If I am capable of inference, I have the capacity to form beliefs on the basis of my beliefs. Groundless self-knowledge exploits this capacity, not to form the belief that *p*-or-*q* on the basis of my belief that *q*, or the belief that *p* in light of evidence that *p*, but to form the belief that I believe that *p* on the basis of my belief that *p*. In doing so, I follow the rule of transparency for belief. The capacity for groundless self-knowledge, then, is a repurposing of the capacity to follow rules of inference. If I am able to make inferences, and I have the concept of belief, I can identify my own beliefs without appeal to evidence.

This picture needs elaboration and defence. To begin with, although it exploits the capacity for inference, I have been careful not to describe the movement of transparency as inferential.[44] Unlike inference in the ordinary sense, it does not draw on epistemic support: the premise of the rule of transparency, that *p*, typically is not good evidence for its conclusion, that I believe that *p*. Also unlike inference, the justification of the conclusion does not depend on the justification of the premise. When I infer from *p* to *q*, my belief that *q* will not be justified if my belief that *p* is not. By contrast, when I follow the rule of transparency, I come to know that I believe that *p* even when that belief is irrational or unjustified.[45] (These facts are related: the rationality of inference depends on the provision of evidence, which unjustified beliefs cannot supply.)

While they clarify the present account, the preceding remarks prompt serious objections. If the rule of transparency is so different from an ordinary rule

43. Evans, *The Varieties of Reference*, 225–226. For this approach see Byrne, "Introspection," 95, to which I am once again indebted. A related view is developed in Moran, *Authority and Estrangement*, but there are differences that affect the generality of the respective accounts. I come back to this briefly in section 3.

44. Compare Gallois (*The World Without, the Mind Within*, 46–47), whose view is otherwise similar to the one expounded here.

45. Again, compare Gallois (ibid., 50–53, 111–112), who struggles to explain self-knowledge of unjustified belief precisely because he treats the rule of transparency as a rule of inference. See also Martin, "An Eye Directed Outward," 110.

of inference, why suppose that the capacity for inference entails a capacity to follow this rule? And even if it does, how is it rational to form the belief that I believe that p on the basis of my belief that p, when the fact that p is not good evidence that I believe that p? Possible or not, this procedure seems epistemically corrupt.[46]

In response to the first objection, note that the claim involved in the account is relatively weak: if one has the capacity for inference, no further *general* capacity is required for other forms of epistemic rule-following.[47] This is consistent with local incapacities, with rules that, for one reason or another, a particular subject is prevented from following. But so is the capacity for inference itself. Although I have this capacity, specific rules of inference may be cognitive blind spots. What I need in order to follow them is training, or instruction, or therapy, or physical repair; not some entirely new psychological power. This is how to read Cognitive Self-Knowledge. If A has the capacity for inference and can ascribe beliefs to others, she has the general capacities required to follow the rule of transparency and thus gain groundless knowledge of her own beliefs, but she may be prevented from doing this by obstacles of various kinds.

Here, as above, I am drawing on a natural picture of inference as the application to evidential rules of a general capacity to form beliefs on the basis of other beliefs. Is there any reason to resist this view? An alternative would hold that inference always turns on the assessment of evidence. If the capacity to infer is the capacity to form beliefs on the basis of prior beliefs about evidential support, it cannot be redeployed in following the rule of transparency, whose premise is not evidence for its conclusion. But this is a dead end. Suppose that, in order to infer from p to q, one must believe that p is evidence

---

46. For this complaint, see Anthony Brueckner, "Moore Inferences," *Philosophical Quarterly* 48 (1998): 366–369; Martin, "An Eye Directed Outward," 110; and Shoemaker, "Moran on Self-Knowledge," *European Journal of Philosophy* 11 (2003): 391–401, 396–398. The problem is taken up in different ways by Moran, "Responses to O'Brien and Shoemaker," *European Journal of Philosophy* 11 (2003): 402–419, 404–406, 409–415; Byrne, "Introspection," 93–98; and Lucy O'Brien, *Self-Knowing Agents* (Oxford, 2007), 103–104, 111–120.

47. Unfortunately, the next two paragraphs are littered with claims about the identity of rational capacities, without the further metaphysics needed to make them precise. The topic is too large and too obscure. My hope is that we can make progress without being more systematic. At any rate, I don't know how to talk about the epistemology of self-knowledge without invoking such capacities and the distinctions between them.

that q. Where does this belief come from? It is a belief about the specific support offered by a specific fact—that there are puddles on the sidewalk, say—for a specific conclusion—that it rained. This is not the sort of claim for which one needs no evidence or for which the evidence is perceptual. It must be acquired on the basis of other beliefs by the use of a rational capacity. And now there is an obvious dilemma. If this instance of epistemic rule-following is subject to the demand for prior beliefs about evidence, we face a vicious regress.[48] If it is not, the capacity for inference after all depends on a capacity to follow epistemic rules without believing that one's premise is evidence for one's conclusion, a capacity that might be applied to the rule of transparency for belief.

Suppose we grant all this. Still, the second objection remains. How can it be rational to form the belief that one believes that p on the basis of one's belief that p itself, when the content of the latter is not good evidence for the truth of the former? As before, however, we should ask for the argument behind the question. What makes this appear irrational? Is it that one's conclusion is not based on evidence? Since our topic is groundless self-knowledge, that much is inevitable, and it would beg the question to doubt its legitimacy. Nor is there a problem about the non-accidental reliability of beliefs about one's beliefs acquired by transparent means. Far from it: no epistemic rule is more reliable than the rule of transparency. In saying this, we do not fall into reliabilism. It is essential that self-knowledge of belief be acquired by the exercise of a rational capacity, not just a causal process. The point of mentioning reliability is to pre-empt any sceptical argument. Compare Evans: "If a judging subject applies this procedure, then necessarily he will gain knowledge of one of his own mental states: even the most determined sceptic cannot find here a gap in which to insert his knife."[49] The claim of necessity may be unduly optimistic, but the second part seems right. It is idle to question

---

48. Mark Johnston, "Self-Deception and the Nature of Mind," in *Perspectives on Self-Deception*, ed. B. McLaughlin and A. Rorty (Berkeley, 1988), 63–91, 87–88; Peter Railton, "How to Engage Reason: The Problem of Regress," in *Reason and Value*, ed. R. J. Wallace, P. Pettit, S. Scheffler, and M. Smith (Oxford, 2006), 176–201; and Paul Boghossian, "Epistemic Rules," *Journal of Philosophy* 105 (2009): 472–500, 492–494; earlier versions appear in Hume's *Treatise* (*A Treatise of Human Nature*, ed. D. F. Norton and M. J. Norton [Oxford, 2000], 1.3.7.5n) and, perhaps, in *Philosophical Investigations* (Ludwig Wittgenstein, *Philosophical Investigations* [Oxford, 1953], §§185–242).

49. Evans, *The Varieties of Reference*, 225.

the epistemic standing of beliefs acquired in this way without identifying serious grounds for doubt, and this has not been done.

A final objection is that the present account gets the phenomenology wrong. Having formed the belief that p, do I really need to engage in epistemic rule-following in order to learn that I believe that p? For the most part, I am not aware of any further step. Asked whether I believe that p, when I do, the answer takes no further thought. This is true, but it does not conflict with our appeal to the rule of transparency. Suppose one has the capacity to make a rational inference from p to q. Having formed the belief that p, say, on the basis of perception, must there be a further temporal step before one believes that q? There is no reason to think so.[50] One's inferential capacity makes it rational to form, on the basis of the relevant perception, the belief that p-and-q. What goes for inference goes for other sorts of epistemic rule-following. If one has the capacity to know that one believes that p on the basis of one's belief that p, one need not wait to exercise it moments after forming that belief. In coming to believe that p, by whatever epistemic means, one is entitled by the rule of transparency to believe that one believes that p. These thoughts need not even be distinct from one another. We commonly form beliefs whose content is self-referential: "I hereby affirm that p" or "p, as I believe."[51] We do so by employing the rule of transparency in concert with our capacity to form the belief that p on the basis of perception, or inference, or whatever. Evans's procedure is performed in anticipation.

Further objections are possible, but they cannot be examined here. It is more fruitful to end by noting, in brief, how the arguments of this section illuminate a pair of tempting claims about the nature of self-knowledge. The first is Kantian:

> It must be possible for the "I think" to accompany all my representations; for otherwise something would be represented in me which could not be thought at all, and that is equivalent to saying that the representation would be impossible, or at least would be nothing to me.[52]

---

50. Gallois (*The World Without, the Mind Within*, 104) makes the same point in defending his "doxastic schema."

51. The importance of such judgements in understanding self-knowledge has been emphasized by Burge, "Our Entitlement to Self-Knowledge," 92–93, and "Individualism and Self-Knowledge," *Journal of Philosophy* 85 (1988): 649–663, 649, 654.

52. Kant, *Critique of Pure Reason*, trans. N. Kemp Smith (New York, 1965), B131–B132.

Whatever exactly Kant meant by this, something similar holds for Cognitive Self-Knowledge. Assuming that I can ascribe beliefs, any belief from which I can make inferences and thus take up in thought is one to which I can attach "I think" by following the rule of transparency.[53] (How far this extends to other representations, perceptual and volitional, will occupy us below.)

The second claim is that we have a way of knowing our own beliefs that is distinctively first-personal and is not available to others. That is precisely what we get by adapting our capacity for inference to the rule of transparency. In doing so, we gain self-knowledge through a rational sensitivity to our own beliefs that we cannot have to the beliefs of anyone else. If this is how I come to believe that I believe that *p*, I am aware of myself "as subject" in Wittgenstein's sense: my belief is "immune to error through misidentification" and there is no room for the question, "Someone believes that *p*, all right, but is it me?"[54] Nor is there a possibility of reference-failure, as there is with demonstrative thought and, perhaps, with bodily self-awareness.[55] These echoes of Kant and Wittgenstein offer confirmation, albeit modest, for the account developed so far.

3. Transparent Intentions

In the previous section, I argued that we need to explain the following principle:

> *Cognitive Self-Knowledge:* If *A* has the capacity for inference and can ascribe beliefs to others, she has the capacity for groundless knowledge of her own beliefs.

We cannot account for the necessity of this conditional by claiming that inference presupposes knowledge of belief; for it does not. Instead, the capacity for inference must be a *source* of groundless and so non-inferential knowledge. That it is rational to follow the rule of transparency explains how this could be.

53. For this connection, see also Evans, *The Varieties of Reference,* 228; and Boyle, "Two Kinds of Self-Knowledge," 160–161.

54. Ludwig Wittgenstein, *The Blue and Brown Books* (Oxford, 1958), 66–67; Shoemaker, "Self-Reference and Self-Awareness," *Journal of Philosophy* 65 (1968): 555–567, and "Self-Knowledge and 'Inner Sense,'" 210–212.

55. O'Brien, *Self-Knowing Agents,* 33–43.

How far do the idea of transparency and the considerations that motivate it generalize? We should not expect them to apply to all mental states, only to those that admit an analogue of the argument about belief.[56] That argument was driven by entailment of the capacity for groundless self-knowledge by other capacities apparently independent of it. That something similar holds for intention is a lesson of section 1. There we saw that even critics of Anscombe should accept the following principle:

> *Non-Perceptual Knowledge:* If *A* has the capacity to act for reasons, she has the capacity to know what she is doing without observation—in that her knowledge does not rest on sufficient perceptual evidence.

According to the sceptic, the capacity for non-perceptual knowledge of action that follows from the capacity to act for reasons is a capacity for inference from intention and ability. Its first-person character turns on the fact that, like the knowledge of belief explored in section 2, self-knowledge of intention is groundless. For the sceptic, then, the capacity to act for reasons brings with it a capacity for groundless knowledge of intention; it is by inference from such knowledge that we are able to know our intentional actions without appeal to evidence of the kind that others need. Those who resist Anscombe's Principle thus concede not only Non-Perceptual Knowledge but the following claim:

> *Practical Self-Knowledge:* If *A* has the capacity to act for reasons and can ascribe intentions to others, she has the capacity for groundless knowledge of her own intentions.

Like the sceptic, though on different grounds, I think this must be true. It is the counterpart of Cognitive Self-Knowledge. Just as it is impossible for a subject

---

56. On the dangers of assuming uniformity in the sources of self-knowledge, see especially Boyle, "Two Kinds of Self-Knowledge." A question of particular interest is whether transparency explains how we know the *reasons* for our beliefs. There would be a problem here if reasons for which I believe that *p* were efficient causes of that belief, since transparency affords no special access to how my beliefs were caused. But that is not what such reasons are. (Here I side with Keith Lehrer, "How Reasons Give Us Knowledge," *Journal of Philosophy* 68 [1971]: 311–313, against Gilbert Harman, "Knowledge, Reasons and Causes," *Journal of Philosophy* 67 [1970]: 841–855, 845.) Instead, reasons for which one believes that *p* consist in what one takes as evidence that *p*. Hence the following extensions of the rule of transparency for belief: If you believe that the fact that *q* shows that *p*, form the belief that you believe that *p* because you believe that *q*; if you believe that the fact that *q* is evidence that *p* and *p*, form the belief that you believe that *p* partly on the ground that *q*.

with the power of inference and the concept of belief to lack first-person access to his own beliefs, so it is impossible for an agent who does things for reasons and has the concept of intention to lack first-person access to what she herself intends.

The correspondence between the two conditionals encourages the extension of the transparency approach. Further reflection demands it. Assuming that the concept of intention does not bring with it a new capacity of epistemic reason, a new way of forming beliefs on a par with perception and inference, the capacity for groundless knowledge of intention is entailed by the capacity to act for reasons. There are two possible explanations of this. On the Presupposition Approach, acting on the ground that p or in order to ϕ presupposes groundless knowledge of intention acquired by other means. But this is no more plausible here than it was in relation to belief. In the simplest case, practical inference, like theoretical, is wholly world-directed, moving from premise to conclusion without self-ascription. I am cooking dinner, for which I need some eggs, so I'll head to the store and buy them. In reasoning thus, I am sensitive to my own intentions and beliefs, but I need not ascribe them to myself. (This point is emphasized in Anscombe's own discussion of the "practical syllogism.") If this is right, the capacity to act for reasons does not rest on a further capacity for self-knowledge of intention. Instead, it must be the source of such knowledge—as the capacity for theoretical inference is the source of cognitive self-knowledge through the rule of transparency for belief. The hard question is *how* to adapt the transparency approach from the cognitive to the practical sphere. As I will argue, there is no way to do this without accepting Anscombe's Principle: the capacity to act for reasons must be a capacity to know what one is doing—not just what one intends—without sufficient prior evidence.

Perhaps the most prominent attempt to generalize the model of transparency is Richard Moran's *Authority and Estrangement*. But his line is unsustainable. For Moran, "transparency requires . . . the deferral of the theoretical question 'What do I believe?' to the deliberative question 'What am I to believe?' "[57] This normative inflection is absent from the rule of transparency pursued in section 2, on which the question "Do I believe that p?" is transparent to the question whether p. In extending his approach, Moran takes the questions "What am I doing?" and "What do I intend?" to be transparent to the normative question, "What am I to do?"[58] But whatever may hold for

57. Moran, *Authority and Estrangement,* 63.
58. Ibid., 124–128.

belief, to determine the balance of reasons for intending or acting is *not* to settle the question of what I intend or what I am going to do. Nor is there any special self-opacity when these questions come apart: along with *akrasia*, there are mundane examples of choice in the face of many permissible options, where I know perfectly well, in the ordinary way, both what I intend and what I am doing.[59]

What we need, therefore, is an explanation of Practical Self-Knowledge that adapts the idea of transparency but does not pursue a normative line. In seeking an alternative, we should go back to Evans, who sketched a view about the self-ascription of perceptual experience, where normative considerations do not apply.

> A subject can gain knowledge of his internal informational states [i.e., perceptions] in a very simple way: by re-using precisely those skills of conceptualization that he uses to make judgements about the world. Here is how he can do it. He goes through exactly the same procedure as he would go through if he were trying to make a judgement about how it is at this place now, but excluding any knowledge he has *of an extraneous kind.* . . . The result will necessarily be closely correlated with the content of the informational state which he is in at that time. Now he may prefix this result with the operator "It seems to me as though . . ." This is a way of producing in himself, and giving expression to, a cognitive state whose content is *systematically* dependent upon the content of the informational state, and the systematic dependence is a basis for him to claim knowledge of the informational state.[60]

This may sound like an implausibly elaborate strategy for discovering how things look or taste. But that appearance is deceptive, as we can see by comparing Evans's procedure with the rule of transparency for belief. The idea behind that rule is to redeploy one's capacity for epistemic rule-following and consequent sensitivity to the belief that *p*, not to make an inference from the premise that *p*, but to form the belief that one believes that *p*. Here, one redeploys one's capacity for perceptual knowledge, not to form beliefs on the basis of how things perceptually seem, but to form the belief that they seem that way. Although we could defend this adaptation much as we did the rule of transparency in section 2, perception is not our principal topic. Instead,

---

59. These objections are made at greater length in Jonathan Way, "Self-Knowledge and the Limits of Transparency," *Analysis* 67 (2007): 223–230.

60. Evans, *The Varieties of Reference*, 227–228.

the moral to be drawn from Evans is that we can tell a story of transparency for any capacity to know the world. For those with appropriate concepts, such capacities contain epistemic resources for self-knowledge.

As I understand it, the capacity to act for reasons is a capacity of just this kind. It is a capacity for non-perceptual, non-inferential knowledge of what one is doing and why. This formula states in epistemic terms what Anscombe meant when she wrote about intentional action as that to which the question "Why?" is given application and what it means to think of intention as desire-like or motivating belief.[61] The paradigmatic exercise of the capacity to act for reasons is a belief about what one is doing and why that has the power to motivate action. "Intention" is a name for this kind of belief, but the terminology is misleading if it obscures the range of conditions to which the relevant capacity gives rise. Here the comparison with perception helps. Although the capacity to know by looking often yields belief, this is not always so. In particular, I may become more confident that p on the basis of visual perception, while remaining quite unsure. Suppose that I am looking at a distant figure in the ocean at dusk. Is it a man or a woman? Swimming toward me or away? Waving or drowning? Perception rationally affects my degrees of belief about these questions in complex interaction with evidence of other kinds. While the capacity to act for reasons is not perceptual, it is similar in this respect. Epistemic right to form the belief that I am doing φ by forming an intention turns on knowing how to φ, not just the general capacity to act for reasons.[62] And even when I do know how, this right may be revoked or undermined: I may have doubts about my own ability or evidence of interfering factors. Like other capacities to know, the capacity to act for reasons can be exercised in conditions that are epistemically flawed. It then contributes to confidence without sufficing for knowledge or belief. This is what happens in the case of paralysis, where I am clenching my fist intentionally but only partly believe that I am doing so, since my recovery remains in

---

61. Anscombe, *Intention*, 9–12; Setiya, *Reasons without Rationalism*, 29–51. Among those who think of intention as being or involving belief are Stuart Hampshire and H. L. A. Hart, "Decision, Intention and Certainty," *Mind* 67 (1958): 1–12; Gilbert Harman, "Practical Reasoning," in *The Philosophy of Action*, ed. A. Mele (Oxford, 1997), 149–177; Pears, "Intention and Belief"; and Velleman, *Practical Reflection*, chapter 4. Critics include Davidson, "Intending," in *Essays on Actions and Events* (Oxford, 1980), 83–102; Michael Bratman, "Intention and Means-End Reasoning," *Philosophical Review* 90 (1981): 252–265, 254–256; and Alfred Mele, *Springs of Action* (Oxford, 1992), chapter 8.

62. Setiya, "Practical Knowledge" and "Practical Knowledge Revisited."

doubt. Such examples do not refute the present conception of the will, any more than examples of perceptual uncertainty refute the idea of perception as a source of knowledge.

If this Anscombian picture is correct, we can adapt Evans on transparency to intention. Roughly speaking, an agent can know what he intends in the following way:

> He goes through exactly the same procedure as he would go through if he were trying to make a judgement about [what he is doing] but excluding any knowledge he has *of an extraneous kind*. . . . The result will necessarily be closely correlated with the content of [his intention.] Now he may prefix this result with the operator "I intend . . .". This is a way of producing in himself, and giving expression to, a cognitive state whose content is systematically dependent upon the content of the [intention], and the systematic dependence is a basis for him to claim knowledge of [what he intends].[63]

This protocol differs from the perceptual one, in which a rational capacity is applied to an existing state. In gaining transparent knowledge of experience, I exploit my capacity for perceptual knowledge, with its sensitivity to appearances, not to form a perceptual belief but a belief about how things perceptually seem. Doing so does not affect the perceptual state itself, to which my thought is merely receptive. In contrast, when I try to make a judgement about what I am doing using only my capacity to act for reasons and excluding knowledge "of an extraneous kind," I am engaging in practical thought: making up my mind about what to do, not tracking how my mind is already made up. It follows that, while the transparency procedures for perception and belief can be utilized after the fact to gain knowledge of how things already seem or what I already believe, the transparency procedure for intention cannot.[64] The picture is rather that, when I employ the capacity to act

---

63. Compare Evans, *The Varieties of Reference,* 227–228, quoted in the text above.

64. This may be too quick. If the capacity to act for reasons entails a capacity for instrumental reasoning, in which I form one intention on the basis of another, that may restore the parallel between intention and belief. Just as the capacity for inference from p to q is sensitive to the belief that p, and can be redeployed in forming the belief that I believe that p, so the capacity for practical inference from intending E to intending M is sensitive to the former intention, and might be redeployed in forming an intention and thus belief whose content is that I so intend. I am not convinced, however, that the capacity to act for reasons entails the further capacity for putting means to ends. If it does, that would simplify some of the arguments in the text—but they do not depend on it. For further discussion, see Anscombe, *Intention,* 30–33; Vogler, *Reasonably Vicious;* and Thompson, *Life and Action,* 106–115.

for reasons in forming an intention and thus acquire some degree of belief—ideally, knowledge—about what I am doing and why, I may at the same time and by the same capacity form the belief that I have that intention. What looked optional in section 2—using one's rational capacity at once to form an attitude and the belief that one has it—is mandatory here. But the crucial analogy holds. If one has the capacity to act for reasons and can ascribe intentions to others, one has everything one needs for groundless knowledge of one's own intentions. Like other capacities for knowledge of the world, the capacity to act for reasons is potentially self-conscious.

While there are differences between the transparency of perception, intention, and belief, in each case we use a capacity for knowledge of one kind in forming beliefs of another. The capacity for inference or epistemic rule-following takes me from the belief that p to the belief that I believe that p, instead of beliefs for which the fact that p is putative evidence. The capacity for perceptual knowledge takes me from the appearance that p to a belief about this appearance, instead of the belief that p itself. And the capacity to act for reasons, as a capacity to know what I am doing by intending to do it, is used to gain knowledge of my intention along with the belief about what is happening that this intention provides. A peculiarity of this case is that, since I come to know what I intend through the capacity to act for reasons, I know it by intention, not mere belief. In effect, when I form an intention self-consciously, it refers to itself: "I am doing ϕ, as I intend."

This claim may seem too weak, since it leaves room—at least in principle—for intentions that are not self-conscious. On the present account, I could act on the intention of doing ϕ, and know that I am doing ϕ, without knowing that I have the relevant intention.[65] The peculiarity of this should fade, I think, when we recognize that the description of what I am doing that figures in the content of my intention is almost always "of a type to be formally the description of an executed intention."[66] Anscombe lists actions one can-

---

65. For versions of a stronger view, on which intentions are *always* self-referential, see Harman, "Practical Reasoning," §II; John Searle, *Intentionality* (Cambridge, 1983), 83–90; Velleman, *Practical Reflection*, 88–90, 94–97, 140–141; and Setiya, *Reasons without Rationalism*, 41–45, 48–49. In the past, I have also claimed that intentions represent themselves as *causing* action. Again, the argument in the text is weaker: when I intend to be doing ϕ self-consciously, I represent myself as doing what I intend—not necessarily as doing it "hereby," or *because* I so intend. As I now recognize, the stronger claim is false; see Harman, "Practical Reasoning," §II.

66. Anscombe, *Intention*, 87.

not perform except intentionally, such as greeting and promising. But the point applies much more widely. Whenever I am doing φ for reasons, part of what I intend is to act for those reasons, and what I know (if all goes well) is that I am doing so, from which it follows that my action is intentional.[67] Only when I am doing φ for no particular reason and what I am doing is not of a type to be formally the execution of intention can I have knowledge in intention that I am doing φ, which does not entail that I am doing it intentionally.

Other objections echo those against the rule of transparency for belief. We can ask whether it is possible to redeploy a rational capacity for knowledge of the world in gaining knowledge of ourselves and whether doing so is epistemically corrupt. But there are no more grounds for doubt at this point than there were before. If I can form the belief that q on the basis of my belief that p, why not the belief that I believe that p? Likewise, if I can form the belief that I am doing φ in practical thought by forming an intention, why not also the belief that I intend to be doing it? So long as we have the appropriate concepts, there is nothing to prevent our capacities for knowledge from being exercised in these ways. Nor is there a problem about the epistemic propriety of the beliefs thus formed. They may not rest on evidence, but we knew that already, since it is groundless self-knowledge we are trying to explain. And since the way in which they are formed is non-accidentally reliable, it is hard to imagine how a sceptical challenge would go.

One virtue of this account is that it extends so readily to prospective intention. If the will is a capacity for non-perceptual, non-inferential knowledge of action, planning agency involves its application to the future: what one comes to know, or believe, is that one is *going* to φ. With the concept of intention, the capacity to form such beliefs by forming prospective intentions can be used to form the belief that one intends to φ, along with the belief about action itself.

Most importantly, the conception of the will as a capacity to know what one is doing and why explains the truth of our conditional:

---

67. For the claim that one's reasons figure in the content of one's intention, see R. J. Wallace, "Three Conceptions of Rational Agency," in *Normativity and the Will* (Oxford, 2006), 43–62, 60–62; Searle, *Rationality in Action* (Cambridge, Mass., 2001), 16; and Setiya, *Reasons without Rationalism,* 39–49.

> *Practical Self-Knowledge:* If *A* has the capacity to act for reasons and can ascribe intentions to others, she has the capacity for groundless knowledge of her own intentions.

If *A* has the capacity to act for reasons, she has the capacity to form beliefs whose contents are systematically correlated with her intentions, since those intentions themselves involve beliefs. If she also has the concept of intention, she has the capacity to incorporate this correlation into the content of the intentions she forms, and thus to know what she intends.

This way of explaining Practical Self-Knowledge entails the truth of Anscombe's Principle: if *A* has the capacity to act for reasons, she has a capacity to know what she is doing that is distinct from both perception and inference. No similar explanation can be had if the capacity to act for reasons is *not* a capacity for knowledge or belief, but for intention as a non-cognitive state. While a capacity for knowledge of one sort might issue in knowledge of another, a capacity for non-cognitive intention cannot be used to form beliefs: attitudes that differ in kind, not just in content. Nor can we follow an epistemic rule that takes us from intention to self-ascription if intention does not involve belief, since the capacity to follow epistemic rules is a capacity to form one belief on the basis of others. For those who reject the conception of the will as a capacity for knowledge, and with it Anscombe's Principle, knowledge of intention must draw on quasi-perceptual evidence, on inference from evidence of other kinds, or on a further rational capacity. Since it is groundless knowledge we are after, perception and inference are out. And the necessity of Practical Self-Knowledge precludes appeal to a primitive faculty of insight: one could have the capacity to form intentions and act for reasons without it. It follows that there is no way for Anscombe's critics to explain why the capacity to act for reasons and to ascribe intentions to others are together sufficient for groundless knowledge of one's own intentions. Self-blindness is, absurdly, possible.

It follows in turn that these critics cannot make good on the promise to explain first-person knowledge of intentional action as a matter of inference from intention and ability. The capacity to know what one is doing without the kind of evidence that others need is contained in the capacity to act for reasons—that was the concession to Anscombe in section 1—while the capacity for self-knowledge of intention, on the critics' account, is not. The upshot is that only the Anscombian view, on which the capacity to act for reasons is a capacity for knowledge of what one is doing distinct from perception and inference, can accommodate first-person access to our own intentions *or* intentional actions. Only this view can explain why such access is entailed by the capacity to act for reasons. Whatever we say about of the rest of *Intention,* Anscombe's starting point was right.[68]

68. Earlier versions of this essay were presented at Stanford University and at a conference on Anscombe's *Intention* at the University of Chicago. I am grateful to Agnes Callard for perceptive comments at the Anscombe conference, and, for further discussion, to Matt Boyle, Michael Bratman, Matthias Haase, David Hunter, Jennifer Hornsby, Patricia Kitcher, Krista Lawlor, John McDowell, Sarah Paul, Sebastian Rödl, Tamar Schapiro, Nishi Shah, Fred Stoutland, Ben Wolfson, and two anonymous referees.

7

Anscombe's *Intention* and Practical Knowledge

MICHAEL THOMPSON

One of the impediments to our comprehension of G. E. M. Anscombe's *Intention* is that it is packed full of bits of jargon and peculiar obsessive theoretic tics that were characteristic of Anscombe's teacher, Ludwig Wittgenstein. For example, the famous dogma about the relation of knowledge to narrowly psychical phenomena like pain or belief and intention itself—the insistence that I shouldn't be said to *know* that I am in pain, or to *know* that I intend this or that, or that I believe one thing or another. Whether my foot *hurts* or whether I *intend* to leave Uppsala some day, or whether I *think* that some day I'll leave Uppsala—these are supposed to be things I *can say*. I cannot myself be said to know them "except perhaps as a joke." (Shooting pains through the leg, you say? Well, you should know . . .)

Insofar as I can make something of this once famous article of the faith, it is a protest against understanding the case in which you come to know that I am in pain, or intend something, from me telling you—it is a protest against understanding this coming to know on your part by a simple reduction the standard case of the spread or movement of knowledge by hearsay, as when I tell you what the weather has been like in Pittsburgh.

In the standard case, you then have secondhand knowledge of the weather in Pittsburgh, and can transmit this important knowledge to your friends—who are evidently moved, like you, by the Love of Truth and the Desire to Know. The sensible formulation of Anscombe and Wittgenstein's point, if they have one, is thus this. In the case where I tell you that I'm in pain or that I *think* that something is wrong with my liver, you don't have it secondhand by simple knowledge transfer; nor, on the other hand, is your knowledge of my pain a mere matter of observation exactly. When it comes to the narrowly psychical features of the speaking animals, the humans—well, there is, among them, a way of coming to know certain propositions about one another from one another that is sui generis, or anyway, in need of another account: it is neither testamentary in any ordinary sense, nor observational, nor is it derived by inference from these things, and so on. That this is what Anscombe at least has in mind is her repeated opposition of the things I can be said to know, and the things I can say.

But the idea that the one from whom and about whom we know in this special way sui generis—namely, the pained intending believer—the one who talks and can talk to us about it—the idea that he does not himself know is quite unnecessary to preserve the distinctiveness of our coming to know from him by

that USE . . . which expresses the psychical,

as Anscombe's translation of her master's *Investigations* puts it.

This particular bit of egregious Wittgensteinism is a buzzing noise that distracts the reader, and may dispirit him or her quite quickly. In my own view, though, it is a sort of obnoxious but superficial terminology that one can replace with one's own, though it takes a little labor. And many features of the book are like this.

But it may also be that when we clear away this detritus, we will find that the essential core of Anscombe's teaching is in some sense dependent on that of the so-called later Wittgenstein. This may or may not be benign, or mostly benign; I cannot say, since I cannot say I understand this Wittgenstein. Of course, I can't claim to understand Anscombe either. But this much seems plain: If Anscombe's *Intention* is a genuine illustration of the mysterious "method" advanced by Wittgenstein in the 1930s and 1940s, still, it is a far better illustration of it than the old man himself ever managed to produce.

I have mentioned the business about knowledge of the inner or psychical, because it will bear on my principal topic, namely, Anscombe's doctrine of practical knowledge, or of my knowledge of what I am doing intentionally, that is my knowledge of what I'm up to.

We today sometimes speak of self-knowledge—as opposed, if you like, to knowledge of something that is other, or other-knowledge. And on a certain going using use of the term, it does not simply mean knowledge that would be put forth with the first person. My knowledge that I have a coffee stain on my shirt, or that I have a little scar on my left knee—these knowledges pertain to me. We should call them cases not of self-knowledge, but rather of knowledge of oneself, or rather as knowledge of oneself *as other,* to put it in the original Aristotelian, a language to which I will return. The possible contents of my proper self-knowledge, on the contemporary conception of it, are things like my pain, my intention, my belief, and so on; not my condition in respect to trouser health and shirt origin.

It may be that I am hearing too much in the contemporary use of the expression "self-knowledge." But if Anscombe could have broken the spell of her master on the points mentioned earlier, she might have employed it to express herself more lucidly. The overarching thesis of *Intention* was that *self-knowledge in this familiar sense extends beyond the inner recesses of the mind, beyond the narrowly psychical, and into the things that I am doing.* One form of self-knowledge, she thinks, is practical knowledge. Or, in a different jargon: one form of self-consciousness is self-consciousness in respect of one's actions. Or again, now in the formula of Sebastian Rödl: one form of knowledge from spontaneity is a form of knowledge of a material process.

Her most famous formula, which appears very early in the book, is this: My knowledge of what I'm doing intentionally, or of what I'm up to, is knowledge "without observation." This is a purely negative specification, though, and one that, as we will see, must be expelled from the final theory; a theory tells us what things are, not what they are not.

On the face of it, there are lots of kinds of knowledge that come to us "without observation," for example, my knowledge of certain familiar facts about the number 17, e.g., that it is prime, that the associated polygon is constructible, that it is $2^4 + 1$. Her point, as I said, is rather that my knowledge of what I'm doing is self-knowledge, alike in this respect to my knowledge of what I think. In alluding to observation, we characterize the intended form of self-knowledge more closely. It is not founded on the knowing and known substances' entering into a relation of intuition of the other by the one; nor even on a special case of this in one individual substance entering into the relation on both sides, which in the Aristotelian jargon would be intuitive knowledge of oneself as other.

In Aristotelian craft, in techné, we have The Craftsman, and that to which he is opposed, really opposed: The Material, the raw materials. In medicine we ourselves give these opposed items the titles Doctor and Patient, still speaking a half-Aristotelian. When the doctor heals himself, the substance comes into both positions and wears both hats. And so the Philosopher says that the physician heals himself, but only *as* other. So it is with empirical knowledge of oneself; self-knowledge is not like that, no more than poésis is like praxis.

But there is more to the contrast with the observation nexus: Anscombe's practical knowledge is precisely self-knowledge in respect of what might in principle be observed. Or rather, it is knowledge of something that is of such a kind as is regularly observed, and, presumably, necessarily typically observable—namely, what someone is doing, what he's up to. This is something that is already encoded in her emphasis on the question, "Why are you doing A?" as I will suggest in a moment.

That is, for the agent herself, the intentional action, what she's up to, is indeed not known "as something alien, from without, through the medium of the senses," as Frege would put it. But on the other hand, her action is not like Frege's numbers, since that is precisely how it really is for others: her action comes to them as something "alien," as pertaining to an *alius,* another, and "from without," and "through the medium of the senses." Frege's numbers are not objects of experience for anybody; we have no *Anschauung* of them, as Frege says, they can't even make a dent; but in the case of someone's action, some of us might have such an *Anschauung.*

Nor, on the other hand, is the agent's intentional action quite like the narrowly psychical determinations mentioned earlier. These too are not given to subject as something alien from without. But they are not properly matters of experience and intuition for outsiders either; they are not contents of simple perceptual knowledge, but enter the outsider's cognition in other ways.

By contrast, Anscombe insists everywhere that an agent's intentional action is just another sort of process in the world, something perceptible and watchable by others. Indeed her first attempt to isolate the category of intentional action, in a section that might easily be overlooked, depends on this. She says that if I ask you to enter a room with some people in it and to report what's up with them, the process-descriptions you return with will mostly be descriptions of intentional actions. When it comes to each other, the process-descriptions to which our perceptual power is especially attuned are just these, the intentional actions.

> I am sitting in a chair writing, and anyone grown to the age of reason *in the same world* would know this as soon as he saw me, and in general this would be his first description of what I was doing. (emphasis added)

Too bad she didn't say: I am sitting in a chair writing, and anyone grown to the age of reason in the same world would get his mirror neurons triggered. Maybe she would have won the Nobel Prize. The kind of "world" she's talking about, if it is a human world, is something that essentially and at one stroke decks its bearers out with a pile of possible objects of volition, or descriptions of intentional action, and possible contents of perception. To paraphrase Parmenides, then, we can say that *they are the same that are for doing and for perceiving people doing.*

Let us leave that thought aside. The connection with observation is why Anscombe's later formulation of her difficulty in comprehending practical knowledge is a bit closer to the core of the matter:

> Now if there are two *ways* of knowing here, one of which I call knowledge of one's intentional action and the other of which I call knowledge by observation of what takes place, then must there not be two objects of knowledge? (51)

Here the contrast is best framed with respect to the inner psychical—pain and belief and so on. We will all or mostly all say that, on the part of their bearer, inner psychical things are "known from within," and not as something alien and from without; they are contents of her self-knowledge or self-consciousness in standard cases; but, for others, on the other hand, as I just suggested, they are not exactly directly intuitable, potentially observable, features, like hair color or posture.

How can something that is captured in an observational concept, as we might put it—something that is such as to be observed, or known from without through the impact of the thing known—in this case something that is happening or going on, a material process—how can such a thing be, at the same time and intrinsically, such as to be "known from within"? It is difficult to combine the two models of knowledge; the idea of self-knowledge seems to draw the thing known into the agent and away from others. And the picture of things knowable from an intuition of an external substance seems to put them at a distance from the cognition even of that substance, if it is a knower. He must look down to see the gravy on his jacket or the coffee stain on his pants.

Now it is, I think, increasingly common for philosophers to attempt to find a place for self-knowledge in respect not just of thoughts and intentions and pains and so on, but in respect of action. But we should see that this was her program all along. Indeed, in the end we may say that her definition of intentional action is in terms of a form of self-knowledge, or self-consciousness: what's up with me is an intentional action precisely where it is a content of specifically practical knowledge, otherwise not. This is the real definition. It is a nominal definition of intentional action that is propounded earlier on in the complicated account in terms of what is known, and non-observationally known, and so forth: a mere fixing of the extension of the term, to put it crudely; something that is to hold the topic in place as we seek to divine this real definition.

A principal difficulty in comprehending Anscombe's teaching on this point arises, I think, from a distorted emphasis in the choice of examples in the literature and also on unnoticed presuppositions of the use of nominal-izations like "action" and "event," which of course Anscombe herself uses freely. Terms like these make the construction of grand philosophical gen-eralizations easy and smooth. But they bring along a danger that we will lose contact with the more fundamental judgments in respect of which we are generalizing, the ones that would exemplify our claims. Thus we will fail to follow the fundamental principle of Fregeanism, of which Anscom-bism is a subordinate sect, in always keeping before our minds a complete thought.

But let us consider some of the complete thoughts that might be at issue. One striking difference between the approaches Anscombe and Davidson respectively take to this material shows up in an apparently subtle feature of their illustrations.

The typical Davidsonian example is in the past tense, the typical Anscom-bian example is in the present. There are exceptions to this rule, in either au-thor, but consider a few familiars from Davidson's great essays on action:

I flipped the switch because I wanted to turn on the light.
Cass walked to the store.
Smith coughed.
Alice broke the mirror.
Brutus kissed Caesar.
I flew my spaceship to the morning star.
Amundson flew to the North Pole.

And everyone's favorite:

> Strange goings on! Jones did it slowly, deliberately, in the bathroom, with
> a knife, at midnight. What he did was butter a piece of toast.

Flipped, Walked, Broke, Kissed, Flew, Buttered, *did*. It is not just that these
propositions all concern the past. They all exhibit what linguists call perfective
aspect. What is represented is represented as a completed whole that falls under a certain heading, whether as switch-flipping, kissing, or buttering toast.
The metaphor of completion and wholeness is what is intended by the word
perfect or perfective.

If, for each verb phrase, we introduce a common noun by nominalization,
and speak of switch-flippings, kissings, and so on, then the *complete thoughts*
Davidson puts before us, the "he did it" propositions, will all entail the existence of something falling under such a noun. That is, they will all entail the
existence of an event of a certain type. And this is indeed Davidson's theory
of what makes the propositions true.

But the class of *complete thoughts* to consider contains some quite different
forms. This is something that E. J. Lemmon pointed out in his comment on
the original essay on Action Sentences, and which Davidson pooh-poohed as
false hairsplitting in his response.

If I may be permitted to superimpose phases of human history, consider
that it might have been like this: at the fateful moment when Brutus kissed
Caesar, or when the kissing occurred, Cass was walking to the store, moseying
along with thoughts of the tobacco he was proposing to purchase. But then
the sight of this same-sex Roman kissing so alarmed his tender modern sensi-
bilities that his heart failed for good there and then.

Or, to superimpose again, it might be that at the moment when I flipped
the switch and there was a switch-flipping, Jones was buttering the toast. The
wiring I triggered was faulty, and so I thereby electrocuted the poor devil, who
was leaning against a copper water pipe. Toast and butter were only a half-
centimeter apart when the knife and toast fell to the ground, and with them
Jones, quite dead.

Let the stories be placed in time definitely past. In that case, we will have to
say that Cass did not walk to the store in fact; Jones precisely did not butter
the toast. Moreover, there was in neither case an event of toast-buttering or
to-the-store-walking. Event is *eventus;* it is what came out, what turned out,
what happened; *X eventus est,* or *X est eventus V,* means: it happened. But a

walk to the store and a toast-buttering are not among the things that happened. The kiss and the flip happened; there were such events. It is true that in Cass's case, a walk to the scene of the kiss happened; and in Jones's case, a beginning of buttering occurred. If the question is, "What happened on that fateful day?; render unto me a syllabus of Events, or *Eventa*," we will get the answer that Brutus kissed Caesar, and that Cass walked to the scene of it, but of course not that Cass walked to the store. If the question is, "What happened on that fateful night," we will get the answer, I flipped the switch, and Jones started to butter the toast, but not Jones buttered the toast.

Nevertheless, the verb phrases "walk to the store" and "butter a piece of toast" have a certain foothold in reality in the two cases. We express this by using imperfective aspect, i.e., as English speakers, with the past progressive. There is thus something that Davidson's doctrine of events or of things that happened is missing, namely, not to put too fine a point on it, the things that didn't happen. That is, he forgets about the things that didn't happen, but were happening. For this reason, I will suggest, he is not capable of properly grasping the nature of what really did happen, that is, of events, especially where these are completed intentional actions. The whole system is formally structured to repel this content.

By contrast, Anscombe's illustrations are unrelentingly present, and for this reason always imperfective in character. Since she is speaking English she expresses the propositions or states of affair by means of the present progressive. There are of course exceptions, but we typically come upon Anscombe's agents in medias res, so to speak, or *in* flagrante delicto: here's a couple of examples from page 35:

> Why are you setting up a camera on that pavement?—Marilyn Monroe is going to pass by.
>   Why are you crossing the road?—I am going to look in that shop window . . . (or more obscurely: Eclipse in July.)

One agent is setting up a camera, the other is crossing the road—we say, speaking progressively. If philosophers perchance arrange that the H-bomb goes off just now, these propositions will not be falsified. But then it will never be true to say that the one *did* set up the camera, or the other *did* cross the road. No such events will have occurred.

I will be laboring the imperfective element in the complete thoughts that we Fregeans must keep ever before us, and also the contrast with Davidson.

But we should bring out immediately that Anscombe's standard examples are not only progressive and imperfective and in medias res, but typically first person in character, or rather, as we might say, first and second person. For example, she begins by describing the man replenishing the house water supply in the third person, "He is moving his hand up and down . . . He is earning his wages. . . . ," etc. But soon enough she *goes Anscombe on us,* and we are asking him, "Why are you moving your hand up and down?" and he is replying, "I'm pumping." Whereupon we ask him, "Why are you pumping?" and he says, "I'm pumping the water supply for the house."

Formally speaking, this interaction is in some sense the fundamental scene Anscombe is working with throughout the book. Although it is of course perfectly contingent whether someone's intentional action ever gets brought up in such an exchange, all of the crucial elements of her thought emerge in it. One human being comes upon another and perceives her doing something, or observes her at it—he is setting up a camera, she is crossing a road, he is moving a pump handle. The enquirer knows by perception, by an intuition or *Anschauung* of the other as other, by observation of her, that the agent is setting up a camera or is crossing a road.

Notice again that this is exactly what is given to the senses of the suitably cultivated observer, even though, of course, a prudent philosopher will arrange that the hydrogen bomb is just now going off; that does not make the perception anything but veridical. In the first instance this empirical knowledge is demonstrative and third person in character. But the difference between the observer's observational thought in the case at hand, and his thought in other cases of observed things happening, like trees falling down, comes next. The observer moves into what we might call a cognitive relation with the agent herself and asks her why she's doing it. He does not do this with falling trees. The mark of the cognitive relation is the use of the second person, "Why are *you* doing A?" That he addresses himself to the observed individual substance is already a clue that something is different.

We should notice that the answer the agent gives will itself frequently supply a first-person–present-progressive formula. The agent might say, "Well, I'm doing B." That is, he might come out with the formula of the type that was contained in the question, but something that is by chance not so readily observed, at least not by the enquirer; it is as it happens not given in her intuition of the agent. Of course not all answers are in the first person of the present progressive: "I'm doing B." Some are like: "He killed my brother," or "I like it, it's fun," or "It befits a Nazi," or "No particular reason." But even some that aren't could be put this way, for example some that take the form, "To do B." Of the one who is doing A, and is asked "Why?" she says (pp. 38–39—I substitute my preferred letters, for her X and Y):

> Let the answer contain a further description B, then sometimes it is correct to say not merely: the man is doing A but also: 'the man is doing B'—if that is, nothing falsifying the statement 'He is doing B' is observed. E.g., Why are you pumping?—'To replenish the water supply'. If this was the answer then we can say: He *is* replenishing the water supply; unless indeed he is not. [Much later it emerges that maybe the pipe is broken and the water is running out.] This will appear a tautologous pronouncement, but there *is* more to it. If after his saying 'To replenish the water supply' we can say 'He is replenishing the water supply,' then this would, in ordinary circumstances, be enough to characterize *that* as an intentional action. . . . Now that is to say, as we have already determined, that the same question 'Why?' will have application to this action in its turn.

Of course, in that case, if we ask him *why he's pumping* he might have just said, "I'm replenishing." And again this use of the progressive would be marked as the sort to which one can annex the question "Why?"

What I observe, on the one hand, and what I am told on the other, are each marked out in the same way, as inviting the question "Why?" in her special employment of it.

This nexus of descriptions, of doing A with doing B and so forth, or rather the nexus that is here given as founding it, the one that might, if you like, be expressed with the infinitival formula

He's doing A in order to do B,

or

He's doing A to do B,

but in many others as well—this is something that Anscombe has just argued is essential to the constitution of her material. This is in the all-important sections 19 and 20. Section 20 begins with the question

> Would intentional actions still have the characteristic 'intentional', if there were no such thing as expression of intention for the future, or as further intention in acting?

The answer is supposed to be "No."

Of course, not everything I do intentionally is done *in order to* do something else; sometimes, as we saw, it's for no particular reason, or because I like it, or because he killed my brother, and so on. Nevertheless, apart from the possibility of this sort of connection—of doing A with doing B, and of doing B with doing C and so on—there could be no intentional doing of anything, no Will and no articulate discourse that latches onto it, as the elements in the fundamental scene do. Consider those rational trees I read about in an essay by Colin McGinn a million years ago, rational, sighted trees who observe sheep moving across their visual fields, and, as it happens, round the hill. They can't go around to the other side, they can't even move their eyes, they peer firmly ahead. Isn't it obvious that they could come to know that the sheep go around to the other side of the hill? (He was giving a counter-example to Michael Dummett's philosophy, securing his position at the head of a then very happening lynch mob.) Anyway, let's expand on the example, and suppose that once in a while, the rational trees just spit, and just for the hell of it. That's all they do and all they can do.

That's impossible, she argues: "Some chains must begin." Piecing these remarks together with the one about the man who keeps answering to do B and then to do C and so on, we can see that Anscombe's proposition, "Some chains must begin," entails the proposition, "Some practical progressives must stack."—or in her jargon, "An A–D order must be possible." This thought is most easily understood if we take her to be characterizing the Will as a capacity or faculty or power, rather than hunting for something to characterize each case of intentional action. The Will is the power to be subject of intentional actions, or, if you like, apt for process ascriptions that can be queried with her question "Why?" Not every exercise of the Will is an intentional action; for example, an intention to do something and a certain sort of wanting to do it are exercises of the same power, and might not accompany any action. Similarly, not every exercise that does take the shape of an intentional action, an action of doing A, say, need be accompanied with other simultaneous exercises that take the shapes of doing B, doing C and doing D, where these are fitted together in what she calls the A–D order. But if this is not possible, there is no Will, no action, no agency.

I propose to piece this point together with the doctrine of practical knowledge.

Now, when Anscombe speaks of practical knowledge, of knowledge without observation of my intentional action, there is a danger of misunderstanding. I said that the word "event" taken as applying to individuals, properly applies to what happened, and not what was merely happening; so the word "action" or "deed," as applied to individual tokens, properly applies to what was actually done, not to what the agent was merely doing; the etymology is similar: *ago, agere, egi, actum*. Our new-modeled Cass did not perform any such ACTION as walking to the store; our new-modeled Jones did not perform any ACTION of toast-buttering. *Nihil actum est*. Nevertheless, each had the knowledge Anscombe is talking about. The late Cass knew that he was *walking to the store;* the late Jones knew that he was *buttering toast.*

The content of Anscombe's practical knowledge is progressive, imperfective, in medias res. Its character as knowledge is not affected when the hydrogen bomb goes off and most of what the agent is doing never gets done. In this respect it is to be compared with the more familiar forms of self-knowledge. I do not have self-knowledge in respect of another person's pain or belief; and I do not have self-knowledge of my own pains and beliefs of another day or week. An affirmation of self-knowledge in the sense in question will be, as is said in a famous passage of Wittgenstein, *the first person of the present tense.* It is here that we find the so-called expression of the psychical.

So it is with specifically practical knowledge, Anscombe's practical self-knowledge. Only here, as with all event-description or process-description, the present tense entails not-yet-completeness and imperfective aspect, and thus (in English) a present-progressive formulation. My thoughts and pains are matters for self-consciousness, only as long as I have them, as long as they are present. It is the same with practical knowledge, and thus since the present in this case must be imperfective, there is practical knowledge only when the thing is precisely NOT done, not PAST; there is more to come, something is missing, and the H-bomb may hit before it does. My so-called knowledge of my intentional action in truth exists only and precisely when there is no action, but only something I am doing.

Now, this might be enough to bring out the defect in a celebrated argument of Davidson's, which unfortunately killed off the sublime topic of practical knowledge for a few decades, until Velleman, in his way, revived it. Davidson considers someone making several carbon copies of a document as he signs it. He needs ten, one for the bank, two for his lawyers, two for the other guy's lawyers, one for the county, and so on. He starts to write his name on the top. He doesn't know, as he writes that first bit, whether he is making an impression on the last copy. But suppose he is and keeps it up through all the letters of his name. In the end he has signed all ten documents, and did it intentionally. But he didn't know it.

Now there are some real estate closings that are like that. But the more ordinary case is like this: you write on the top sheet, trying to make a good impression to get through all the carbon, then look to see if your impression made it through to all of them. If it did, you stop. If it didn't, you remove the last properly impressed sheet and begin again. If necessary, you repeat. Even the man who has to go through five stages is all along, from the first feeble impression, making ten copies of the document, and he knows it, all along.

The one who doesn't know it, Davidson's man, must be under some strange mafia threat: he gets one chance, no checking, and he's dead if he doesn't manage it. Well, for him, the making of the inscription is like the buying of a lottery ticket. You can say he made ten copies intentionally if you like, but it will not be an illustration of the topic of Anscombe's book, any more than lottery-winning is when you bought the ticket with that aim.

The failure to perceive this comes from failing to meditate on the progressive, on the fact that the content of practical knowledge is something present, and thus something of which more is to come, perhaps including several attempts at it or some part of it.

8

Two Forms of Practical Knowledge and Their Unity

SEBASTIAN RÖDL

Introduction

At a crucial point in *Intention*, G. E. M. Anscombe suggests that the nature of intentional action is shrouded in darkness for modern philosophy because modern philosophy no longer comprehends what ancient and medieval philosophers knew as practical knowledge. Following St. Thomas Aquinas, Anscombe explains, "Practical knowledge is 'the cause of what it understands', unlike 'speculative' knowledge, which 'is derived from the objects known'" (87).[1] She could have followed Kant, who represents the will as a power of practical knowledge, distinguishing practical knowledge from speculative knowledge in the same way as Anscombe does: Kant defines the power of desire as the power of a living being to be, through its representations, the cause of the existence of the objects of these representations, and argues that the will, the power of practical knowledge, is a power of desire in this sense.

For Kant and Anscombe alike, practical knowledge is distinguished, on the one hand, from speculative knowledge as a form of desire—and thus as

---

1. Bare numbers refer to the pages of G. E. M. Anscombe, *Intention,* 2nd ed. (Cambridge, Mass.: Harvard University Press, 2000).

efficacious, or practical. It is distinguished, on the other hand, from other forms of desire as knowledge. Anscombe emphasizes the practical character of practical knowledge, its causality in respect of its object. This does not mean she disregards the character it bears as knowledge. She says not only that practical knowledge is the cause of what it represents; she says it is the cause of what it understands. A representation is a desire if it represents its object in such a way as to cause it; a desire is knowledge if it causes its object in such a way as to understand it. This is why Anscombe says, "The notion of 'practical knowledge' can only be understood if we first understand practical reasoning" (57). For, practical knowledge causes its object through reasoning, and this is how, here, causing the object is understanding it. This thought, too, Anscombe shares with Kant. Kant argues that the will is nothing other than practical reason because it is the power to act according to principles, and acting according to principles is deriving actions from principles.[2] While deriving in general is reasoning, deriving an action is reasoning practically. Kant says the will is a power to act through practical reasoning.

Anscombe seems to be recovering Kant for modern philosophy. This may surprise, because Anscombe is known to reject Kant's moral philosophy. And it is natural to suspect that, even though *Intention* remains outside the field of ethics, her opposition to Kant is not unrelated to the thoughts put forth in this essay. Indeed, her account of practical knowledge may seem to stand opposed to Kant's: practical knowledge, in *Intention,* is knowledge of what one is doing, which is a form of knowledge of what is happening and thus knowledge of something actual. By contrast, Kant holds that practical knowledge is of the pure form of practical reason and on that account not knowledge of anything actual. It is knowledge of what is good to do and as such knowledge of what one can and must do, but not knowledge of what one does or is doing. However, I shall argue that the semblance of opposition is an illusion, which arises from the fact that Kant and Anscombe attend to distinct aspects of the will.

Anscombe attends to the character of the will according to which it is knowledge of something actual, while Kant's interest is in the character according to which it is moral knowledge. However, these are not only not in tension, but essentially united in the will. Hence there is nothing that prevents Kant from embracing what Anscombe says about the form of practical

2. Immanuel Kant, *Grundlegung zur Metaphysik der Sitten,* 412.

knowledge that is her main topic. On the contrary, we shall see that the very consideration that shows how the will is a power of knowing what one is doing entails that moral knowledge has no material content, but is knowledge of the pure form of practical reason. Developing the account of practical knowledge of *Intention* is one way to bring out the soundness of Kant's moral philosophy.

As the essay traverses a considerable distance, it will be helpful to have a description of the whole, which may orient the reader, providing her with a schema that acquires content as she progresses. The will—this is our point of departure—is a power of knowledge in virtue of being the cause of its object through reasoning. I shall argue that the form of practical reasoning is this: it derives from an act of the will (first premise), by way of an act of the intellect (second premise), an act of the will (conclusion). Now, as a premise of reasoning of this form an act of the will is knowledge in two ways, the difference between them reflecting the difference of the first from the second premise: an act of the will is knowledge insofar as it itself, the first premise of practical reasoning, is valid; and it is knowledge insofar as it governs a valid second premise. It is moral knowledge as it is a valid first premise. It is knowledge of something actual as it is joined together with a valid second premise. These are ways in which an act of the will is knowledge as an act of the will. Hence we can with justice speak of practical knowledge with regard to both. This common name signifies a real unity. A given act of the will may be knowledge in the one way, but not in the other: it may be moral knowledge without being knowledge of something actual, and vice versa. However, the two forms of practical knowledge spring from the same power. Their unity is the unity of practical reasoning, the unity of its two premises, which unity is the nature of the will.

In the first section I lay out the form of practical reasoning. In the second section I explain why willing to do something, in virtue of being a first premise of reasoning of that form, is knowing that one is doing it; in the third section why it is knowing that it is good to do.[3] In the fourth section I say why Anscombe's thought that the will is a source of knowledge of what is

---

3. As the topic of this essay is the will—a power—I speak (must speak), here as elsewhere, only of acts of willing that are perfect as willing, that is, of acts that reveal the nature of the power. It is irrelevant that I may want to do something I ought not to do, or may fail to be doing what I want to do.

happening cannot only be conjoined with, but confirms Kant's thought that moral knowledge is knowledge of nothing but the form of the will.

1. The Form of Practical Reasoning

1.1 Action

Following Aristotle, I distinguish two forms of action: poiesis and praxis. These are a special form of movement (kinesis) and activity (energeia), respectively, namely, movement and activity whose temporal unity is constituted by reasoning. The respective forms of practical reasoning differ, but share an abstract structure. I first define movement and activity by their temporal unity, then action by a special form of that unity; finally I link the form of temporal unity that defines action to practical reasoning and thereby to practical knowledge.

1.1.1 MOVEMENT AND ACTIVITY. Aristotle defines kinesis, or as I shall translate, movement, by a form of predication: a movement concept is predicated under the contrast of perfective and progressive aspect. "S was doing A" does not entail "S has done A"; S may have been doing A without ever completing the act.[4] Hence, a concept of interruption applies: if S was doing A, but never did, the movement was interrupted. This shows that a movement is not a heap, but a unity of phases. A movement concept is a rule of temporal synthesis, which joins phases that accumulate as S is doing A and until it has done it.

The unity of a movement may be the cause of what it unites. Then a phase is explained by being located within the relevant unity, for example, "The stork is flying to its nest because it is feeding its young". If we call a unity that is the cause of its elements an end, we can say that the movement bears a teleological structure: what is explained is a means, what explains it an end. When a movement concept is of an end, I call the rule of temporal synthesis a principle of temporal unity. For a principle is a cause and provides an explanation.

Energeia, too—or as I shall translate, activity—Aristotle defines by a form of predication. An activity concept is predicated in such a way that the

---

4. All references to Aristotle in this section are to *Metaphysics,* book 9, chapter 6, 1048b23–34.

progressive judgment entails the perfective judgment: being doing it, I have done it. This may appear not to distinguish activity from state. Activity predication and state predication share in common that they do not oppose perfective and progressive aspect. But while a state is below the contrast of aspect, an activity is above it. A state concept is predicated only under a contrast of tense: so it was then, so it is now. Thus a state concept is no rule of temporal synthesis; a state is a heap, not a unity of phases. The concept of interruption does not apply. Of activity, Aristotle does not say there is no aspect. He says the progressive entails the perfective. The opposition of aspect is, we might say, sublated in a higher unity: the character expressed by aspect, temporal unity, is there, but freed from a limitation. An activity concept designates a principle of temporal unity, but one whose power to unify does not exhaust itself. The concept of interruption applies; indeed, it never ceases to apply. An activity is such as to go on indefinitely.

Of movement, we said its temporal unity may be the cause of what it unites. Of activity, we must say that it is. If it were not, an activity would not be such as to go on forever. So here, too, a phase is explained by being located within the relevant unity. Therefore, here, too, the unity is an end. However, the end, here, is not the limit of the means to it. The end is not outside the means, but inside. An activity exhibits internal purposiveness. According to Aristotle and Kant, the primitive form of internal purposiveness, or activity, is life and its unity a life form.[5]

I.I.2 MOVEMENT AND ACTIVITY CONSTITUTED BY A CONSCIOUS-NESS OF THEIR PRINCIPLE. We described the temporal unity that defines movement in general, and a kind of movement whose unity is the cause

---

5. A note on a way of speaking: I distinguish movement concepts "do *A*" from the concept of movement. The latter is defined in terms of a form of predication and is a formal concept. A movement concept is a concept of something that bears this form; it is a material concept. I sometimes speak of a material movement concept. This is a *hen dia dyoin*: a movement concept, in contrast to the concept of movement, is a material concept. *Mutatis mutandis* for activity. (There may be an exception: there may be an energeia concept that is nothing other than the concept of energeia—an activity that is activity itself. We have no reason to rule out this possibility, but it will not concern us.) I shall suppose that in applying a material concept, I apply the corresponding formal concept, as well. For example, predicating a movement concept, I apprehend that of which I am conscious in this predication as bearing the form of a movement.

of what it unites and which therefore is an end. Now we can frame the idea of a movement that is an end and whose unity is constituted in a special fashion: the movement bears a teleological structure in virtue of the moving subject's representing this very structure; the phases of the movement are united under its principle in virtue of the subject's subsuming them under it. In this case, there is no difference of the principle from the subject's consciousness of the principle. For, the principle is the cause of what it unites in virtue of the subject's representing it, bringing under it what it thereby unites; the causality of the principle—the teleological order of the movement—consists in the subject's representing it in this way. Thus the subject's consciousness of the principle constitutes it as the principle of her movement.

Consider, for example, "She is crossing the street because she is getting bread". In ordinary circumstances, this describes an act in which means are ordered to an end through the subject's consciousness of this order. The subject understands the nexus of means to end: she who is crossing the street because she is getting bread recognizes that she can get bread by crossing the street (and doing further things such as opening the door to the bakery). And her grasp of the teleological nexus and its actuality in her act do not come together *per accidens*. It is not that she is crossing the street because she is getting bread, this being one reality, and realizes that crossing the street (together with doing suitable further things) is a way to get bread, this being a further reality. She would not be crossing the street because she is getting bread did she not see that crossing the street was a way to get bread. Her taking the means to her end is her subsuming the means under the end.

We defined a form of movement by its form of temporal unity: the principle of its unity is the cause of what it unites in virtue of the subject's representing the principle, bringing under it what it thereby unites. This definition is silent on whether the temporal unity of which it speaks is limited or unlimited. It abstracts from what distinguishes movement from activity. Thus we can use the same form of words to define a form of activity: the principle of its unity is the cause of what it unites in virtue of the subject's representing the principle, bringing under it what it thereby unites. A subject of such an activity represents a principle of temporal unity that does not give out. In the fundamental case, such a principle is a life form, a manner of living. The subject represents this principle; she brings under it what it unites; and the principle is the cause of what it unites in virtue of being so represented. The subject's acts exhibit a unity in accordance with the principle; she understands this; and that she understands this is the source of the actuality of this unity in her acts.

Consider, for example, "She is giving M a bottle of wine because he helped her". Unless circumstances are special, this explanation represents the subject as exhibiting gratitude and thus as acting well. And acting well is acting from an idea of acting well, which in the given case includes the notion that one gives thanks for help. The subject acts from this idea. It is not that she is giving M a bottle of wine because he helped her, this being one reality, and recognizes that it is good to do that, this being a further, distinct reality. Rather, she would not be giving him a bottle of wine because he helped her, did she not recognize that to do this was to act well. The subject's exhibiting gratitude and thus acting well is her subsuming her act under her idea of gratitude and her conception of acting well.[6]

I.I.3 SPECIFICATION OF THE CONSCIOUSNESS IN QUESTION AS REASONING. We can give a more specific description of the consciousness of temporal unity that constitutes that unity: it is an act of reasoning. For example, she who is crossing the street because she is getting bread reasons in this way: wanting to get bread, she thinks the fact that the bakery is across the street is a reason to cross the street. She reasons from her end (getting bread) to the means (crossing the street).

> I want to get bread.
> The bakery is across the street (entailing that crossing the street is a way
>   to get bread).
> ∴ Let me cross the street.

> I want to do A.
> Doing B is a means to doing A.
> ∴ Let me do B.

The unity of the movement represented in "She is doing A" is constituted by reasoning of this form: she is doing A by holding together in one con-

---

6. It might be objected that I need not possess the concept of gratitude and relate my act to it in order to exhibit gratitude in acting as I do. This is true; a general sense of acting well is enough. Yet, it is no accident that wherever there is human life there are concepts that articulate aspects of acting well, virtue concepts. Such concepts articulate an understanding contained in acting well.

sciousness her idea of doing *A* and her idea of doing *B,* being conscious of their nexus.

Or, she who is giving M a bottle of wine because he helped her thinks the fact that he helped is her a reason to give him a bottle of wine. Thinking this is a reason is thinking it shows that giving him a bottle is acting well, or, perhaps more specifically, is an act of gratitude. So she reasons:

> I want to be grateful (act well).
> He helped me (entailing that giving him a bottle is acting gratefully and
>   thus well).
> ∴ Let me give him a bottle of fine wine.

> I want to act (live) in such-and-such a way.
> Such-and-such is the case (entailing that doing *A* is acting (living) in this
>   way).
> ∴ Let me do *A*.

The unity of the activity represented by "She is acting (living) in such-and-such a way" is constituted by reasoning of this form: she is acting in such-and-such a way by holding together in one consciousness her idea of acting in such a way and her idea of doing *A,* being conscious of their nexus.

Movement and activity whose unity is constituted by reasoning spring from the will, for the will is a power to act through reasoning. Following Aristotle, I call a movement that springs from the will "poiesis", an activity "praxis". It will be helpful to have a generic concept that covers both poiesis and praxis. I use "action" for this purpose.[7]

1.2 The Elements of Practical Reasoning

In order to see how the will is a power of knowledge, we need to consider more closely the reasoning that constitutes the unity of actions.

The first premise of practical reasoning is the subject's consciousness of the principle of her action. This consciousness is not, and does not purport to be, speculative knowledge. It does not derive from the object: the subject's application of the concept of doing *A* in the first premise is not derived from the fact that she is doing *A*. On the contrary, she is doing *A*—that fact

---

7. In line with the usage described in footnote 5, I speak of poiesis concepts and praxis concepts, which are material concepts, and the concept of poiesis and the concept of praxis, which are formal concepts. Generically, I speak of action concepts and the concept of action.

obtains—as she reasons from the movement form *do A* to means to doing that. Hence, the first premise is a desire as Kant defines it: a representation through which its subject is the cause of the existence of its object.

The second premise of practical reasoning is a statement of independent fact; it purports to be (in the good case it is) speculative knowledge. Doing something serves a given end not on account of my, or anyone's, thinking that it does so. I do not bring means into existence by thinking that something is a means. Rather, my thinking that something is a means to my end is valid depending on whether it is in fact a means. If my thinking is knowledge, it is "judged as such by being in accordance with the facts" (57).

This difference of the first premise from the second premise—the first premise is a desire, the second premise a statement of fact[8]—marks the will as finite. It reflects the fact that, in realizing its object, the will depends on conditions that are not its own deed. It depends on a matter in which to realize itself. And only on that account does the will realize itself; otherwise, the will would rather be reality. However, then it would not even be a will. There is no such thing as an absolute will. The contrast of will and intellect, of practical and speculative knowledge, is the mark of the finite mind. Divine thought is not theoretical, for it does not depend on the existence of its object. Neither is it practical, for it is not the cause of the reality of its object, but is its reality. The will, insofar as it is finite, is not always already the reality of its object, but realizes its object. And the reasoning through which it realizes its object reflects this finitude. It does so by distinguishing within itself the will from the intellect, the will being the source of the first premise, the intellect that of the second premise. In its own act the will distinguishes itself from the intellect and in this way marks itself as finite.[9]

The conclusion of practical reasoning is again an act of the will. This is evident from the fact that it is such as to be a premise of a further practical

---

8. Aristotle makes this distinction when he says that the premises of action are of two kinds, the one relating to the good, the other to the possible (*De Motu Animalium*, 701a23ff.); Hegel makes it asserting that practical knowledge distinguishes the "immediate relation to the good end" from the "external means deployed against an external reality", represented in the first and second premise of the "Schluß des Handelns" respectively *(Wissenschaft der Logik)*.

9. That the will is conscious of its relation to, and unity with, the intellect, is the reason why Hegel presents it as the higher form of the idea of knowledge. It is the reason why, according to Kant, the practical use of reason is higher than its theoretical use.

inference. The conclusion of an inference whose first premise is an application of an energeia concept may apply a (more specific) energeia concept; or it may apply a movement concept. By contrast, on a first premise that applies a movement concept only a conclusion applying another movement concept can depend. A movement may be an element of an activity, but not vice versa, because the unlimited temporal unity of an activity cannot be contained within the limited temporal unity of a movement.

2. Knowledge of What One Is Doing

2.1 *The Account and an Objection*

We specified the form of reasoning that is the unity of action. Now we must see how, in virtue of being a premise of reasoning of this form, an act of the will is knowledge. It may seem that our account of the nature of action already shows that the will is a power of knowing what one is doing. If I am doing A in doing B, C, D, etc., and this is an action, then I join the idea of doing A with the idea of doing B (C, D, etc.), reasoning from the one to the other. This consciousness of the unity of doing A and doing B constitutes their nexus in my action. And as this consciousness is conscious of its practical character, that is, is conscious of itself as constituting the teleological order of my action, it is knowledge of the reality that it constitutes. For example, I am getting bread in crossing the street only if I am conscious of crossing the street in the service of getting bread, that is, only if I know that, in crossing the street, I am realizing my will to get bread. So, if I am getting bread in crossing the street, then I know that I am getting bread in crossing the street. In general, if I am doing A in doing B, C, D, etc., and this is an action, I know that I am doing A in doing B, C, D, etc.

This account attracts an objection. We said, if I am doing A by reasoning from the idea of doing A to something in doing which I am doing A, then I know that I am doing A (and know that I am doing it in doing whatever it is I derive from the idea of doing A). So, *if I am doing A (through reasoning)*, then I know that I am doing A. Now it will be objected that this does not show that the will is a source of knowledge of what one is doing, for the will does not provide for the antecedent: it does not provide for the fact that I am doing A (through reasoning). The will would provide for this if reasoning practically from a will to do A were doing A. But it is not, for I may reason practically from willing to do *A* and yet fail to be doing *A*. Reasoning is one thing, acting, another.

The objection asserts that the will is not, and cannot know itself to be, the sufficient cause of the action that it wills. The will accounts for the existence of its object only together with something other than it. Therefore, willing to do something is not on its own knowing that one is doing it, but only when conjoined with a consciousness of this other factor, for example, with the experience that, when I will to do something, I tend to do it. Anscombe calls this a mad account (52). However, to see that the objection entails a mad account is not yet to reveal the error in the objection. This is the aim of the present section.[10]

Before we inquire into the error underlying the objection, we must give a better statement of it. For, as it stands, it is easy to rebut. In general, a power of knowledge does not yield knowledge when its exercise is impeded. And it may be that the will is impeded in its proper exercise in cases in which one fails to do the thing from the willing of which one reasons practically. Then the fact that it may happen that I reason practically from my will to do *A* without doing *A* has no tendency to show that, when in fact I am doing *A* through reasoning, my reasoning does not on its own account for this.

However, the objection reasserts itself when we consider the cause of the failure. I fail to be doing what I think I am doing (reasoning from my end to suitable means) when I deploy a false second premise: I think that doing *B* is a means of doing *A* when in fact it is not. Anscombe has these examples: I think I am replenishing the water supply in operating the pump. In fact, I am not replenishing the water supply: the pipes are broken. Or, I think I am pushing button *A* in pushing this button. In fact, I am not pushing button *A*: this button is button *B* (56–57). Now the second premise, the one at fault in these cases, is a statement of fact. I fail to be doing what I want to do (and thereby think I am doing) on account of a failure not of the will but of the intellect. Hence, it is not that I am not doing what I want to do because there

---

10. In order for the will to know itself to be the sufficient cause of the action, it is not enough that it represent itself as efficacious. For this does not show that the representation is knowledge. Nor is it enough that there be some connection among its representation of efficacy and its efficacy, for this does not entail that the connection is known in one of its terms, the representation of efficacy. Rather, the efficacy of the will must be nothing other than the representation of its efficacy. Our account of the will as a power to act through reasoning satisfies this requirement.

is an impediment to the proper exercise of my will. Whether I am doing what I want to do depends on the validity of the second premise through which I act, and as it is an act of the intellect, the will does not through its proper exercise secure its validity. Therefore, knowledge that I am doing what I want to do cannot be attributed to the will.

2.2 *The Practical Form of the Second Premise*

There is something right in the objection above, and we shall come to it in section 3. In this section, we need to say why it is wrong. It is wrong because the will is not only the source of the first premise of a practical inference; it is the source of the inference. And this entails that there is a sense in which the second premise, too, has its source in the will: the will is its formal cause.

In order to see this, we must appreciate that an inference is not only a unity of premises and conclusion, but a consciousness of this unity. It is not only a unity of acts of the mind; rather, this unity is itself an act of the mind. In the case of practical reasoning, this act—the unity of premises and conclusion—is an act of the will: the unity of a practical inference is the work of its first premise. (This is why we call it the first premise.) For, an act of the will is a desire that causes its object through reasoning. And in order so to cause it, it requires a second premise by which to determine itself to an act of will that is subordinate to it as means to end. Therefore, an act of the will does not happen to encounter a suitable second premise. It attracts it according to its nature: its attracting a second premise is an aspect of its causality in respect of its object, because this causality is constituted by reasoning. Thus the will is not only the source of the first premise; it is thereby the source of the inference, of the consciousness that conjoins premises and conclusion.

This entails that the will is the formal cause of the second premise. For, the unity of an inference underlies its elements as their form. Anselm W. Müller develops this idea as follows.[11] It may happen that, without any thought of doing A, I contemplate the fact that doing B is a means of doing A. In that case, if indeed I want to do A, a further act of the mind, in addi-

---

11. In "How Theoretical Is Practical Reasoning", in *Intention and Intentionality: Essays in Honour of G. E. M. Anscombe*, ed. C. Diamond and J. Teichman (Brighton, U.K.: Harvester, 1979), 91–108, as well as in *Praktisches Folgern und Selbstgestaltung nach Aristoteles* (Freiburg: Alber, 1982 [habilitationsschrift], §§23–25.

tion to my thought that doing A is a means of doing B, is required to relate that thought to my end of doing A. In this further act, I recognize that my idle speculation of how to do A can be brought to bear on my end of doing A and be put to use in pursuing it. However, this cannot be the general case. It cannot be that, in general, a further act of the mind—a recognition that my insight that doing B is a means to doing A is helpful to reach this end and do A—is necessary. If it were, a regress would ensue, and there would be no such thing as practical reasoning. It follows that it is internal to the second premise—it is its form—that through it I am doing A. It is internal to it that it constitutes the causality of my will.

We already said this when we introduced the temporal unity of actions: we said the subject's thought that doing B is a means to doing A constitutes the teleological order that obtains as she is doing B because she is doing A. Another way to describe this character of the second premise is to say that the subject expresses the same thought saying "Doing B is a means of doing A" and explaining "I am doing B because I am doing A". There is no step from the one to the other, no act of the mind that connects them. Rather, it is the inner character of the thought—the form that it bears as a second premise of practical reasoning—that it is a thought thinking which the subject is doing A. Yet another way of expressing the point, of which we shall make use in what follows, is to say that the second premise applies the formal concepts of action. A formal concept of action is nothing other than the consciousness of the corresponding form of practical reasoning. As the will is the source of practical reasoning, the formal concepts of action have their source in the will. They are formal concepts of the will not only in the sense that they describe the reality that springs from the will according to its form, but in the sense that they are themselves acts of the will. Indeed, they are concepts of the will in the former sense because they are concepts of the will in the latter sense. Hence, if the second premise applies the formal concepts of the will, it is in this respect an act of the will.

Müller's argument applies the insight of Achilles and the Tortoise to practical reasoning: the consciousness of the unity of premises and conclusion cannot be a further premise; the unity of the inference must underlie its elements as their form. (An analogous—considered at a suitable level of abstraction, the same—insight is Frege's, that the unity of elements in a thought cannot be a further element, but must underlie the elements as their form.) If the reasoning is practical, this means that it must be internal to—define the form of—the second premise that it is the causality of the desire that is its first premise.

The will, being the source of practical reasoning, is the formal cause of the second premise of practical reasoning. This does not make that premise an act of desire: it does not turn it into a representation through which the subject is the cause of the existence of the represented object. The will, as finite, acts through knowledge of means, which is knowledge of independent facts.

2.3 Powers and General Knowledge of Means

It might appear that, even as the second premise bears a practical form, it represents a content whose primary form of representation owes nothing to the will; the practical form is imposed on this content as it is caught up in practical reasoning. However, the dependence of the second premise on the will reaches further. When we reflect on the source of a second premise of practical reasoning, we find that, in the fundamental case, it lies in general knowledge how. Such general knowledge constitutes the material concepts that figure in it and thus in acts of the will.[12] And the will, being the formal cause of the second premise, is the formal cause of such general knowledge. So, as these material concepts depend on a representation that applies the formal concepts of action (namely, the general knowledge in which they figure), it follows that their material content is inseparable from their practical form. For example, if the concept of an arm figures in general knowledge how to move one's arm, then the concept of an arm is not independent of action concepts articulating ways in which one can move one's arm. Knowledge of means depends on the will for its form; the will depends on knowledge of means for its matter; the matter is inseparable from the form. This unity of wanting the end and knowing the means, of first and second premise, constitutes the will as a power of action and thus is its nature. At least this is what I will seek to establish in this subsection. I first introduce the notion of general knowledge how and show how practical reasoning depends on it, and then explain how general knowledge constitutes the elementary powers of

12. Anscombe maintains that many descriptions "doing *A*" depend "for their own sense" on the form of explanation that defines intentional action (85). Equivalently, they depend for their sense on their use in practical reasoning. This does not seem to be an accident. It appears to be necessary and have a sufficient ground. The aim of this subsection is to articulate this ground.

movement that are the primary matter that the will informs as a power of action.

2.3.1 KNOWLEDGE HOW BY APPLICATION AND BY CALCULATION.

The second premise says by what means, or how, something can be done. If it is knowledge (as opposed to error or opinion), then it is knowledge how to do what one is doing. Now there are two forms of knowing how to do something, distinguished by the form of the value of "do something": the expression that specifies what one knows how to do either contains a reference to particulars or is completely general, for example, "split that block of wood (with that axe)" as distinct from "split blocks of wood (with an axe)", or "break out of this prison cell", as distinct from "break out of a prison cell". If the expression is general, then so is the knowledge: the values of the letters in the statement, "One can do A (i.e., break out of a prison cell) by doing B, C, D", all are general. And if the expression contains reference to particulars, then the knowledge does so, as well: the values of the letters in the statement "I can do A (i.e., break out of this prison cell) by doing B, C, D" all contain a reference to particulars. I call the former general knowledge and the latter specific knowledge.[13] Poiesis, as movement, or change, relates to particulars. So does praxis insofar as it involves movement. Therefore, actions contain specific knowledge how. General knowledge does not constitute an action.

Specific knowledge how to do something, insofar as it is an element of practical reasoning, is a practical representation in the sense that in virtue of its form it is the manner in which the subject's will realizes itself. The same holds of general knowledge insofar as it is the source of specific knowledge that figures in practical reasoning. General knowledge how, too, is an irreducibly practical representation; it, too, deploys the formal concepts of action, which spring from the will. Thus, while general knowledge how to do something does not constitute an action, it constitutes a skill, a craft, a technique, a practice, a life. Indeed, as an act of a skill is, as such, an act of applying the corresponding general knowledge, and vice versa, we can identify the skill with the knowledge.

The specific knowledge that an action contains as a second premise of reasoning that constitutes its unity is either general knowledge applied to

---

13. Anton Ford, in conversation, alerted me to the importance of this distinction. See also Doug Lavin, "Basic Action" (unpublished manuscript), 22–23.

given particulars (particular terms of a change, instruments, material) or thought out on the spot in the light of those particulars. In the latter case, the teleological nexus that the knowledge represents is in the first instance specific: it conjoins action forms that contain a reference to particulars. ("If I suspend this here, then that will be dislodged from its support when he comes in, so that, when at that moment I push that a little, this touches that, so that . . . he is dead".) In a second step, one may find something general in this, which can be applied to other cases. Or one may not. By contrast, in the former case the teleological nexus is in the first instance general; the specific nexus obtains as an instance of a general nexus. When Kant introduces the notion of a priori knowledge, he defines a broad sense according to which knowledge is a priori if it is derived from general knowledge.[14] If we adopt this use of the term, we can say that specific knowledge that applies general knowledge is a priori: I do not think out the teleological order of my act in the light of the particulars of the situation. I know it prior to encountering these particulars; I bring it to them. If we call thinking out how to do something in the light of given particulars "calculating", then specific knowledge is either by application and a priori, or by calculation and a posteriori.

Knowledge by application is prior: knowledge by calculation depends on knowledge by application, while the converse does not hold. Specific knowledge by calculation arrives at a statement of the form "I can do A by doing B, C, D". This is knowledge how to do A only if the subject knows how to do B, C, D. Her knowledge how to do B, C, D may also be by calculation, but at some point calculation must come to an end. If calculation did not come to an end—if there were no such thing as its coming to an end—then there would be no such thing as calculation. Hence, where there is calculation, there are end points of calculation: things the subject knows how to do without calculation. She knows how to do them a priori, applying general knowledge.

2.3.2 ELEMENTARY POWERS OF MOVEMENT. In the fundamental case, practical reasoning is not calculation; its second premise applies general knowledge. Then the subject need not ask "How do A?" She already—a priori—knows how to do it. Where calculation comes to an end, practical reasoning need not. For a carpenter, making a cabinet is an end point. A carpenter who, building a cabinet, is doing B because he is doing A, knows that doing B is a

14. Immanuel Kant, *Critique of Pure Reason*, B2.

means of doing A (we are speaking of specific knowledge: all letters contain a reference to particulars), and only because he knows this is he doing B because he is doing A. He did not think it out on the spot, but knows it a priori.

Some end points of calculation hold a special position in that they are not specially acquired, but constitute the subject as the moving substance that it is. We may call them elementary powers of movement. (That a power is elementary does not carry the suggestion that it does not relate the subject to things other than herself. On the contrary: a moving substance is as such in relation to something other. So, for example, an elementary power may be the power to push something.) As an act of a craft applies general knowledge how, so does the exercise of elementary powers of movement. And as a craft, elementary powers of movement are general knowledge.

Before we consider the implications of this fact, we need to confront an objection. It might be held that in acts of elementary powers, not only calculation but also practical reasoning comes to an end: their acts are not constituted by reasoning. Then elementary powers would not be knowledge, and we would have to abandon our starting point: Anscombe's and Kant's notion that the will is a power of practical knowledge in virtue of being a power to act through reasoning, for, acts of elementary powers are actions. If they are not constituted by reasoning, then either they are no object of practical knowledge, or one does not have practical knowledge in virtue of acting through reasoning.

An act of a craft such as carpentry contains reasoning that applies general knowledge. We are considering the thought that this is not true of acts of elementary powers such as the power to move one's arm. It is not obvious what the ground of this thought might be. Does not a subject of practical reasoning, in having the power to move her arm, possess general knowledge how she can move her arm? And is not this general knowledge operative whenever she does something that involves moving her arm?[15] However, we can give the objection a logical ground. We said the fact that I am doing A in doing A' (a phase of doing A) consists in my knowing that doing A' is a means of doing A. Since this entails that my doing A' is an action, the fact that I am doing A' in doing, say, A'' (which is a phase of doing A') consists in my knowing that

---

15. It has become fashionable to say, in contexts such as this one, that this falsifies the "phenomenology" of skillful action. This presupposes that the presence of knowledge in action would make itself felt in the manner of a sensation. But knowledge has no "phenomenology". Descriptions of how it feels to do something one knows well how to do are irrelevant to our inquiry.

doing A'' is a means of doing A'. And so on. This entails that doing anything is knowing an infinite number of facts. And this is absurd. Hence, practical reasoning is not in general the unity of an action; practical reasoning, and with it the knowledge how that it contains, comes to an end.

However, a subject can know an infinite number of facts if all of them are contained, and known by the subject to be contained, in something she knows. So it is in the present case. Suppose I am moving my arm from here to there (imagine a context that confers a meaning on these indexicals), applying general knowledge how to move my arm. This knowledge contains the formal concept of poiesis. Therefore, in applying it, I conceive of my movement as exhibiting the temporal unity of a poiesis: a unity consisting in consciousness that unites the phases of the movement under the whole. It follows that I always already relate any phase of my movement to my end of moving my arm to there. For any "here" between beginning and end of my movement that I may choose to consider, I always already think that moving my arm to here is a means to moving it to there. (I may be wrong: it may be that I cannot move my arm there by moving it here.) Consider the following story. In anger, I mean to kick a box I happen to pass. However, as it happens, I hit a glass wall between me and the box. I am surprised. This shows that I thought I could kick the box by moving the leg to where I now learn the wall is (and then moving it further), and now find that I cannot kick the box in this way. (There is no limit to how close the glass wall may be to the beginning of the movement of my foot. I may have begun to kick the box before I began to move my foot: I got ready for kicking, adjusting my posture.) The case is not like one in which I am surprised that the movement of a ball is broken by a glass wall I failed to see. The ball's path is broken whether I am surprised or not. By contrast, if I am not surprised that my foot meets resistance where it does, then I was not kicking the box, but, perhaps, the glass wall. And then the movement of my foot was not broken. This shows that the thought that underlies the surprise is internal to the movement of my foot and constitutes its unity.

Elementary powers of movement that are powers of action are general knowledge. This knowledge applies the formal concepts of action, which, being nothing other than the consciousness of the corresponding forms of practical reasoning, spring from the will, which is the source of practical reasoning. In this way, the will constitutes these powers as the powers that they are: as powers to act through reasoning. Hence, these powers cannot exist without the will. This does not mean that they are willed into existence; I do not have the power to move in a certain way by thinking that I do. The elementary powers of movement of a subject of will depend on the will in respect of their form.

2.4 The Unity of Wanting the End and Knowing the Means

It defines the form of the second premise of practical reasoning that it is an element of practical reasoning: the second premise represents an independent fact, but it does so in an irreducibly practical manner. The first premise, as well, essentially is an element of practical reasoning, for, it is a representation through which its subject is the cause of the object of this representation. And I am the cause of my doing A through my will to do A as I derive from my end means that are sufficient to realize it. It may be that I want to do something that I do not yet know how to do, and thus that there is not yet an act of practical reasoning through which I am doing it; the act of will is not yet integrated into practical reasoning. However, it is only true to say that I want it if I can calculate how to do it—even if, in the case at hand, I have not yet found a way. But someone who can calculate—someone such that there is such a thing as his calculating—has end points of calculation; that is, there are things he knows how to do not by calculating how to do them, but by applying general knowledge. In this case, which is the fundamental case, the action concepts that are applied in the act of the will that is the first premise are constituted by the general knowledge how that is the source of the second premise. We can say that these concepts, material action concepts, provide the primary matter of the will. It is the primary matter because, insofar as it has material content, any concept that determines the will is internally related to these elementary concepts of action, the concepts of the elementary powers of movement. For these define the space of calculation to which willing an end necessarily relates that end. Hence, while general knowledge how depends on the will for its form, the will, as a power of action, depends on general knowledge how for its matter. Both enter the scene—can only enter the scene—together.[16]

16. This illuminates the way in which a man knows himself as a subject of movement. A man's elementary powers of movement are elementary in the sense that a man acquires them in coming into his mode of living at all. In the case of a man, who, as man, is a will, possessing these powers is having knowledge how he can move. As this knowledge depends on the will

This is the necessary unity of wanting an end and knowing the means, which constitutes the will as a power of action. The error of the objection with which we began this section lies in this: that it fails to appreciate this unity and that it is founded in the will. We said: if I am doing A by reasoning practically from a will to do A, then I know that I am doing A, and know I am doing it through reasoning. The objection was that the will does not provide for the truth of the antecedent. Whether in fact I am doing A, reasoning practically from my will to do A, depends on the truth of the second premises I employ. And, as a second premise is an act of the intellect, the will does not through its proper exercise secure its validity. Therefore, the will is not a power of knowledge of what one is doing. However, we now see that there is a sense in which the will provides for the truth of the second premise: in general, a subject of will knows how to do what she wants to do. For there is a necessary and a priori unity of wanting the end and knowing the means. And this unity, being the very nature of the will, must be attributed to the will. The will as a power of action is the ground of its own unity with the practical representation of general knowledge. Therefore it is no accident if someone who wants to do A is doing A. Rather, wanting to do A, reasoning practically from it, she is doing A. And when she is doing A in this way, she knows that she is. Wanting to do A, she knows that she is doing A. Since the reason why this is so lies in the will, the will is a power of knowing what one is doing.

3. Knowledge of What Is Good to Do

The will fails when the subject is not doing what she wants to do (and thereby thinks she is doing) on account of the falsity of the second premise through which she acts, for, even though the second premise is an act of the intellect, its falsity is a failure of the will insofar as the will is a power to act through reasoning. As the will acts through knowledge of means (which in the fundamental case is a priori and constitutes the material concepts applied in the act of the will), a subject of will knows what she is doing. Knowing what one is doing is a manner of knowing what is happening; it is knowledge of some-

---

for its form, and the will on the knowledge for its matter, a child grows into the will and into such knowledge in one motion. Thus a man knows himself as a moving substance primarily through his will, or power to act; primarily, because the will provides the form of representation that enters into the constitution of his elementary powers of movement.

thing actual. This is one way in which the will is a power of knowledge. It is the one Anscombe has above all in view.

An act of the will is knowledge in this way on account of the validity of the second premise of the reasoning through which the subject acts. This suggests that there may be a second way in which an act of the will is knowledge, namely, on account of being a valid first premise of practical reasoning. As a valid first premise, it would be knowledge not of what is happening, but of what is good to do.

I shall seek to establish this conclusion along the following path. I begin by introducing the notion of a valid first premise of practical reasoning and the associated form of knowledge. Then I show that this notion has application: acts of the will are subject to a measure of validity; moreover, the measure is such that conformity to it qualifies an act as knowledge. This shows itself in the fact that acts of the will enter into a certain form of unity of consciousness, namely, inference. An act of the will, then, as a valid first premise of practical reasoning, is knowledge. The relevant knowledge, knowledge of the good, originally is moral knowledge and is understood as such in the pre-philosophical use of virtue terms. So the will is a power both of knowledge of what is happening and of knowledge of what is good to do. We end by seeing that, as anticipated above, this is no accident. A power of knowing what is good to do necessarily is a power of knowing what one is doing, and vice versa. Although a particular act of knowledge of what is good to do may fail to be knowledge of what one is doing, knowledge of what one is doing does not spring from a self-standing power that is only accidentally related to the good.

3.1 The Idea of a Valid First Premise of Practical Reasoning

It is a failure of my will when I am not doing what I want to do (and thereby think I am doing). However, and this is what was right in the objection we considered above, there is a sense in which my will is not at fault: that I am not doing what I want to do does not show that I go wrong in wanting it. I reason from an erroneous second premise; yet the first premise of my reasoning may be sound. Thus, even as my will fails as a power of knowledge of what is happening, there is a respect in which it need not have failed. The converse holds as well. That I am doing what I want to do (and thereby know I am doing) does not show that I do well to want it. The second premise of the inference through which I act is sound; yet my first premise may be foul. Thus, even as my will yields knowledge of what is happening, there is a respect in which it may have failed.

If an act of the will were knowledge on account of being a valid first premise of practical reasoning, then the will would be a power of knowledge of a different kind from the one we considered so far. The measure according to which an act of the will is valid is not the measure by which we judge the validity of a second premise of practical reasoning. That premise is valid depending on whether things are as it says, whether what it represents as a means in truth is a means. Truth is the measure of acts of the intellect, which purport to be speculative knowledge. A valid act of the will is not true, but good. It is good as that which it is a will to do is good to do. There can be good willing that is not knowledge of what is happening; there can be willing that is knowledge of what is happening and not good. The knowledge that springs from the will insofar as it is a source of a valid first premise of practical reasoning is not knowledge of what one is doing and how one lives, but knowledge of what to do and how to live.

3.2 An Act of the Will as Conscious of Its Validity

When we explained in the preceding section how willing to do something is knowing that one is doing it, we did not touch the question of how it can be knowing that it is good to do. Our account of how one knows what one is doing in virtue of reasoning practically from a will to do it left it open whether this will is valid or not. Following Anscombe, whose ideas we sought to explicate, we remained outside the field of ethics. Indeed, it might seem that our account of practical knowledge of what one is doing leaves it open whether the idea of validity applies to a first premise of practical reasoning at all, let alone whether its validity is of the kind enjoyed by knowledge. However, it only seems that way. In truth, our account of the will as a power of knowing what one is doing, although it does not explain the idea of a valid act of the will, settles it that the notion of validity applies to acts of the will; indeed, it settles it that the validity of an act of the will is such as to qualify it as knowledge, for, we said that willing to do something is knowing one is doing it in virtue of being a first premise of practical reasoning. And a premise of reasoning as such is not only subject to a measure of validity; it is subject to a special kind of validity: a valid premise of reasoning is valid in such a way as to be conscious of its validity. And this is the kind of validity signified by the generic concept of knowledge.

3.2.1 INFERENCE. It will be helpful first to consider judgment and the character in virtue of which it is such as be a term of reasoning. The first thing to note about judgment is this: in judging, one represents one's judgment as true. The representation of one's judgment as true is not a further judgment over and above the judgment represented as true. It cannot be a further judgment because the representation of the judgment as true constitutes the judgment as judgment. A judgment and its representation as true are one and the same act. We can express this by saying that the judgment represents itself as true. Now a true judgment is as it should be as judgment; a true judgment is a valid judgment. A judgment is conscious of its own validity.

This character of judgment underlies its capacity to be the conclusion of an inference. For, inferring something from given premises is not just thinking it because one holds to the premises. It is thinking it on account of one's recognition that the premises provide sufficient grounds for thinking it. This recognition is not, nor can it be, a further premise. Rather, it is the consciousness of the unity of premises and conclusion that constitutes this unity as the unity of an inference. So the conclusion of an inference contains a consciousness of itself as resting on the premises and as valid on that account. This consciousness is not part of its content, but its form as conclusion. It follows that only an act that is valid in such a way as to be conscious of its validity can be the conclusion of an inference. Moreover, the conclusion of an inference can be conscious of its validity only if rests on a premise that is so conscious. Hence, a judgment is a term of reasoning, premise, or conclusion, in virtue of its character of being conscious of itself as valid.

Inferring something from other things is not just thinking it because one thinks those other things, but thinking it in recognition of the fact that those other things provide sufficient grounds for thinking it. This describes reasoning in general. It is by recognizing this manner of dependence, this form of unity, among acts of the mind in the form of thought that constitutes the unity of actions that we are licensed to speak of practical reasoning: when I want to do B because I want to do A, and this nexus is constituted by reasoning from a will to do A to a will to do B, then not only is it the case that my wanting to do A explains my wanting to do B. It does so on account of my recognition that there is sufficient ground to do *B,* lying in the fact that doing it is a means to doing *A.* (This requires that there be sufficient grounds for doing *A*.[17]) In general, the consciousness of the validity of the conclusion of a practical inference is not part of the content of the conclusion, but its form as a conclusion. Hence, the capacity of an act of the will to be the conclusion of an inference reveals it to be the kind of act that is conscious of its own validity. Now the conclusion of an inference can be conscious of its validity only if rests on a premise that is conscious of its validity. Indeed, it is in the first instance the premise that exhibits this character and on that account the conclusion. Hence, an act of the will, in virtue of being a premise of practical reasoning, is conscious of itself as valid.

3.2.2 KNOWLEDGE. An act of the will is a term of reasoning. Hence it is an act that is conscious of itself as valid. We now inquire what this shows about the will. To this end, it will again be helpful first to consider judgment.

A judgment is conscious of its own validity. This shows that the measure of validity to which it refers itself in this consciousness is inherent in the nature of judgment: a judgment is subject to this measure not in virtue of any circumstance in which it may find itself, but simply as judgment. Now when we think of an act simply as a judgment, we refer it to the power as an act of which it is a judgment: the power of judgment. Hence, the measure of validity of judgment is nothing other than the power of judgment. A judgment, being conscious of its validity, refers itself to the power from which it springs (as, e.g., St. Thomas Aquinas observes).[18]

It follows that any judgment contains a representation of the power of judgment. This representation of the power is the same in any act of that power. Therefore, it is a consciousness of the unity of the acts of this power (the unity they possess in virtue of being acts of the same power) that is a priori contained in all of them. This entails, further, that this consciousness of the unity of all judgments, which is contained in any one judgment, is nothing other than the unity of which it is the consciousness. It is not the case that there is a unity among acts of the mind by which they all are judgments, of

17. It might be thought that we must require further that doing *B* is compatible with any end that limits the pursuit of doing *A.* However, this is unnecessary because the limitation will define, and thus be contained in, the end of doing *A.*

18. *De Veritate,* Quaestio 1, Articulus nonus.

which the subject in addition happens to be conscious. Rather, acts of the mind are united under the power of judgment in virtue of the consciousness of this unity, namely, of the power of judgment, that is contained in them. A consciousness of a unity that is nothing other than that consciousness is self-consciousness. So the power of judgment is a self-conscious power.

A judgment's consciousness of its validity constitutes it as a judgment. Hence, the representation of the power of judgment contained in any judgment constitutes this power as the power that it is: the power of judgment. It follows that the power of judgment is nothing other than that representation of it. And as this representation of the power of judgment must itself be assigned to that power, the power of judgment is self-constituting in the sense that it is its own act: it is its act of representing itself. (In this act, the contrast of power and act collapses: the power is nothing other than this act.) The power of judgment is self-constituting because it is self-conscious: any power a representation of which is contained in any of its acts is self-constituting in the sense that it is identical with this representation of it, which representation is its own act.

Therefore, the power of judgment is spontaneous in the sense that it is not determined to act by something other; rather, it and it alone is the sufficient ground of its acts. This is evident with regard to its original act of representing itself, by which it constitutes itself as the power of judgment. But it also cannot be determined by something other to any specific act. If it were, then a judgment would be valid, not absolutely, i.e., simply as an act of the power of judgment, but in relation to that which determines the power to that judgment. Consequently, the consciousness of its validity would have to refer the judgment not only to the power, but in addition to that which determines the power to this particular act. As that thing is, *ex hypothesi*, something other than the judgment, the consciousness of the validity of the judgment could not be that very judgment. However, the identity of a judgment and the consciousness of its validity defines judgment. Hence, the power of judgment is self-determining.

We said a judgment is conscious of its validity. We could have said it is conscious of itself as necessary and general. This is how Kant describes judgment.[19] Its necessity lies in this that the power of judgment is not determined to act by something other. Insofar as nothing impedes its proper exercise, the

---

19. Kant, *Critique of Pure Reason*, B 139–142.

power of judgment, and it alone, is the sufficient ground of any judgment. This constitutes the judgment as unconditionally necessary. And as any judgment refers itself to the power of judgment as to its ground, it is conscious of this necessity. The generality of judgment lies in this that she who judges is, really, the power of judgment: the "I" contained in any judgment—the consciousness of unity that is the unity of which it is conscious and therefore is self-consciousness—is the power of judgment. Nothing that is particular to a material subject of judgment and distinguishes her from other such subjects can determine her to judge as she does. The ultimate ground of any judgment is the same in every material subject; it is the power of judgment. In this sense, it is the power who judges. If you and I share the power of judgment, then, insofar as its exercise is not impeded, there can be no disagreement among us. And as this understanding of the power is contained in any judgment, a judgment as such is conscious of its generality.

We argued that a judgment, because it is conscious of its validity, originates in a self-conscious, self-constituting, self-determining power. As the argument nowhere depended on any other character of judgment, in particular not on any character that distinguishes it from an act of the will, it holds generally of any act that is conscious of itself as valid, and in particular of acts of the will. The will, as its acts are such as to be terms of reasoning, is a self-conscious, self-constituting, self-determining power. As an act of will is a desire, the will is a self-conscious, self-constituted, self-determining power of desire.

If we abstract from the difference of judgment and will, and consider what they have in common insofar as they can be terms of reasoning, we can say: they are valid in such a way as to be conscious of their validity. If we call an act that enjoys this form of validity knowledge, then there is theoretical and practical knowledge. An act is knowledge insofar as it is conscious of its validity; it is practical or theoretical depending on how it relates to its object: as the cause of its existence or as depending on its existence.

3.3 *Moral Knowledge*

A valid act of the will is not true, but good; it represents its own validity in representing something as good to do or a certain manner of acting as acting well. An act of the will as an act that is conscious of its own validity is knowledge of the good.

An act of the will insofar as it is a conclusion of practical reasoning depends for its validity on the validity of both the first premise and the second premise: supposing that I am reasoning from a will to do A, it is not good to do *B* if doing it does not further the end of doing *A;* and if it is not good to do *A,* then the fact that doing *B* is a means to doing *A* does nothing to show that it is good to do *B.* However, we can isolate in a valid conclusion the aspect of its validity that it owes to the validity of its first premise. This is the validity that an act of the will exhibits (not insofar as it is also a conclusion, but only) insofar as it is a first premise of reasoning, and it depends solely on the ultimate first premise in the series of inferences whose final conclusion it is and is independent of the validity of any mediating second premise anywhere in this series. Hence, the validity in question is in the first instance the validity of an ultimate first premise of practical reasoning.

It is natural that philosophical reflection should introduce a word for that kind of validity. It is called moral validity. Pre-philosophical practical thought recognizes terms that represent this sort of validity: terms designating a manner of acting that is such that whether someone is acting in this manner does not depend on the validity of second premises he deploys in so acting.[20] These are virtue terms. (This defines a concept of virtue.) For example, someone who, out of kindness, seeks to repair the tire of the bicycle of his neighbor acts kindly regardless of whether he manages to repair the tire; indeed, he acts kindly even if, inadvertently, he enlarges the hole in the tire by his efforts.

A valid act of the will is knowledge of the good. It is original knowledge of the good if it is an ultimate first premise of practical reasoning; it is derived knowledge of the good if it is also a conclusion. Original knowledge of the good is—according to the above-introduced philosophical usage of this term—moral knowledge. Derived knowledge of the good depends on and thus contains knowledge of means, and insofar as it does so, it is more than moral knowledge. However, its standing as knowledge of the good depends solely on the ultimate first premise on which it rests and thus on the moral knowledge it contains.

The will as a power to act through reasoning is a power of two forms of knowledge: it is a power to know what one is doing and a power to know

20. We are supposing that the error in the second premise is not traceable to moral imperfection.

what is good to do or how to act is to act well. Perfection in the will comprises the attainment of knowledge of both forms. However, although knowledge of the goodness and knowledge of the actuality of the deed are both perfections of the will, they do not relate to the will in the same way. An act of the will is knowledge of the good insofar as it itself is valid. It is knowledge of something actual insofar as it attaches to itself a valid act of the intellect, namely, knowledge of means, through which it realizes its object. Hence, although it belongs to the will both to pursue valid ends and to act through valid judgments of means, the former is a perfection that it has in itself, while the latter is a perfection in its relation to circumstances of its realization that are not its own deed and in this sense other than it. (This takes nothing away from our thought in section 2, that it is the nature of the will as a power of action to be related to what is other than it.) "Good" in general signifies perfection. Here it is proper to reserve it for the perfection that the will possesses in itself. The good will is the will so constituted as to give rise to knowledge of what is good to do; the perfect will is the will that, on the one hand, is good, and that, on the other hand, realizes itself through knowledge of what is other than it.

A conclusion of practical reasoning is knowledge of what is good to do insofar as it depends on a valid ultimate first premise. Hence, a will is revealed as good by the ground of its determination in respect of its ultimate first premises. As transpires from our general reflections on the kind of validity that is conscious of itself, the will is a source of knowledge if its ground of determination is nothing but itself, the self-conscious, spontaneous, self-determining power of desire.

An act of a power of knowledge is necessary because its source is nothing but the relevant power. Insofar as an act of the will is knowledge of the good, it is necessary in this way. In the primary instance knowledge of the good is an ultimate first premise of reasoning, and an ultimate first premise is necessary. An act of the will that is not an ultimate first premise is knowledge of the good and hence necessary insofar as it rests on knowledge of the good and, that is, on a necessary first premise. However, in such an act, a second premise has related the will to circumstances that are not its own deed. Insofar as the determination of the will depends on these circumstances, it need not be necessary; if it is, that is accidental to it and has nothing to do with its standing as knowledge of the good. Ends are necessary; means rarely are. Almost never is there only one way.

3.4 The Unity of the Two Forms of Practical Knowledge

The will yields two forms of practical knowledge: knowledge of what one is doing and knowledge of what is good to do. A given act of the will may be knowledge of what is happening without being knowledge of the good. This follows from the difference of the first premise from the second premise of practical reasoning, which marks the will as finite and, that is, as will. However, this does not mean that there can be a power that is a power of the one form of knowledge, but not of the other. Rather, in fact, a power of knowing what one is doing as such is a power of knowing of what is good to do, and vice versa.

It is obvious that there can be no power that yields knowledge of what is good to do (or how to act is to act well) without yielding knowledge of what one is doing (or how one acts). For knowledge of the good is a first premise of practical reasoning. Hence the power of knowing what is good to do is a power to act through reasoning and therefore, according to the argument of section 2, a power to know what one is doing.

It might seem that there may be a power that yields knowledge of what one is doing, but not knowledge of what is good to do: it might seem that the first premise of practical reasoning may be provided not by a spontaneous power of desire, but by a receptive power, a power determined to act by affection. Then the subject may reason from this first premise, using a sound second premise, and thereby have knowledge of what she is doing, without so much as possessing the idea of something good to do. However, this is incoherent. For, what the subject does is reasoning only if it exhibits the unity of reasoning: the conclusion is conscious of itself as valid on account of resting on the premises. And this is possible only if the first premise, too, is conscious of itself as valid, which means that it springs from a spontaneous—a self-conscious, self-constituting, self-determining—power.

4. The Content of Knowledge of the Good

The will is a power of knowing what one is doing on account of the necessary and a priori unity of wanting an end and knowing the means. This unity notwithstanding, knowledge of means is never, cannot be, the ground of determination of the will. My knowledge of how to do something is not the source of my wanting to do it. This holds of general knowledge no less than it does so of specific knowledge. The existence of a craft presupposes a general determination of the will to pursue the object of the craft. General knowledge how is knowledge of something actual (that is, is knowledge) only on account of a general desire to do what it is knowledge how to do. General knowledge how bears an a priori nexus to the will to do it, but it is not the source of this will to do it. The source of the unity of wanting the end and knowing the means, the unity of the first and the second premise of practical reasoning, is the will.

Hence, an account of how the will is a power of knowing what one is doing and how one lives is no account of how it can be a power of knowing what to do and how to live. It presupposes that such an account can be given. For only because the will acts through practical reasoning is it knowledge of what one is doing; and insofar as the will is a source of a first premise of practical reasoning, it is a power of knowledge of what is good to do. So, an account of the manner in which willing to do something is knowing that one is doing it presupposes as its foundation an account of the manner in which willing to do something is knowing that it is good to do.[21]

Thus we know that the will is a source of knowledge of the good. We do not know how it can be. Our reflections show that, in order to reveal that on account of which an act of the will is knowledge of what is good to do, we must abstract from everything that pertains to it in virtue of the subject's knowledge how. For, as we said, knowledge how, as such, can never be a source of knowledge of the good. Now we saw that the will depends on general knowledge how for the material content of its determination. Hence, if we abstract from everything that pertains to an act of will in virtue of the subject's knowledge how, we abstract from its material content. The material content of an ultimate first premise of the will depends on knowledge how of the subject. And the character in virtue of which it is knowledge of the good does not depend on knowledge how of the subject. Therefore, its material content can be no part of what qualifies it as knowledge of the good. It follows that what so qualifies it can be nothing other than its form, the form that it bears as an act of a power of knowledge of the good, and that is, as an act of a spontaneous power of desire. An act of the will is knowledge of the good insofar as it conforms to this form.

---

21. This remains true when, as in section 2, Anscombe's account of knowledge of what one is doing is extended to knowledge of how one lives. The difference of the first premise from the second premise is not obliterated when the first premise applies a praxis concept.

Original knowledge of the good—moral knowledge—is knowledge of that form alone and does not have any material content. Any act of the will that, through practical reasoning, rests on knowledge of the good is itself knowledge of the good. Insofar as it contains knowledge of means, it is more that moral knowledge. However, its standing as knowledge of the good depends only on the validity of the first premise on which it rests, independently of the validity of second premises, which account for its material content. Thus, any act of the will is knowledge of the good only insofar as it contains knowledge of the form of the will. This gives a sense in which knowledge of the good exhausts itself in knowledge of this form, and is not of anything actual. Kant's thesis thus transpires to be a consequence of the account we gave of the will as a power of knowledge of what one is doing. The very consideration that shows the will to be a power of knowing the actuality of the deed (namely, the insight that the material content of acts of the will depends on general knowledge how) entails that, insofar as an act of the will is knowledge of the good, it is not knowledge of anything actual.

This is no account of how the will is a power of moral knowledge. It is unclear how the mere form of the will can be its principle and the measure of its goodness. However, this is what an account of the ground of the possibility of moral knowledge must render intelligible.

9

Backward-Looking Rationality and the Unity of Practical Reason

ANSELM WINFRIED MÜLLER

1. Background to the Topic

Rationality, as a mark of our species, is manifested, *inter alia,* in the rationality of what we do, and this in turn is, at least in part, a matter of the reasons on which we act. A large part of Anscombe's splendid book *Intention* is concerned with such reasons. But it ties the *rationality of actions* to the operation of reasons that are, or could be, made explicit in *practical reasoning;*[1] and she claims that only teleological or forward-looking reasons—reasons supplied by further intentions—contribute to actions' rationality in that sense.

In what follows I hope to show that this claim is ill-founded; that the operation of backward-looking reasons—and, in particular, reasons that manifest motives[2] such as gratitude or revenge—is actually a *basic* component of

---

1. My formulation takes account of the fact that, in general, human beings act on reasons which they can articulate, in a truthful answer to the relevant question "Why?" by means of something like a practical syllogism, even though they have gone through no "process of deliberation".

2. All motives are, or can be formulated as, reasons. A motive, whether backward- or forward-looking, is always an *ultimate* reason. However, there seem to be non-motivational

our rationality;[3] and that this fact must not be ignored in any attempt to give a unitary account of practical reason.

In order to provide a little more background for the discussion, let me begin by calling to mind (in the first two subsections) the positions taken up with regard to the function of practical reason by Aristotle and Anscombe, respectively, and (in section 1.3) some questions suggested, by the latter's account, to the inquisitive student of forward- and backward-looking reasons.

1.1 Aristotle on Practical Rationality

Aristotle's conception of practical rationality is teleological. It is purpose-oriented not only in the platitudinous sense that, on this conception, practical reason is *applied for the sake of* a purpose, or *telos*, viz., ostensibly good action and a good life. Rather, Aristotle teaches also that the practicability of a (practicable) *telos* is invariably constitutive of *the content, or topic,* of any piece of practical reasoning. And it is this doctrine that I am here going to call a "teleological conception".

To Aristotle, it must have seemed not only true but utterly *obvious* that when you act on a reason, that reason, the action's *dia ti*, cannot be but a *telos*, an ostensible good to be achieved by that acting. Everything he says about action, not to speak of deliberation and prudence, presupposes that assumption. As far as I can see, however, he does not as much as *state*, let alone argue for or question, it.

This may be due to the fact that he thought of practical reasoning as somehow analogous to the kind of theoretical (or epistemic) *teleological syllogism*

---

ultimate reasons, too, such as the judge's reason for sentencing the criminal (see section 3.2(d)).

3. I am saying that we misrepresent human rationality if we neglect the occurrence or importance of backward-looking patterns of practical reasons. I am not of course implying, concerning any particular such pattern, e.g., revenge, that its deployment is part of human rationality. Revenge may be said to give you no reason (or a bad reason) for killing X. But if you do kill X from revenge, some injury you think you have suffered is *your reason* for doing so: you are necessarily *taking* that pattern plus the (ostensible) injury to give you a (good) reason for killing X. Moreover, "I killed X because X killed my father" exemplifies an *intelligible* pattern, whereas, e.g., "I killed X because grass is green", as it stands, does not. See my "Was heisst Praxis begruenden?" in *Gute Gruende. Zur Bedeutung der Vernunft fuer die Praxis,* ed. K. Rothermund (Stuttgart, 2003), 123–171, esp. 143–145.

that several explanations make use of in his biological works.[4] In any case, the teleological conception of practical reason is a plausible *pendant* of the teleological account of nature and, particularly, of life, that we find in his works.

It is not, however, in any way tied to such an account. On the contrary, it is *opinio communis* among philosophers, including those who give teleology no chance outside the sphere of practical deliberation and deliberated practice. Moreover, like phenomenalism, universal scepticism, ethical subjectivism, utilitarianism, and Humean accounts of causation, the teleological conception of practical reason is one of those ineradicable philosophical views that, once admitted into an otherwise innocent mind, are extremely difficult to get rid of—a circumstance which may suggest that the supposed mental innocence is in fact marred by some cognitive variant of original sin.

1.2 Anscombe on Practical Rationality

Even Anscombe's account of practical reason is not entirely unaffected by this lamentable infirmity. More precisely, she is in two minds about the Aristotelian identification of reasons for action with its objectives.

In some contexts she expressly endorses the teleological conception. Thus, when considering, in section 3 of her book, the suggestion that "an expression of intention is a description of something future in which the speaker is some sort of agent", she explains "reasons for acting", at least provisionally, as "reasons why it would be useful or attractive if the description came true". In section 22 she speaks of "the answer to the question 'Why?' as mentioning an *intention*", i.e., a purpose. And when, in the hope of elucidating the notion of practical knowledge, she starts an investigation of practical reasoning (§§32–46), her model is Aristotle's "practical syllogism": no backward-looking reasons are considered for the role of giving rise to a piece of practical reasoning, i.e., of providing an ultimate answer to the question "Why?"

In other places, however, she denies that reasons must be purposes, or further intentions. Thus she says in section 5 that "if you ask 'Why did you kill him?' the answer 'He killed my father' is surely a reason rather than a cause, but what it mentions is previous to the action". So, although not criticizing Aristotle

---

4. Cf. A. W. Müller, *Praktisches Folgern und Selbstgestaltung nach Aristoteles* (Freiburg, 1982), esp. 44–61 and 72–85.

for ignoring backward-looking reasons, and following him in admitting only forward-looking reasons *as components of practical reasoning,* she does seem to diverge from him by *recognizing* them. Such reasons she examines more closely in sections 13–15 under the head of "backward-looking *motive*".

1.3 Questions Concerning the Unity of Reason

Although Anscombe's book treats backward-looking reasons as a side issue, what it has to say about them raises important questions concerning the nature and, in particular, the unity of practical reason. Here are some of these questions:

What is the essence of the difference between backward- and forward-looking reasons, and what are the criteria for backward- and forward-lookingness, respectively?[5] Do forward-looking reasons in any sense *contain* backward-looking components, or vice versa? Can no reason count as both backward- and forward-looking? Are there transitions between the two kinds of reason? Is there any way of reducing one of them to the other? Does the distinction represent an exhaustive division of practical reasons? If not: how is the line to be drawn between backward-looking reasons or motives and what Anscombe calls interpretative motives or motives-in-general? Is it true that our notion of an intentional action presupposes not only that we act on reasons but also that the reasons on which we act are not in general, or not always, backward-looking ones (as Anscombe holds in section 20)? What is the precise relation between reasons and motives (cf. fn. 1)? And, of course: What account should be given of the unity of practical reason?

I am going to touch only on some of these questions. My aim will be to argue that in following Anscombe's account of rationality as it stands, we are

---

5. I submit that it is somewhat misleading to mark the difference in terms of tense. The deeper rationale of the distinction Anscombe has in mind seems to be the difference between, roughly speaking, (a) one's being *prompted* by an ostensible *fact* that is seen to call for a response, and (b) one's being *attracted* by something ostensibly *good* that is seen to require implementation. For obvious reasons, the relevant facts must, in general, be past or present, and the goods in question present or future. We nevertheless *understand* agents such as Hippasos, who, according to one version of the Pythagorean legend, killed himself because there were (tenselessly!) irrational numbers; or people who curse God because he will (!) allow them to die; and, on the other hand, the parents who pray for their daughter not to have been (!) involved in the railway accident reported on the wireless. For the purposes of the present enquiry, *forward-* and *backward-looking* will do as provisional labels.

likely to risk achieving a unitary picture of rationality and practical reason at the cost of neglecting the important role that backward-looking reasons actually play in our language and in our lives.

2. Unwarranted Neglect of Backward-Looking Reasons

As far as I can see, Anscombe is the first philosopher to introduce and make use of the concept of a backward-looking reason. (Many philosophers have of course *treated* backward-looking considerations such as *having promised* or the *"sense of duty"*, as genuine reasons for action; but we do not seem to meet with the *classification* and the discussion of its significance before Anscombe.) On the other hand, she leaves this concept somewhat unclear; her application of it is excessively restrictive, and its role in her account of practical reason unduly limited. Let me spell out these complaints.

2.1 *The Unresolved Status of Backward-Looking Reasons*

Even if we ignore the straightforward incompatibility between Anscombe's provisional account of reasons for acting and her eventual recognition of backward-looking reasons (cf. section 1.2), there is surely some tension between the admission of such reasons, on the one hand, and the refusal to consider them as potential ingredients, or rather starting points, of practical reasoning, on the other. What is clear is that in her account of practical reason forward-looking reasons enjoy pride of place, while backward-looking ones are a side issue. Her arguments in favour of this unequal treatment, however, will be seen to be rather weak.

True, Anscombe's book is about *intention;* her account locates the centre of this notion in that of a *further intention,* or "intention with which" (cf. §20); and in a discussion of *this* notion one will inevitably find oneself talking about forward-looking reasons, not about backward-looking ones. But this is no excuse for discriminating against the latter when their contribution to *rationality* is in question.

If backward-looking reasons do not enter practical reasoning, on what grounds should they be called, and treated as, *reasons* at all? Well, in section 5 we are told that revenge is a case of acting for a (backward-looking) reason *rather than from a mental cause.* A fuller account of this opposition is given when Anscombe returns to the topic in section 13. In addition to revenge, her examples here are the motives of gratitude, remorse, and pity. Where any of these are at work, there (in answer to the relevant question "Why?") "something that *has happened* (or is at present happening) is given as the ground of an action or abstention that is good or bad for the person (it may be oneself, as with remorse) at whom it is aimed". And in section 14, "the way in which good and evil are involved in" these motives is invoked in order to explain why in their case "the past event (or present situation) is a reason for acting, not just a mental cause".

Thus, backward-looking motives are classified as reasons on account not of what they share with forward-looking reasons, but of what seems to set them off from *other things past or present* that may be mentioned in answer to the question "Why?"

Anscombe's test for intentionality seems to yield a somewhat negative definition of "*reason or motive* for action": a definition in terms of all those answers to the question "Why?" which do *not* refer us to evidence or to a mere (mental) cause. According to section 16, such answers "may *(a)* simply mention past history, *(b)* give an interpretation of the action, or *(c)* mention something future". This sounds more positive; but it is an enumeration—and how can we be sure that it is complete until we are in a position to consider those answers in the light of a positive and, hopefully, unitary understanding of what a reason is?

Anscombe does not in section 16 specify any aspect shared by the three kinds of answer beyond their responding to the question "Why?" There is no *common* feature to distinguish them from answers that refer us to evidence or a cause. Nor do I find any other passage in the book that might explain *why* (a) should be grouped together with (c) as articulating *reasons*. The absence of any such explanation is particularly noteworthy in view of the fact that the remaining type of answer, viz. (b), is said to articulate an interpretative *motive* (or motive in general), but *not* a *reason* for action.

2.2 *Backward-Looking and Interpretative Motives*

This observation also raises the question on what grounds Anscombe excludes motives of this latter kind, e.g., admiration and friendship, from the class of *backward*-looking ones (§13). Her arguments in favour of this restriction are sketchy and do not seem cogent. Would she deny that "good and evil are involved in" the motive of, say, friendship, or that they are involved "in the right way"? Does anything she says give us grounds for treating motives like jealousy, or envy, as interpretative rather than, like revenge, as backward-looking? If the distinction between (a) and (b) were to turn out to be spurious, this would mean that Anscombe fails to acknowledge as reason-giving a host of motives that ought, by rights, to be treated as yielding backward-looking reasons.

Let us look at an example of hers: "Consider the statement that one motive for my signing a petition was admiration for its promoter, X. Asked 'Why did you sign it?' I might well say 'Well, for one thing, X, who is promoting it, did . . .' and describe what he did in an admiring way. I might add 'Of course, I know that is not a ground for signing it" (§13). Here, "not a ground" surely means: *not a reason*. But do I not, *in signing the petition because I admire X for φ-ing*, at least *treat* X's φ-ing as a *reason* for signing—much as the avenger treats Y's bloody deed as a reason for killing X? According to Anscombe herself, X's φ-ing may here be "one of the things that most influenced me" in my decision to sign the petition. But, surely, it does not just *cause* me to do this! No, it is *consideration* of X's φ-ing that makes me sign. So what kind of "influence" is in question here if not a reason?

2.3 Homeless Motives and Reasons

There are other reasons and motives beside "interpretative" ones that seem to be unfairly excluded from enjoying the status of backward-lookingness. When Anscombe lists gratitude, revenge, remorse, and pity under the head of backward-looking motives, there is no "and so on"; nor yet does she say that the list is meant to be exhaustive. So we do not know which further motives, if any, she would have classified as backward-looking. There are, however, in any case, non-teleological motives that do not look obviously like siblings of either the four she classifies as backward-looking or the ones she calls interpretative.

Here are some of these: obedience ("He told me to φ, so I φ-ed"); truthfulness ("I did not believe that p, so I refused to sign any declaration that implied that p"); justice ("The bicycle isn't mine, so I'll return it"); solidarity ("They do not provide free transport for black people, so I won't make use of it either", uttered by a white person); further: impatience, generosity, hatred, envy, jealousy, love.[6]

---

6. We may add to the list more dubious reasons expressed by such explanations as "Because everybody does it" or "Because we have always done it". In "Sylvie and Bruno" (in *The Works of Lewis Carroll* [London, 1965], 471; see also 474), Bruno finds the crocodile's default reason

One reason for regretting the neglect of this group of motives is the fact that some of the motivational patterns that I have just indicated are characteristic of important ethical virtues (cf. sections 3.2 (d) and 3.4).

2.4 "No Reasoning from Backward-Looking Reasons"

As I have already noted, Anscombe's investigation of practical *reasoning* takes no account of backward-looking reasons. The chains of reasons that she considers invariably lead from an action description back, in the end, to a desirability characterization (§§37–39), never to a backward-looking motive. And in section 35 we read that "not everything that I have described as coming in the range of 'reasons for acting' can have a place as a premise in a practical syllogism. E.g., 'He killed my father, so I shall kill him' is not a form of reasoning at all"—though she allows that reasoning, or "calculation", does take place where the avenger treats the revenge that he desires as a (forward-looking) reason for choosing appropriate ways and means of revenge.

On Anscombe's account, then, the motive of revenge gives you not just a bad reason but no reason *to reason from*. By analogy, the motive of gratitude, though presumably giving you a good reason to act from, does not give you a reason to reason from. But this means—if rationality in the sense of Aristotle's *phronêsis* is a matter of good or sound practical reasoning—that your *rationality* could depend on ultimate *purposes* that you pursue but not on the kind of backward-looking reasons, or motives, on which you act. And this seems to be a mistake.

3. A Defense of Backward-Looking Rationality

So much then for an exposition of my complaint that Anscombe is unfair to backward-looking reasons. I am now going to defend the view that good backward-looking reasons are at least as much part of practical rationality as forward-looking ones. I'll proceed by considering and rebutting *objections* to this view.

---

for doing things thoroughly plausible: "I *heard* it say: 'Why *shouldn't* I walk on my own forehead!' So of course it *did*". Even if you are right to deny that any of these three "considerations" give you reasons to do anything whatsoever, you have to treat them as occupying the place of a reason in explanations such as "X φ-ed because everybody φ-ed". See footnote 3.

3.1 No Rationality without Teleology?

The first of these objections says: Backward-looking reasons for ϕ-ing do not tell us what is the good of ϕ-ing; but the rationality of anyone's ϕ-ing depends on their ϕ-ing with a view to what is the good of it; so backward-looking reasons can do nothing toward establishing an action's rationality.

This objection is really no more than the prejudice that only a teleological conception of practical reason on the lines of Aristotle's account (cf. section 1.1) *can* be correct. It seems to be one of the "musts" that Wittgenstein holds are the roots of many philosophical misunderstandings. The prejudice is a deep-rooted one, and this suggests that it is the distortion of a deep truth, which might be brought to light by a thorough investigation into the nature of human reason. Even so, the objection is a prejudice. I know of no good argument in its favour. On the contrary, there seem to be good reasons for rejecting it.

First, a reason that represents a backward-looking (or, for that matter, interpretative) motive tends to make an action *intelligible* in precisely the same sense in which a *purpose* of the agent's would make it intelligible. How, then, could it be true that such a reason does "nothing towards establishing an action's rationality"? (Cf. my "argument from competition" at the end of section 3.3.)

Second, not only do backward-looking reasons make actions intelligible. They are moreover characteristic of certain ways of acting well whose *goodness* depends on specific backward-looking motives (cf. section 3.2(d)). And such goodness is surely at least a *component* of practical rationality. In these cases, then, there must be ways in which backward-looking reasons for ϕ-ing are related to whatever is the good of ϕ-ing.

Third, appeal to purpose does *not* seem to be of the essence of good reasons. To see this, consider the operation of *theoretical* reason. The rationality of a judgement that p often depends on its being based on good reasons. But such reasons are typically provided by evidence, not by any purpose you may pursue in judging that p. Why, then, should rationality not be secured by non-purposive reasons also for *doing things other than judging?* What, however, it may be objected, if the rationality of these "other things", actions for instance, is the work of practical rather than theoretical reason? Well, the idea that "practical" here entails "appealing to purpose" is just what I am disputing; so it should not be assumed.

3.2 No Teleology in Acting on Backward-Looking Reasons?

Although I know of no good reason for claiming that practical reasoning must be teleological in *content,* it may well be that it is of the essence of practical (and theoretical?) reason to be related to ends in *other* ways—apart, that is, from the obvious fact that, qua practical, it exists and operates *for the sake of practice.*

(a) Let us return to the objection, raised in the last subsection, that there is *no* room for teleology in things done from a backward-looking motive. To get clearer about the limitations of this objection, let us compare two patterns of acting on reasons.

Suppose first that your reason for φ-ing is of the forward-looking kind, say a further intention to ψ. We can then ask: "Why ψ?" in order to learn about a yet more *remote* reason you may have for φ-ing. If this reason is also a forward-looking one, i.e., a purpose for which you intend to ψ, then this purpose will enter the teleology of your φ-ing as well. (We may call this connection the transitivity of intentional teleology.)

Suppose, on the other hand, that your reason for φ-ing is not of the forward-looking but of the backward-looking kind. In this case, the question "Why φ?" receives an answer to which we can*not* in turn apply the question "Why?" This kind of answer simply does not relate to anything in the way of an action or activity or achievement that a further request for a reason of the relevant sort might latch on to. In other words: a backward-looking reason for φ-ing is always an ultimate reason; it leaves no room for an ulterior, more remote reason and, therefore, in particular, no room for a reason that might confer any teleology on φ-ing.

While this argument is (I think) valid, it *does not show that backward-looking reasons for φ-ing do not contribute to the teleology of φ-ing,* let alone that there is no teleological aspect to acting for backward-looking reasons. In fact, there are at least three ways in which backward-looking reasons may be involved in the teleology of an agent's φ-ing, or at any rate contribute to the achievement of practical *telê.*

(b) First, nothing that has been said here—or indeed in Anscombe's book *Intention*—excludes the possibility that an action has a *telos,* or purposive orientation, that simply *does not depend* on its being performed for an agent's (forward-looking) reason. This kind of teleology is actually displayed by judgements. In judging that p, you aim at truth (and, I should add, knowledge); you

could even be said to judge that p "with a view to" forming a legitimate judgement as to whether p. Yet the hope and purpose of correctly judging whether
p (or of knowing whether p) does *not give you a reason for* judging that p rather
than not-p (or vice versa). So, why shouldn't actions other than judgements
exhibit a comparable inherent teleology that is not conferred on them by the
reasons, backward- *or* forward-looking, that an agent may happen to have for
performing them?[7]

Remember also that when you do have a reason for judging that p, it is
typically evidence for p and that this resembles a backward-looking reason
for acting rather than a forward-looking one. Now, judging that p *because of
evidence for p* is not only *compatible* with the inherent teleology of that judgement: going by that evidence is actually what tends to *achieve* the judgement's *telos*. So why should there not, similarly, be backward-looking (and
possibly other non-teleological) reasons of a kind such that certain actions
achieve some inherent *telos* in virtue of being performed for those reasons?

(c) Let us now turn to a second way in which backward-looking reasons are
involved in the achievement of a practical *telos*. Although it has been shown
that such reasons are necessarily ultimate and exclude any (so to speak) *linear
reiteration* of the question "Why?" this leaves open the possibility of asking
someone who φ-es for a backward-looking reason *why* he or she *practises, or
implements, the motivational pattern* that is displayed in his or her φ-ing for that
reason. Thus, we may ask: "Why do you act gratefully?" i.e., roughly: "Why do
you respond to undeserved benefits received from X, by doing things welcome
to X?"

Or consider the case of truthfulness: "Why do you avoid telling lies?" i.e.,
roughly: "Why do you treat the fact that you do not believe that p as a reason
not to assert, or imply, that p?" Here, your answer may be "In order to be a
decent human being", or "It will earn me the joys of heaven", or "I have a
poor memory, so I avoid telling lies in order not to get confused about whom
I told what", or . . .

Any one of these answers states a forward-looking reason; not, however, a
reason for refusing, on a particular occasion, to make a particular assertion.
Your reason for *that* is simply the fact that the assertion in question would

---

7. Aristotle and the scholastics may have had this kind of teleology in mind when claiming
that *omne agens agit propter finem*. Cf. also my "Mental Teleology", *Proceedings of the Aristotelian Society* 92 (1992): 161–183.

not match your beliefs—a backward-looking reason! But the *policy of acting on that reason in the way you do,* the habitual practice of that backward-looking motivational pattern: *that* is also pursued for a reason. And if *this* reason is of the forward-looking kind, it confers on that practice a *telos* which is achieved by your acting on the backward-looking reason characteristic of truthfulness.

As I have said, your reason for treating something as a reason for φ-ing is not itself a reason you have for φ-ing. It might be called a *background reason* relative to your φ-ing. If it is a teleological one—as are the three alternative motives I mentioned when exemplifying reasons for the policy of truthfulness—we may now ask: Does it confer a *telos* also on your φ-ing?

Well, not, of course, in the sense of constituting a *further intention with which* you φ. Thus, the prospect of eternal rewards isn't your (ultimate) reason for deciding not to say that p, if in fact you so decide *because you do not believe that p.* On the other hand, we ought not to deny that, if rewards motivate you to treat this fact as a reason, they are in a way responsible for your declining to say that p—and, indeed, responsible in the way of a *final cause.* In this sense, but only in this sense, could one say that the *telos* of your policy of φ-*ing from such-and-such backward-looking motives* also provides your φ-ing itself with a *telos;* and that your immediate backward-looking motivation, in virtue of mediating the connection between your φ-ing and its forward-looking background motive, serves the purpose of achieving those rewards, which provides that background motive.

(d) There is yet a third way in which backward-looking motivation contributes to actions' teleology. I mean the obvious benefits that result from a widespread customary practice of certain ethical virtues such as honesty, justice, gratitude, generosity, or compassion. These virtues are habits of implementing characteristic backward-looking patterns of practical inference and motivation (cf. (c) and section 2.3).

We have already looked at the pattern operative in the case of truthfulness, and seen that it consists in refusing to say what one does not believe, for the reason *that one does not believe it.* We have also seen that this backward-looking rationality of truthfulness does not prevent the existence of a forward-looking background motive—a *telos* that provides the agent with a reason for the policy of treating lack of belief as a reason against assertion. What I am pointing to now is a *telos* of acting that does *not* similarly depend on the agent's own practical thought and (background) motivation. Rather, it is identical with the "natural" *function* of that kind of policy and of virtue quite generally, viz., something like the flourishing of human lives.[8]

Another instance of functional teleology attaching to acting on backward-looking reasons is found in the legal institution of punishment. This *institution* seems to exist for, and be justified by, the purpose of deterrence. But no such purpose ought to enter the judge's reason for condemning any particular criminal to whatever penalty. If the punishment is to be just, that reason must be retributional, and hence backward-looking: it must be supplied by the criminal's transgression, and nothing else.

So much about a third way in which backward-looking reasons are involved in the teleology of human action.

3.3 No "Calculation"?

As I suggested at the beginning of this essay, Anscombe may have written *Intention* under the spell of Aristotle's exclusively teleological conception of rationality. Whether or not this is the case, her professed reason for excluding backward-looking reasons from the realm of rationality seems to be that "there is no calculation", or "reasoning", in a thought such as "He killed my father, so I shall kill him" (§35). But what is to count as *calculating* in the context of considerations in whose nature it is to lead to action?

Calculation of the relevant sort is presumably going on when you intend to kill X and, reflecting that aiming at X with a gun is a means to killing X, you aim at X with a gun. Now this kind of calculation concerning means to ends may take place whatever your *more remote* reason for aiming the gun at X—even where *this* reason is a backward-looking one (§35).

Let us, however, first suppose that the more remote reason is of the *forward*-looking sort; i.e., you kill X in order to, say, inherit his money (cf. pattern I in section 3.5). By this supposition we have, as it were, expanded our account of your calculation by the addition of a premise which says that killing X is a promising means to inheriting X's money.

But could we not be said in an analogous manner to *expand* our account of your *calculation* by adding a different kind of premise, viz., a *backward*-looking one, such as "X killed my father" (cf. pattern II)? And why not say

---

8. Cf. P. R. Foot, *Natural Goodness* (Oxford, 2001), esp. 38–80.

that this premise *plays a part in your calculation* just as much as, on the previous supposition, does a premise such as "Killing X is a means to inheriting X's money"?

Of course, if "calculation" is simply another word for "means-ends reasoning", it is trivially true that from a backward-looking reason you do not calculate—not, that is, until your considerations reach the point where you wonder how to implement the kind of response that that reason is a reason for. If, however, "calculation" means something like *reaching a result by putting things together in thought,* it is less clear that the avenger does not calculate in his backward-looking considerations.

3.4 Mere Reaction?

But isn't he just *reacting?* Is backward-looking motivation more than an instance of the pattern of stimulus and response?

Well, it might indeed be said that, in the life of adult human beings, acting on backward-looking reasons largely *supersedes* reacting to stimuli (such as the dog's cocking its ears at his master's voice) in the life of brute animals. (In both cases, a situation recognized by but *external* to the agent prompts a *response.*) But, then, it might be said with equal justice that, in the life of human beings, doing something for a purpose takes the place that instinctive behaviour (such as food seeking) occupies in the life of brute animals. (Here, the behaviour is *spontaneous,* not occasioned by an external factor, in both the human and the animal case.) In other words: Action on backward-looking reasons is not "just reaction"; it can be viewed, rather, as the form that reaction typically takes in a rational animal—much as action on forward-looking reasons can be viewed as typically taking the place, in a rational animal, of spontaneous instinctive behaviour.

It is indeed typical of human beings that *their* "food-seeking" behaviour—what they do in order to have a meal—is (or can be represented as) the result of *reasoning.* My point, however, is precisely that the same must be said about what they do in response to situations that supply them with backward-looking reasons for action, for the pattern to which the response conforms is not a causal law. It is at work, rather, in the agent's *conceptions and considerations.* An act of revenge (or of gratitude, impatience, obedience, etc.) requires both (a) the general conception of a specific type of situation S *as* calling for (i.e., requiring or inviting) a characteristic type of action R, and

(b) the subsumption under S of a given actual situation. Thus, the avenger has to "put two and two together"—viz., to infer the need for some version of R from a consideration of (a) and (b). In other words: A piece of *reasoning* (possibly implicit) does precede the practical syllogism that *then* leads him from the specification of R as his purpose to something he can do here and now to promote it.

3.5 Lack of Complexity?

There is more than one legitimate way of articulating, and parsing, any piece of practical reasoning.[9] Neither Aristotle nor Anscombe follow a canonical pattern when giving examples of the practical syllogism. We can, however, characterize the essential components of the simplest form of Anscombian practical reasoning that leads you from a desirability characterization to an action, by means of pattern I:

> I. (a) You view something, D (e.g., living in comfort), as in itself desirable and achievable in your life.
> (b) You judge that something achievable, ψ (e.g., inheriting X's money), is constitutive of or conducive to D (now or at some later time).
> (c) You judge that something, ϕ, that you can do immediately (e.g., aiming a gun at X), contributes to ψ.
> (d) You ϕ.

Since your conception of D may be highly implicit, (a) and (b) will sometimes collapse into your acceptance of ψ as an end. And because of the "transitivity of intentional teleology" (section 3.2), the combination of (b) and (c) could be either replaced by your more immediate conception of ϕ itself "as constitutive of or conducive to D", or else expanded into a longer chain of teleological judgings to connect D with ϕ.

    What about the essential components of a train of thought that leads from a *backward-looking* reason to action? They might plausibly be represented by pattern II, as follows:

---

9. Cf. my "How Theoretical Is Practical Reason?" in *Intention and Intentionality: Essays in Honor of G. E. M. Anscombe,* ed. C. Diamond and J. Teichman (Brighton, 1979), 91–108, esp. 100–103.

II. (a1) You adopt an inferential pattern, P, that provides for an R type response to an S type situation (such as: proportionately to harm X in response to X's having harmed you or . . .).

(a2) You judge that your present situation, Σ (X's having killed your father), is of type S.

(b) You judge that, given Σ, P provides for response ψ (killing X) (as appropriately instantiating R now or . . .).

(c) You judge that something, ϕ, that you can do immediately (such as aiming a gun at X), contributes to ψ.

(d) You ϕ.

The two schemata agree in the teleological inference represented in lines (c) and (d). But where forward-looking reasoning requires, as a starting point, the (implicit) acceptance of D as an ultimate type of end (cf. I.(a)), backward-looking reasoning requires the acceptance of an inferential (and motivational) pattern P (cf. II.(a1)) *together with* the recognition that one's situation is of a relevant type (cf. II.(a2)). From this point of view, acting from backward-looking reasons might be said to provide practical reason with a *more* demanding, i.e., more complex, task than acting from forward-looking reasons does.

3.6 No Equal Standing?

The best argument I can think of to show that backward-looking reasons are on a par with forward-looking ones is an argument from competition: They get in each others' way. Let me explain.

One important aspect of the unity of practical reason is surely the *defeasibility,* in principle, of any practical inference. ("In principle", allowing for the possibility of reasons that are never defeated.) If a promise to ϕ gives you, *pro tanto,* reason to ϕ, and your sister's sudden predicament gives you, *pro tanto,* reason not to ϕ, you want to know how to act *omnibus perpensis.* Wisdom disposes you to choose correctly (or it sanctions both options). If practical reason is *one,* it does not place equally valid but irreconcilable claims on the agent. Politicians who declare that *raison d'état* and moral considerations are incommensurable have given up on this unity. So have philosophers who believe that different virtues may make tragically incompatible demands on you with no chance of your escaping guilt.

My point, however, does not concern exceptional or dramatic contexts. There is nothing remarkable, e.g., about the fact that the prospect of *pleasure* may give you a reason to φ, while it seems *safer* not to φ. Here at most one of two forward-looking *pro tanto* reasons can be acted on *omnibus perpensis*. The same holds of the two backward-looking reasons cited in the last paragraph: If you ought, *tout court,* to keep your promise to φ, it is not the case that, because of your sister's predicament, you ought not to φ—and vice versa. Here, considerations of justice and reliability *compete with* considerations of, say, loyalty, and in general at most one side will supply the reason on which you ought to act *omnibus perspensis.*

It should, however, be obvious that, equally, forward-looking considerations of pleasure, safety, or what not, and backward-looking considerations of gratitude, reliability, loyalty, etc., may compete for *omnibus perpensis* supremacy *with each other.* If, inferring from considerations of, say, safety, you are led to φ, while, for reasons of justice (which you play down), it would be better for you not to φ, your *reasoning* is at fault. And how could that be if practical reasoning were as such limited to teleological considerations?

3.7 No Important Role for Backward-Looking Reasons?

A friend of the teleological conception may feel compelled to admit that backward-looking reasons have to be admitted as starting points of practical reasoning, and yet doubt their *importance* for an adequate account of rationality.

There is, however, a clear sense in which backward-looking reasons, far from being of minor importance, are in fact more basic than forward-looking ones. As we have seen in section 3.2(a), a backward-looking reason for φ-ing is by its very nature an ultimate reason. This is true, in particular, of Anscombe's four (paradigmatic) backward-looking motives, but also of her "interpretative motives", and of the homeless ones mentioned in section 2.3. When a backward-looking reason is mentioned in answer to the question "Why φ?" the pursuit of *this* question has struck bedrock (though there may be *background* considerations that motivate one's sensitivity to that reason; cf. section 3.2(c)). There is nothing, on the other hand, in the nature of a *forward*-looking reason that prevents it from representing a purpose that is instrumental to some ulterior purpose.

What then about desirability characterizations? Do not they articulate forward-looking reasons that are as such ultimate? Well, they do. And the recognition of desirability characterizations does commit us to the recognition of certain forward-looking types of reason that are, in a sense, essentially ultimate. But they are ultimate, not qua forward-looking but rather qua referring us to goods that it is in the nature of human beings to desire. Nor are they ultimate in the sense that they could not, on occasion, be wanted as means to ends.

If it be said that the essential ultimacy of backward-looking reasons gives them a merely formal sort of priority over forward-looking ones, I should point out that, on the contrary, ultimacy is reflected in the role that explanation in terms of such reasons plays in our lives.

Read any novel, and you will find that backward-looking motives provide the characters with ultimate reasons for what they do at least as frequently as general ends such as survival, knowledge, pleasure, or other items form some list of "basic goods" or desirables (cf. *Intention* §37). Nor does actual everyday motivation seem to be much more teleological.

Moreover, as we have seen (section 3.2(d)), backward-looking reasons are at work in the practice of many *virtues*. Let me add that they also determine the specific character of *vices* such as revengefulness, arrogance, envy, and impatience. To the extent that morality is a matter of being motivated and not being motivated by these kinds of reason, there can be no doubt that they play a fundamental role in human life.

3.8 A Teleological Interpretation of Backward-Looking Motivation?

Let me consider one more objection to my position. It consists in the claim that there may be reasons for acting that can be viewed both as forward-looking and as backward-looking. Consider the following case:

X φ-es in fulfilment of a promise to φ. Asked why he φ-es, X may reply: "I am keeping a promise (to φ)". The reason thus given for φ-ing seems to be forward-looking in a relevant sense. Admittedly, keeping a promise is not a future state of affairs to be brought about by φ-ing, but if X φ-es *in order to* keep a promise, he is doing so for a purpose, a *telos*. Indeed, φ-ing seems to be constitutive of, and in this sense instrumental to, keeping a promise to φ in much the way that *lying on a bed* is constitutive of and instrumental to *doing Yoga* in one of Anscombe's nice examples (§22). If it can *also* be said of the promising case that the past promise, or X's having promised, is a backward-looking reason for X to φ, that only goes to show that the very same reason can be viewed both as forward-looking and as backward-looking.

So much for the objection. To answer it we must distinguish between two ways of acting in accordance with, or fulfilling, a promise. One of these consists in doing what one has promised, for whatever reason (and being aware of doing as promised); the other in doing the same thing *because* one has promised to do it. Since the first possibility leaves open the question of one's motivation, it obviously admits of forward-looking reasons such as a wish to escape legal measures for breach of contract. (The law, as opposed to the virtue of justice, is not concerned with your motivation.)

With this kind of promise-keeping, the promise itself may just play the role of one of many components in one's situation that have to be considered, with a view to their possible consequences, in a piece of purely *teleological* practical reasoning. (The promise creates a threat of sanctions that you *aim to* escape.) Hence, so far I see no need to acknowledge the existence of reasons for acting that can be viewed both as forward-looking *and as backward-looking.*

It may be said that *the task of keeping it* is itself one of the consequences of one's having made a promise; and that if you φ in order to fulfil that task, your reason for φ-ing is both teleological ("first possibility") *and* up to the requirements of virtuous motivation ("second possibility"). This is correct. But to what extent does it "show that the very same reason can be viewed both as forward-looking and as backward-looking?" We shall obtain an answer to this question by examining the second way of acting in accordance with a promise.

Here, in order to *be keeping a promise,* you must be motivated to φ by the fact that you have promised to do so—the kind of motivation required not by the law but by the *virtue* of justice. Now it seems that if the promise is your reason to φ, you cannot also φ as a means to, or a way or part of ψ-ing (though you will of course φ as a means to ψ-ing if you φ because you promised *to* ψ). Maybe, however, the case where "ψ" stands for something like *keeping a promise to* φ should be treated as special; i.e., Why should not φ-ing for a backward-looking reason (such as having promised) itself be viewed as an aim to be achieved by φ-ing? Do we not use locutions of the form: "X φ-ed in order to keep a promise (to φ)"?

Well, you may say that here we have a kind of reason that can be conceived of both as forward-looking and as backward-looking. Note, however, that the two conceptions of your reason for doing what you promised are not on a par. The *teleological* interpretation of promise-keeping identifies an aim of φ-ing—viz., keeping the promise—that can itself be specified only in terms of an *already acknowledged backward-looking reason.* In the specification of this *backward*-looking reason, on the other hand, no comparable reference to a forward-looking reason is involved. Even if the rationality of promise-keeping is viewed as forward-looking, the priority of its backward-looking rationality has to be acknowledged. To this extent it is wrong to claim that "In φ-ing I am keeping a promise" should be understood on the model of "In lying on a bed I am doing Yoga".

What has been said about the keeping of promises is equally true of other practices such as obedience, punishment, revenge, or thanking. I agree with Anscombe that *returning a favour,* or *taking revenge,* can be the *telos* that initiates a (forward-looking) practical syllogism. But for reasons explained in section 3.3, I hold that "the primitive, spontaneous, form [that] lies behind the formation of the concept 'return', viz., 'he was nice to me—I will visit him'" (§35; cf. also §13) is itself a pattern of practical inference. It is *presupposed as such* in the notion of *returning,* and therefore not superseded by the possibility of reasoning teleologically about ways of returning a favour.

It is thus a mistake to think, e.g., with Anthony J. P. Kenny,[10] that backward-looking reasons or motives are *reducible* to forward-looking ones. If you φ *in order to* show gratitude, or keep a promise, or avenge yourself, your purpose *is* to respond appropriately to backward-looking reasons supplied by a benefit you have received, a promise you have given, some injury you have suffered. The very conception of the reason-giving *telos* is the conception of doing something for a *backward-looking* reason.

4. Contribution: A Curious Pattern of Backward-Looking Rationality

Having defended, in section 3, the respectability and irreducibility of obviously backward-looking answers to Anscombe's question "Why?" I now wish

---

10. In *Action, Emotion and Will* (London, 1963), he says about actions done from motives such as "friendship, obedience, admiration, and gratitude" that here "instead of an action done with a certain intention exemplifying a pattern, we have an action done *with the intention of exemplifying a pattern.* . . . We can talk of an action being done to *show* gratitude, or obedience, or friendship" (97). But what is thus exemplified, or shown, is itself a pattern of *backward-looking motivation.* Hence, if you try to *explain,* rather than merely *represent,* such motivation in terms of an intention to exemplify the pattern, you are moving in a circle. See footnote 13.

to draw your attention to a kind of action that *seems* to be justified teleologically, whose rationality, however, while generally accepted, must appear quite mysterious as long as we do not understand that it relies on a backward- rather than forward-looking pattern of inference. What I have in mind is behaviour that *contributes* toward a *combined effect*.

4.1 The Paradox of Cooperative Rationality

The kind of practical inference that my considerations are chiefly going to rely on is an extremely common one. It is at work wherever some benefit promises to accrue to a group of people in case a more or less large proportion of the group contribute or cooperate to bring that benefit about. If applied where it should be applied it manifests what I'll call *cooperative rationality*.

In the present context, "contribution" is to be understood in the sense in which each of the famous twelve cellists of the Berlin Philharmonic contributes to their music when they play in *unison,* not in the sense in which an individual cellist contributes to the performance of a string quartet. In the second case, the contribution is indispensable for the result, while in the first, any one of the players may fail to contribute without spoiling the result.

Contexts that require the latter kind of contribution are not only, as I said, extremely common. They have also captured the interest of philosophers and social choice theorists. Yet the deeper problem created by cooperative rationality for a one-sidedly teleological conception of rationality seems to have escaped their notice.

What they have noticed is a kind of paradox that may be summarized by saying: In cooperative situations everybody gains if everybody contributes rather than opts out, but everybody loses by contributing rather than opting out (nobody gains by contributing). This kind of situation gives rise to the practical *problem of free riding;* but also to the question, half practical, half theoretical: Has anyone got a *reason* to contribute?

In what follows I am going to take it for granted that human beings need to cooperate, and that contribution is therefore, in principle, rational. This seems to entail that individual agents do have reason to contribute to certain projects.

I further assume, what is less obvious, that the rationality in question does not involve the agent's expectation that his or her contribution is going to make a difference to the result to which it is a contribution.

This sounds paradoxical: how can it be rational for you to pay the costs of contribution if you expect the contribution to have the same result as free riding? And, if it really is rational: What *kind* of reason do you have for contributing if the result you hope for is not affected, or is extremely unlikely to be affected, by your contribution? To get clearer about these questions let us look at the example of a democratic election.

4.2 An Example: Elections

Suppose that you wish the liberals to get into parliament because you think that would be good for you or for the community. It seems reasonable, then, for you to vote liberal when the occasion arises.

Now, being a rational voter, you cannot be said to *intend* to influence politics by your vote for a particular candidate or party, since a rational person will not *expect* such an influence. You cannot, sensibly, reason, e.g.: *In order for X to get into parliament, I must vote for X;* so I'll vote for X, for the premise is just not true. Your voting for X is neither necessary nor sufficient for X to get into parliament, nor is there a likelihood worth speaking of that your vote will make a difference to the outcome of the election. Hence you have no teleological reason for voting.

It may be objected that your vote is indeed extremely unlikely to influence the outcome, and we must not speak of your *intending* it to do so, but your *wish* that X get into parliament as a result of your participation may provide you with a teleological reason for going to the ballot.

Now, I am not at all sure that a representative of the teleological conception should be allowed to speak of a reason here, for, when reasoning practically, you are reasoning with a view to acting in a way such as to *achieve* what you want. The practical syllogism is about what you can do *in order to*—i.e., with an intention to—bring it about. But, for the sake of the argument, let us grant the rationality of some such inferential pattern as: *There is a chance, perhaps ever so slight, that my φ-ing will make a desirable difference to whether p; so I'll φ.*

Even so, your going to the ballot may not be rational from a teleological point of view, as we must distinguish between reasons *pro tanto* and reasons *omnibus perpensis* (cf. section 3.3). The validity of a non-deductive inferential *pattern* does not guarantee the rationality of conclusions drawn in accordance with it *in given circumstances*. Hence the alleged teleological reason for going to the ballot may not save you from being irrational in acting on it. On the contrary, the reasons against may well be strong enough to be overriding. If, for instance, you take the trouble of going to the ballot, you and your children may thereby be deprived of a relaxed Sunday morning; and the near-certainty of such comfort would not be outweighed by the extremely small probability of a beneficial influence of your vote on the election's outcome, let alone on the resulting politics. (It has in fact been argued that the probability of such an influence is, generally speaking, smaller than the probability of your being struck by lightning on your way to the ballot.)

4.3 How Voting Can Be Rational

What then shall we say about the rationality of voting?

So far I have tried to show that no teleological pattern of inference can render your contribution rational; and that, even if there were a valid pattern of the kind envisaged, it would scarcely provide you with an *omnibus perpensis* reason for voting. This does not mean that you *cannot* reason: "My voting for the liberals would enhance their success, which would be a good thing; so I'll vote for them". As Lucy observes in answer to Charlie Brown's assertion that you cannot subtract a larger number from a smaller: "You can if you are stupid". What, however, if you are not?[11]

Let's try this: You say to yourself that if nobody accepted success of the liberals as a reason for going to the ballot, nobody would be motivated to go, so nobody would go, and the liberals wouldn't get in. Hence, in spite of appearances to the contrary, the teleological motivation for voting liberal *must* be rational. Indeed: why not accept its pattern on the basis of treating the notorious "If everyone did that!" as a background motive for accepting it?

This argument is mistaken in assuming that it must be the possible good effects of *your act of voting* that should move you to go to the ballot; and we may improve on it by assuming that it is the prospect of a *collective* effect that should do this. Note, however, that in following this suggestion our understanding of cooperative rationality is going to move outside the framework of what I have called the teleological conception (section 1.1). For, as has been argued in the previous section, this conception does not provide for a derivation of *your* ϕ-ing from premises relating to a desirable result that *you* cannot

11. What is here given as a reason for voting is not a good reason; but it is intelligible, or conceivable, in a sense elucidated in footnote 3 and exemplified in footnote 6.

(however indirectly) *achieve by* φ-ing. We might put this by saying: The *collective effect* of actions performed by a number of agents cannot be *intended;* for on the one hand, there is no such thing as a "collective subject" that could, literally, intend them;[12] and more relevantly, on the other, the individual subject's intention cannot take a collective effect for its object.

Should we then conclude that "cooperative rationality" is really a kind of irrationality? By no means. Instead, we should give up the attempt to understand it in terms of forward- as opposed to backward-looking reasons. The prospect of a desirable collective effect of liberal votes does indeed enter your reason for going to the ballot, but it does so indirectly, not as an *aim of yours.* Instead, your reason might be articulated in premises stating that (a) the liberals ought to get in, (b) they will not do so unless many of their adherents vote for them, and (c) there is a chance that many will in fact do this so that the liberals will get in.

More generally, cooperative rationality must be understood in terms of an inferential pattern that, roughly speaking, provides for premises that (a) specify a desirable effect, (b) state its dependence on cooperation, and (c) give such cooperation a good chance of success, i.e., of achieving that effect. (*Desirability, dependence,* and *chance* must here be taken to correspond to the *situation of the agent.* If, e.g., you are certain, for some reason, that the election's outcome is already settled before you have voted, the (a-b-c) pattern no longer applies to your situation qua voter: from *your* point of view, the liberals' victory is *now* no longer something that may or may not come about, and hence no longer a "desirable" effect in the relevant sense; and questions of its "dependence on cooperation" and cooperation's "chance of success" no longer arise for you.)

A precise account of an inferential pattern of cooperative rationality will have to formulate (b) and (c) as somehow matters of degree; otherwise it might seem that it is more rational, e.g., for you to go to the ballot when your candidates can be expected to win by a landslide than when they haven't much of a chance. (I am grateful to an anonymous referee of the publisher for drawing my attention to this problem.) On the one hand, greater likelihood of the desired result means *less* dependence on cooperation (requirement (b)), and therefore weakens your (cooperative) reason for voting. On the other hand, smaller likelihood of the desired result means a *lesser* chance for coop-

12. See, however, A. W. Müller and C. Friedrich, *Demokratie—Illusionen und Chancen* (Freiburg, 1996), 67–100.

eration to be effective (requirement (c)), and therefore, again, weakens your reason for voting. (Such "weakening" means: more weight for countervailing reasons—cf. section 3.6.) Thus, if (b) and (c) are suitably quantified, cooperation turns out—other things being equal—to be most rational where security of success and danger of failure balance out. And this seems to agree with our intuitive idea of rational cooperation.

A set of premises in accordance with an (a-b-c) pattern on the lines I am proposing is suited to articulate a *backward-looking* reason in the wide sense (cf. footnote 5). As we have seen, the rational voter, for instance, is not acting on a forward-looking reason: he is not voting *in order to achieve* some ostensible good; he is, rather, *prompted* to vote by the consideration of *facts* (including prospects) that he takes as given. The rationality of his action is that of a response, not of an appropriate instrument. We may of course wish to set cooperative rationality apart from the rationality of responding to "something that *has happened* (or is at present happening)" (§13). But no harm seems to be done by using the label "backward-looking" for the wide class of reasons constituted by considerations that are calculated to prompt action without relating such action to a purpose to be attained by it, until we have a *principle* by which to draw plausible distinctions within that class.

If it be said that a backward-looking consideration of the cooperative sort is not going to give you a good reason for going to the ballot, I have to say three things in reply.

First, you are not going to get a better one. There is no chance of replacing that kind of consideration by a teleological reason: the liberals' getting into parliament just isn't a *telos* in the sense of a purpose that you can reasonably intend to attain by voting.

Second, reasonable people do not in fact try to justify their voting behaviour by pointing to its infinitesimal chance of making a difference to the election's result. Instead they will say things like: "What if everyone stayed at home because his vote won't make a difference?" And this thought is in fact the seed of the backward-looking justification that I am arguing is reasonable.

Finally, if in accordance with section 3.2(d), we agree that a good practical reason is, roughly, one acting on which contributes to the quality of human life, then it is entirely plausible to hold that the kind of backward-looking pattern that I claim is constitutive of *cooperative* rationality provides us with perfectly good practical reasons—reasons just as respectable as considerations of justice, gratitude, and other virtuous kinds of backward-looking motivation.

4.4 Cumulative Rationality

In the last subsection I denied that there could be a "collective *target*" that would be realized by the collective effect of many agents' actions. Now, *collective* effects are not the only kind of summative outcome, and I wish to draw your attention, in particular, to what I am going to call *cumulative effects*. A cumulative effect is one that results from a great number of actions, perhaps of one and the same kind, performed by a single agent. Such an effect—as opposed to a collective one—may well be *intended*. Yet this intention cannot provide the agent with a teleological reason for performing any one of the actions that contribute to the intended effect.

You may, for instance, intend to reduce your weight, and therefore start on a programme of slimming by foregoing sweets and drinks. Here, the actual refusal of this or that piece of chocolate on this or that occasion is by itself just as ineffectual as the particular vote cast by this or that particular liberal voter. Moreover, even without any weird metaphysics of a continuum of instantaneous selves, it is easy to see that the structural analogy between the two contexts is relevant to the topic of teleological *versus* non-teleological reasons.

Suppose now that I catch you in an acratic moment and, in reply to my remonstrations, you say that one little piece of chocolate more or less is not going to make a difference to the result of your overall conduct. Well, I should have to admit that you are perfectly right. It would be wrong for me to argue that you should have refused *this* piece of chocolate *in order to achieve* the desired effect. So do you have a reason for refusing to eat chocolate but no reason for refusing any particular piece of chocolate?

This, too, seems wrong. What we should say instead is that the reasons are *not the same* for the two refusals. The *policy* is pursued *for the sake of a purpose* (loss of weight); but this is not, strictly speaking, true of any one of the individual *steps* that, as a rational agent (!), you take in pursuit of the policy. Your reason for refusing *on a particular occasion* will be, rather, the fact that this refusal is a *contribution* (in the special sense explained at the beginning of section 3.1) to the intended loss of weight.

In analogy with the rationality of your going to the ballot, your rationality in refusing a particular piece of chocolate on a particular occasion, may be said to rely on premises stating that (a) you ought to lose weight, (b) you won't do so unless you refuse to eat chocolate on many occasions, and (c) there is a chance that you will in fact refuse often enough to lose weight.

These premises do *not* represent your refusal of a particular piece of chocolate as a practicable means to an end of yours; rather they state *other facts* about it as well as about that end: they give expression to a backward-looking, not a forward-looking reason, in Anscombe's sense.

5. The Respectability of Backward-Looking Reasoning

As far as I can see, a critical examination of Anscombe's account of practical reason gives us grounds for claiming that backward-looking reasons are on all fours with forward-looking ones, as far as their contribution to rationality is concerned. It might even be suspected that the former could claim a kind of priority over the latter as it might be possible to view ordinary practical thinking of the teleological kind as a *limiting case* of cooperative or cumulative rationality, whereas we have seen no way in which backward-looking reasoning might be shown to be a form, or limiting case, of forward-looking rationality.

However, reducibility of forward-looking to backward-looking reasons is no part of my argument in this essay (nor do I advocate it). All I am claiming is that (a) there is quite a variety of motivational patterns that have to be classified as backward-looking, some of them rather unexpected, and (b) we must accord a more prominent place to backward-looking reasons, in our conception of rationality, than Anscombe does in *Intention*[13] and most of us are used to doing in our picture of practical thinking. The second of these claims is relevant to ethical theory since, as I have hinted, the rationality of fundamental virtues such as justice, truthfulness, gratitude, generosity, or compassion essentially involves the rationality of certain types of irreducibly

---

13. In later years, she might have been sympathetic to this demand. After giving this essay at the Chicago conference, I came across a passage in the "Introduction" to her *Ethics, Religion and Politics (The Collected Philosophical Papers of G. E. M. Anscombe*, vol. 3 [Minneapolis, 1981], viii), where she says of some of the essays on "general questions of moral theory" that they "represent a struggle to treat all deliberate action as a matter of acting on a calculation how to obtain one's ends. I have now become rather doubtful about this. Of course, it is always possible to force practical reasons into this mould, constructing descriptions of ends like 'not infringing the regulations about traffic lights', 'observing the moral law', 'being polite', 'playing a game according to its rules', and so on. But it now seems to me that there is a contrast between such constructed descriptions of ends, and the means-ends calculations which really do—at least implicitly—take their starting point from some objective which one has" (see section 3.8 above).

backward-looking reasons. The motivational patterns of those virtues as well as what I have called cooperative rationality cannot be interpreted in terms of intentional teleology.

What then becomes of the unity of practical reason? Is there no prospect of reducing all types of reason for action to a basic common pattern? Well, *must* we seek that unity in a reduction of this kind?

IO

An Anscombian Approach to Collective Action

BEN LAURENCE

1. Introduction

Everyday speech is replete with sentences formed by combining a plural noun phrase and a verb denoting a type of action. "We dragged him for 20 yards." "They just kept riding up and down in the elevator." "The Smiths throw a lovely Christmas party." "Several of the girls are looking for eggs." "Dr. Lau and the innkeeper inspected the scroll." And so on. In many, but not all of these cases it is natural to say of the individuals referred to by the relevant plural noun phrases that they *act together*. But what is it to act together and how does this differ from acting alone? And if, as is usually the case with a phrase freshly lifted from natural language, several phenomena are gathered under this locution, which, if any, are of philosophical significance?

Many contemporary philosophers addressing this question take for granted a familiar conception of solitary action, or of *acting alone*. On this conception, a solitary intentional action is a species of event that is caused in some special way by the psychological states of its agent.[1] When they turn to the topic of

---

1. The "standard story," as it is often called, is associated with Donald Davidson, "Actions, Reasons and Causes," in his *Essays on Actions and Events* (New York: Oxford University Press, 1980), 3–23.

collective action, these philosophers typically begin by noting that there is no one mind shared by a collective agent that might serve as the subject of psychological states standing in the relevant causal relation to the relevant worldly events. They are therefore led to ask how the psychological states of individual agents must be related to the actions of a group in order for that group to be said to "act intentionally" or "share an intention."[2] Their thought is that if we outfit individual agents with psychological states having an elaborate enough content and make these states jointly cause an event in the right way, then we will have accounted for collective action. In this way, they attempt to extend the standard paradigm to the case of collective agency.

The resulting theories of collective action are predictably individualistic and psychologistic in character, for in the end they boil collective action down to the psychological states of individuals and their causal combination. Collective action brings with it no essentially new forms of explanation or agency; its account requires nothing more than a baroque redeployment of the same materials that account for solitary action. We might therefore say that these views treat acting together as though it were only a very complicated case of acting alone.[3] In essence, they attempt to tame collective action by reducing it to the more familiar solitary paradigm.

Anscombe famously rejected the psychologistic account of intentional action in the case where an agent is acting alone.[4] Instead, she attempted to isolate a form of rational explanation to which intentional actions are subject. On her view, a solitary action is intentional if and only if it is subject to a certain sense of the question "Why?" the answer to which provides an expla-

2. See John Searle, "Collective Intentions and Actions," in *Intentions in Communication,* ed. P. Cohen, J. Morgan, and M. Pollack (Cambridge, Mass.: MIT Press, 1990), 401–415 at 404; and Michael Bratman, "Shared Intention," *Ethics* 104 (1993): 97–113 at 99. For a variant see J. David Velleman, "How to Share an Intention?" *Philosophy and Phenomenological Research* 62 (1997): 29–50. Velleman argues that shared public representations—like speech acts, or written documents—can play the relevant causal role.

3. This can be said even of a view like Searle's, which is self-consciously anti-reductive in that the content of the psychological states it posits as causally operating in collective action includes an element (the first-person-plural pronoun) that is not to be found in the individual case. Nonetheless, the form of explanation Searle posits in the collective case is the same as that found in solitary action, differing only in the details of its content.

4. See G. E. M. Anscombe, "Practical Inference," in *Virtues and Reasons: Essays in Honor of Philippa Foot,* ed. G. Lawrence, R. Hursthouse, and W. Quinn (New York: Oxford University Press, 1995), 1–34 at 2–3.

nation for acting that is available to the agent without observation.[5] And according to Anscombe, the same explanatory structure is also to be found in a practical syllogism. That is, the explanations that hold together the elements of an action, relating them all to an end pursued, can also be represented as rational transitions in a course of reasoning about what to do.[6] Anscombe's thought is that action is an exercise of the power of practical reason and is structured by the forms of explanation characteristic of such reasoning.[7]

It is time to consider an Anscombian approach to collective action. Such an approach would differ substantially from the standard approach by accounting for collective agency in terms of novel forms of collective action explanation and practical reasoning, not found in solitary action. It would thus hold out the promise of a theory of collective action that is neither individualistic nor psychologistic. In this essay I make an initial contribution to this project. I begin in section 2 by raising some initial puzzles about collective action. In section 3 I consider Anscombe's account of the form of explanation that characterizes solitary intentional action, and argue that a parallel, although crucially different, form of explanation provides an account of collective action that addresses these puzzles. In section 4 I raise the question of the relation of this form of explanation to practical knowledge and the practical syllogism. Finally, in section 5 I briefly try to undermine the suspicion that such an account must be committed to the existence of a group mind.

2. Some Puzzles about Collective Action

Following Searle, let us begin by considering two pairs of contrasting scenarios.[8] In each pair, the first scenario offers us an example of collective action, whereas

---

5. Sections 5–17 of *Intention* are devoted to isolating the relevant sense of the question "Why?"

6. See G. E. M. Anscombe, *Intention,* 2nd ed. (Cambridge, Mass.: Harvard University Press, 2000), §§32–44.

7. Such an account of solitary action, in contrast to the standard view, is anti-psychologistic, because it finds the same structure of rational connections in worldly events as in the minds of the agents bringing those events about. The psychological and the worldly items are therefore to be comprehended as two sides of the same rational coin. For an Anscombian account of solitary action that highlights this anti-psychologistic feature, see part two of Michael Thompson's *Life and Action* (Cambridge, Mass.: Harvard University Press, 2008), 85–148.

8. See Searle, "Collective Actions and Intentions," 401–403.

the second does not. We may suppose, however, that they would be indistinguishable to the eye of an innocent observer.

(1a) A and B plan to deliver a message in private to the ambassador's son. With this goal in mind they arrive at a party where he is talking to a Swedish diplomat. B distracts the Swede while A delivers the message to the ambassador's son.

(1b) A and B arrive at a party where the ambassador's son is talking to a Swedish diplomat. A intends to deliver a message in private to the ambassador's son, but B knows nothing about this intention. B happens to want to talk to the Swede, and approaching him, does so. A seizes on this opportunity to deliver his message in private to the ambassador's son.

(2a) A band of robbers plans to knock over Mellon Bank. The getaway driver sits in an alley behind the bank with the engine idling, while inside the safecracker listens to the safe with a stethoscope. While the safe is being cracked several burly men stuff money from the teller's drawer hastily into sacks. When everything is loaded up the car speeds away.

(2b) A man happens to be parked in an alley behind Mellon Bank with his engine idling. Among the sidewalk pedestrians, several men carrying sacks and one with a stethoscope—all total strangers—happen to be passing by the bank at the time when another man opening the bank door yells "It's a stick-up!" Pushing inside, each man hopes to get some money for himself. While the man with the stethoscope listens to the safe the other men stuff money into sacks. When they all have whatever they can carry they rush outside and each pushes into the car that happens to be sitting in the alley. The driver is told to drive away, which he does.

In both these contrasting pairs of cases the same actions (in some sense) were performed with the same outcome, but still there remains an inner difference. In the first of each of these cases we have a group of agents acting together, while in the second of each of these cases we have a mere diversity of agents acting on their own. What could account for this inner difference?

Let us begin by considering some quick and intuitive, but ultimately unilluminating, attempts to capture the difference, and so to account for the nature of collective action.

Begin by noting that in cases (1a) and (2a) there is a shared intention between the agents in question. As Anscombe pointed out, the word "intention" has several different but related uses.[9] When we say that the agents in question

9. Anscombe, *Intention*, §1.

share an intention we might mean "intention" in the sense of *the intention with which* they act: some objective they're after in acting now. Alternately, we might mean an intention to perform an action sometime in the future, where no means to that action need now be underway. Finally, when we say that the agents in question share an intention we might mean merely that they act together intentionally.

Focusing on the first alternative, we can note that in cases (1a) and (2a) the agents all share the intention of knocking over Mellon Bank or delivering the private message. Taking a clue from this feature of the cases, we can say that we have a collective action whenever an action is performed with an intention that is shared by several agents.

Unfortunately, this sharing of intentions is, philosophically speaking, rather mysterious. To bring this out, consider that in case (2b) each individual robber acts with the intention to steal money from Mellon Bank. So they too "share an intention," *in a sense:* each has an individual intention with the same content as the individual intentions of the other agents acting. But we're interested in a thicker sense of sharing an intention, a sense in which agents in (2a) share an intention while those in (2b) do not, and in virtue of which the agents of (2a) can be said to act together.

To try to distinguish the thicker sense we might say that in (2a), unlike in (2b), the agents don't merely share intentions with the same content; rather, they have a share in one and the same intention. But it is not any easier to understand what it is for several agents to share in one and the same intention than it is to understand what it is to act together. The problem posed by our second pair of contrasting cases is precisely to say what the difference is between a bunch of agents each individually performing the same action, e.g., robbing a bank, and what it is for them to have a share in a single action together.[10] It would seem that this approach has merely transposed the question

10. It will not help here to bring in what linguists call distributivity. If five boys laugh then each of the five laughs. In this case to say that the group is doing X is to say that each of the group's members is doing X; the predicate "is Xing" distributes to each of them. By contrast, if a crowd is pouring into a room, each member is not pouring into a room. Perhaps we can distinguish cases (2a) and (2b) by saying that in (2b) robbing the bank is to be understood distributively, whereas in (2a) it is not? This will not work. First of all, I think we *can* say in (2a) that each member of the band is robbing the bank, and so this does not distinguish it from (2b). (What is A, in particular, doing right now? He is, precisely, robbing the bank.) To the extent that we refuse to say this about (2a), I believe that it is because we are using the

we began with into a mental idiom, with intentions substituted for actions. But the problem remains even when the terms have been changed, for it's no easier to see how an intention can be shared (in the thick sense) than to see how an action can be performed together. Indeed, it seems like practically the same question.

Nor will it help to appeal to the other use of intention, where "intention" means intention to act in such-and-such a way in the future. Although in (1a) and (2a) the parties involved know what they're getting into ahead of time, and have worked out a plan, it is perfectly possible to do something together in the relevant sense *on the fly*. There is no need to share an intention to do so ahead of time. For example, seeing you with your shoulder to a stalled pickup truck I might spontaneously pitch in, and help you push it to the gas station. Here there was no plan and neither of us knew we were going to do anything together at all, until I began playing The Good Samaritan.

Finally, I hope it is obvious that the third sense of intention, namely, that of acting intentionally, will be of no help here. Saying that the agents in (1a) and (2a) share an intention in this sense is just to say that they act together intentionally—which is exactly what we are trying to account for.

But perhaps we can distinguish the cases in this way. In cases (1a) and (2a) we have some kind of *group* acting together. In case (2a) there is a standing body of agents—the band of robbers—that is performing the heist. And while there is no standing body to be found in case (1a), nonetheless, we do still have a group of people doing something *as a group*. In cases (1b) and (2b) there are no similar phenomena: instead of acting as a group, everyone is on his own. Meditating on this difference we might say that cases of genuine collective action involve action by a special kind of agent: a group. We might capture what's special to this kind of agent by saying that it consists of other agents. When we have a collective action, as we do in case (2a), we have an action being performed by such an agent. When we do not, as in case (2b), there is no such special agent; the agents in question are not part of such a larger acting whole, and that's what it means to say that they are acting on their own.

---

locution to mean that each member of the band is robbing the bank *all by himself.* Here we merely import the idea that we are struggling to elucidate. If "each" just means "individually" then to point out that in (2b) "each" robs the bank, whereas in (2a) "each" does not, is to make no advance in understanding.

Even leaving aside anxieties about the idea of a group agent (more on this in section 5), and supposing this criterion of collective agency extensionally correct, we are still left largely in the dark. Like the notion of a shared intention, this relationship of agents is something that cries out for philosophical elucidation. We can bring out this problem by noting that there are various wholes composed by the agents in (2b): the group of people in the bank, those stealing money from the bank, etc. These groups—like the band in (2a) and the pair in (1a)—can be said to *do* various things: they can serve as the grammatical subjects in sentences predicating action verbs of them. For example, one group of people in the bank in (2b) can be "standing around," and another group "robbing the bank." But nonetheless, in those cases everyone acts individually. As we might put it, although we have various groups of people acting, we do not have people acting *as a group*.

The sense, therefore, in which the group is acting in (1a) and (2a) is thicker than the sense in which they act in (1b) and (2b). It is acting as a group, and this corresponding thicker sense in which a group can be said to act, that interest us. But isn't "acting as a group" just another way to say, "acting together"? And isn't the question of collective action with which we began the question in what sense a group can be said to act? If so, then no advance in understanding has yet been made; the same problem has once again been posed in a new idiom: that of "the group."

Having come full circle, we are left with the question: How are we to explain what it is for action to be collective?

3. An Analogy between Individual and Collective Agency

To make some progress and break into this circle of concepts let us employ a comparison with individual action. Since we want to know what kind of unity is found among actions performed as a group, in virtue of which the members of the group can be said to be doing some one thing together, let us begin by asking what the unity is to be found among actions performed by an individual such that they can be said all to add up to his doing some one thing (alone). And since we want to know what it is to share an intention in acting, let us begin by considering what it is for an individual, doing various things, to have a single intention in so doing.

Expanding on an example from Anscombe, we may consider a case where a man is making tea.[11] Let us suppose he (1) fills up the kettle, (2) turns on the stove, (3) puts the water on to boil, (4) places a tea bag in each of several cups, (5) waits for the kettle to whistle, and then (6) pours the boiling water into each cup. All along as he does first one thing and then another the man is making tea: there is some one thing he is doing throughout; when he is finished doing them all he will have made tea. So here we have several actions the performance of which adds up to the performance of a single action. And, furthermore, they all are done with the intention of making tea. So here, also, we have several actions that "share" an intention. But what is involved in this?

Let us consider it from the perspective of the explanation of action. The sort of explanation we are interested in here is the one investigated by Anscombe in which an explanation cites the agent's reasons for acting. The question "Why?"—heard in the right way—is a request for such an explanation. If we ask our man why he is filling the kettle he might say he is heating some water. And when we query this in turn, he might say that it's because he's making tea. Here we see a nested set of explanatory relations. For example, (1) and (2) are explained with reference to (3), and (3) as well as each of the other items on the list—including (1) and (2)—can be explained by adverting to the fact that the man is making tea: the reason the man is doing all those things is that he is making tea. The several actions thus share an explanatory unity: they are all to be explained as phases or elements of tea-making.[12]

We could gesture at the same explanatory point by saying that it is *no accident* that the man is filling the kettle—he is filling the kettle precisely because he's heating water. And it is *no accident* that he's heating water—he is doing that precisely because he is making tea. Unlike a random collocation of actions, perhaps culled haphazardly from a list of actions performed by an agent on one particular day, these actions are not arbitrarily related, but rather are *fit together* in a unified explanatory series as elements of the action they serve.

11. See Anscombe, *Intention,* §§22–23. The reason that I am not focusing on the case she gives most attention to—that of the pumper—is that it is an example not of many actions all done with the same further intention, or all adding up to a single action, but, rather, of one action that has many *descriptions.* It is, therefore, not apt to shed light on the case of acting together, where we consider several agents acting, and so, *a fortiori,* several different actions too.

12. This follows closely what Anscombe says about the A–D order in §23 of *Intention.*

Notice that the explanations of action that we are considering can also be given a purposive, or teleological formulation. We can say not only that the man is filling the kettle, or turning on the stove *because* he is making tea, but also that he is doing so *in order to* make tea, or *with a view to*, or *for the sake of*, or *with the purpose of* making tea. These possible teleological renderings mark these explanations as what Michael Thompson calls "straightforward rationalization," and I will call "straightforward instrumental rationalization."[13] This sets them apart from other, indirect instrumental rationalizations the man might offer for what he is doing, like "because it's the maid's day off," or "because the kettle is empty." In explanations like these, what are on offer are facts about the agent's situation, facts which in some way bear on what the agent has to do to get what he wants, or how he has to do it. Such indirect rationalizations do not make reference, however, to what the agent is after in acting. Since, of course, in the case we are considering the agent has the purpose of making tea, when he gives one of these indirect rationalizations for filling the kettle a straightforward one will be hovering in the background. It would move into the foreground, if we pressed for a fuller statement of the relevance of the facts cited to the performance of the action. ("Yes, fine, the kettle is empty, but why should you want to fill it up?"—"Oh, because I want to make tea.")[14]

It is the fact that an explanation is a straightforward instrumental rationalization that fits it to serve as a statement of the intention with which someone is acting. If I do something with the intention of doing something else, then I do it in order to do that other thing, or for the purpose of doing it. So we can put the point that all the actions on our list are done with the intention of making tea in terms of the availability of a certain teleological rendering of their explanations. All of our tea-maker's actions are done with this intention because they are all subject to straightforward instrumental rationalization in terms of tea-making.

Consider now a collective action, like that in (2a). Let us focus on the activity of the individuals pulling off the heist. A is bent over the safe with his

13. See Thompson, *Life and Action*, 89.

14. I am not claiming that a straightforward rationalization is available for every action. Clearly the chain must come to an end somewhere with a non-instrumental reason. All I am claiming is that when someone acts with a further purpose in view then a straightforward instrumental rationalization will be available.

stethoscope, listening carefully as he turns the dial. Why? Well, it's no accident that he is listening to the safe with a stethoscope: he is, after all, cracking the safe. Here we have merely the explanation of the sort characterized in
our discussion of the tea-maker, one thing A is doing being explained in
terms of another. However, let us extend our familiar chain of queries one
link further and ask, "Why is he cracking the safe?" *Because the band of robbers is knocking over Mellon Bank.* Here we have an explanation of the action
of A with reference to an action undertaken by the band of robbers. We
jump, as it were, from the individual to the group. This is something new,
with no parallel to the situation of our homemaker and his rudimentary cu-
linary activity. But while A is cracking the safe, B is scanning the street with
a pair of binoculars from an adjacent rooftop. Why is he doing that? Because
he's watching for approaching police cars. And why that? *Because the band is
knocking over Mellon Bank.* Once again, we have the same transition from
individual to the group, from robber to robbers. The actions of A and B are
not related in a haphazard or accidental fashion: they are tied together by a
single explanatory nexus; they are both subject to rationalization in terms of
the activity of the group. This same explanatory connection seems to hold in
case (1a) as well, where the actions of A and B can each be explained by the
fact that *they* are delivering a message to the ambassador's son.

What we find here could be characterized as a form of explanation of the
singular by the plural. This is clear in case (1a) where the subject of the *explanandum*, the action of A or B, is grammatically singular and the subject of
the *explanans* plural. But it is true in case (2a) as well, even though the fact is
thinly masked by the grammatical singularity granted in American English
to noun phrases naming standing groups, e.g., "the band," which we would
refer to as "it" rather than "they" were we to use a pronoun.[15] The band is
plural, metaphysically speaking, for the simple reason that it has more than
one member. Where there is collective action, change involving a singular
agent can be explained with reference to change involving a plural agent.

But this is not all. In collective action we must look not only vertically—
from part to whole—but horizontally—from part to part as well. For in (1a)
B is distracting the Swede because A is speaking to the ambassador's son.

---

15. Note that speakers of British English tend to treat noun phrases like "the band" as
plural, and so would count as unproblematic the sentence "The band are robbing Mellon
Bank."

And in (2a) A is on the roof watching for the police because the rest of the band is doing the dirty work downstairs, some, in turn, keeping their guns trained on bank workers and clientele because others are stuffing money into increasingly heavy burlap sacks, or cracking safes. Here we have explanation member-to-member rather than member-to-group. In this case, although the subject of the *explanans* and the *explanandum* differ, their number need not.

And finally, we find explanation of the plural by the plural. So we can imagine the manager of the bank, emerging innocently from his office during the robbery and stumbling across A with his stethoscope to the safe, asking over his shoulder: "What are you doing?" And we can imagine A answering with exasperation, "We're cracking the safe because we're robbing the bank; get over there with the others." Here, as in the member-to-member case, we have action-to-action explanation with subjects of the same number, with the crucial difference that it is now the same subject in each case, and it is plural.

In collective action we find, therefore, three varieties of action explanation characterizable in terms of their numbers: (1) singular to plural, (2) singular to singular, and (3) plural to plural. In (1) and (2) we find the further peculiarity of action explanation with differing subjects of *explanans* and *explanandum*. Of course they are not *just* different subjects: in (1) the subject of the *explanandum* is included in the subject of the *explanans,* and in (2) the subjects of both the *explanans* and *explanandum* are included in an unmentioned group that might itself serve as the subject of an *explanans* as in (1).

In the individual case we saw that the unity binding many parts of an action into one underwrites a certain teleology, marked in the possibility of purposive renderings of straightforward instrumental rationalizations. These were to be contrasted with indirect instrumental rationalizations, in which the reasons for action were reasons precisely because they bore on the furthering of the agent's purposes, without themselves being purposes. Can a similar distinction be made out in the collective case? And if so, are the forms of explanation we have been considering straightforward, or somehow indirect?

Consider the relation that the actions of the robbers in our pretender case (2b) bear to one another. As far as the lone safecracker from (2b) is concerned, the actions of the other agents composing the group of people who happen to be in the bank make up the circumstances of which he's taking advantage; the fact that someone is waving a gun around is an opportunity he's exploiting. These actions can only explain his action in the way in which a description of the opportunities and obstacles he finds himself confronted with sheds light on what he does. And of course, each person in the group robbing the bank is in the same position vis-à-vis the others. The activity of the others is part of the circumstance in light of which each calculates. It is clear, therefore, that the relationship of the action of each individual bank robber in (2b), both to the action of the group and to those of his individual peers, is that of indirect rationalization. A's safecracking is explained by what the group is doing in the way that the fellow's putting on the tea kettle is explained by the fact that it is his maid's day off. The different actions are not drawn together as parts of a single rational order. The unity of the explanation stems only from the fact that all the agents calculate in light of the same situation; they share an indirect instrumental rationalization.

In (2a), by contrast, we have a single action, knocking over Mellon Bank, the performance of which, like that of making tea, consists in the performance of a great many actions. But in this case the actions that are sub-phases of the overarching process are split up among a diversity of agents. What provides for explanatory unity in this case is not individual calculation in light of common circumstances, but rather the unity of an action through all of its sub-phases. They are, for this reason, drawn together in a single rational order. Each can be explained with reference to the overarching process for the sake of which it is performed. In short, here we have what appears to be straightforward instrumental rationalization.

What emerges from the comparison of individual to collective action is that when a group is acting together, the actions of the individual group members can be straightforwardly instrumentally rationalized by an action being performed by the group. If this is correct then we should expect a teleological transposition of explanation by the group to be available in the first of each of our pair of cases. Consider the explanation from (1a):

> B is distracting the Swede because he and A are delivering a message to the diplomat's son.

This explanation can be transposed into a purposive form, as in:

> B is distracting the Swede for the sake of (with the purpose of, with a view to, etc.) delivering a message to the diplomat's son.

So it is also with the two explanations of action drawn from (2a):

> Agent A is cracking the safe because the band of robbers is knocking over Mellon Bank.

Agent B is scanning the streets because the band of robbers is knocking over Mellon Bank.

Which can be transposed, respectively, into:

Agent A is cracking the safe for the sake of (with the purpose of, with a view to) knocking over Mellon Bank.

Agent B is scanning the streets for the sake of (with the purpose of, with a view to) knocking over Mellon Bank.

So the expectation is justified: teleological renderings for the explanations are indeed available in the collective cases. We are dealing here with straightforward instrumental rationalization.[16]

I am now in a position to offer a preliminary account of collective agency. People are acting together intentionally *if and only if their actions can all be straightforwardly instrumentally rationalized by the same action.*

This account distinguishes neatly between our two pairs of scenarios; for in (1a) A and B can each be said to do what they do because *they are delivering the message.* It is clear, furthermore, that this explanation is a straightforward instrumental rationalization, for A and B each act with a view to delivering the message. Contrast the situation in (1b). There, neither A nor B does anything because the pair of them is doing something. There is no explanation of action in terms of the group at all. So the account seems to distinguish the first pair of cases nicely.

What about the second pair of cases? In (2a) the actions of each robber can clearly be explained by the fact that the band is knocking over Mellon Bank.

---

16. Let me address the sense someone might have that these transpositions are fishy. The reason for this sense, I believe, is this: although in some conversational contexts they are natural, in others they are misleading. When the group is salient they will do just fine. But when the conversational context is such that it is not clear whether the agent in question is acting alone or with others, it is true that the purposive sentences may seem to imply that the whole purpose mentioned is being attributed to the lone agent that is their subject. We will tend to correct this impression either by inserting some qualifying phrase, e.g., "for the sake of helping to . . . ," or by clarifying at greater length with an explicit reference to the group, e.g., "He's doing it with a view to knocking over Mellon Bank. His band is robbing the bank right now." Does the occasional need for this clarification or qualification somehow show that these sentences are not genuinely purposive? On the contrary, the qualifying phrase seems an utterly superficial amendment not touching on the purposive form, and the clarification is nothing but an explicit transposition of the purposive judgment into its non-purposive cousin. Once we have in this way cancelled awkward conversational implicatures, the purposive credentials of these explanations are perfectly legitimate.

Furthermore, these explanations can clearly be provided with a purposive rendering: each robber acts for the sake of the heist. So once again we have a unitary straightforward instrumental rationalization of the actions of each robber. Now in (2b) there is a sense in which each individual's actions can be explained with reference to the actions of the group of people robbing the bank, for each exploits the same situation of group chaos as an opportunity to get some cash for himself. But this unitary explanation in (2b) is clearly not a straightforward instrumental rationalization because, as we saw, the individuals do not act for the sake of the group's doing anything at all. So, as in the first pair of cases, the availability of a single straightforward instrumental rationalization distinguishes (2a) rather neatly from (2b).

Using this account it is also possible to account for the features of collective agency to which the failed explanations considered in section 2 drew our attention. One explanation started from the fact that when people act together they act as part of a group, a group that can itself be said to act. The problem with this was that it left unclear what it is to act as a group, and also in what more emphatic sense a group can be said to act. But now a clear account can be given of both phenomena: people act as a group when their actions are all subject to the same straightforward instrumental rationalization. And a group acts, in the richer sense, when it is the subject of actions that straightforwardly instrumentally rationalize the actions of a diversity of agents.

We are also in a position now to shed light on the idea of sharing an intention in acting. The problem here was to distinguish what it is to share a single intention in a thick sense, where this entails not merely having an intention with the same content, but having a share in one and the same intention. But now we can say simply that two agents share an intention in acting when each of their actions can be straightforwardly instrumentally rationalized by the same action. The bank robbers in (2a) share an intention in acting because all of their actions can be explained by a single further action being undertaken by the band of robbers, which explanation can be given a purposive formulation.

4. Action Explanation and the Practical Syllogism

Thus far, the prospects for an Anscombian approach to collective action look promising. We have located a distinctive form of explanation through which it appears we can characterize collective action. But this is only half of the project. If we are to provide a truly Anscombian account, we will need to consider the connection of these novel forms of explanation to practical reasoning. To make a start on this, let us consider what Anscombe says about the connection of action explanation and the practical syllogism in the solitary case.

As Anscombe argues, for a solitary action to be intentional it must be one about which the agent has, in several respects, knowledge without observation.[17] For instance, if when asked why I am standing on the hose I reply, "Oh I didn't realize I was," I thereby indicate that I was not doing it intentionally. In general if I don't know at all that I am performing an action, or only know by in some way noticing, observing, inferring that I am, then that action is not intentional.[18]

But this is not all. Except for very special cases, it seems that if an action is an intentional one, I am also able to answer the question why I'm performing it without further ado. If in knowing what accounts for my action I am forced to speculate, or appeal to some body of esoteric knowledge, then the question is being rejected in yet another way. So, for example, although I know without observation that my body just gave an odd jerk as I dozed off, I may have no idea how this occurred, or if I do it will only be through highly rarified and esoteric neurophysiological doctrine. If my wife, believing that I'm fussing, asks me, "Why are you jerking like that?" I answer a question with a different sense than the one she was asking by saying, "I'm not sure; I think it's something about electrical discharge in the brain." If I caught the sharp tone in her voice I might have denied her question application by saying, "I'm not doing it intentionally."

We might put the point generally by saying that intentional action is a manifestation of self-consciousness. When I act intentionally, special cases aside, I know what it is I'm doing and why I'm doing it. For this reason, when one person attributes an intentional action to another person, he presupposes

17. Most philosophers of action have followed her in this, accepting her claim or a suitably qualified version of it. The examples that follow are all drawn from Anscombe, *Intention*, §§6–17.

18. There are complications here involving a counter-example offered by Davidson that involve an agent attempting an action under conditions that are uncertain, where she must check to see whether or not she is actually accomplishing what she is setting out to do. For some thoughts about how someone sympathetic to Anscombe's approach might treat this purported counter-example, see the essays by Kieran Setiya and Michael Thompson in this collection.

that the very thing he puts forward in his attribution is grasped by the agent acting; his third-person attribution presupposes the possibility of a corresponding first-person self-attribution.[19] So it is too with any explanation of action that means to capture the reasons for which the agent acts. Such an explanation must be available to the agent acting as well if the action is intentional and the explanation is correct.

A way to see the importance of this point is to consider the connection Anscombe finds in an individual's action between the rational order present in intentional action and the practical syllogism; for she claims that what emerges in her account as a series of answers to the question "Why?" asked with its special sense could also be laid out as a practical syllogism where "the premises shew what good, what use, the action is," thereby displaying the rational order in action as the product of the practical reason of the agent so acting.[20] This is the heart of her account.

Suppose I want to show what the point is of turning on the stove. I can display its point by showing how the considerations I am acting on recommend the action I am undertaking. This can be represented as a kind of argument. Starting from a final objective, by means of some factual premises, an action is justified.[21] Consider the following bit of practical reasoning.

> Objective: I want to make tea.
>> Pouring boiling water into this cup with a teabag will make tea.
>> Turning on the fire under this kettle will boil water.
>> So: I'm turning on the fire.

It is plain that the structure displayed here is the same as that given in the series of explanations given above. Just read the chain of propositions downwards and you have a syllogism, starting from the objective of making tea, and moving by way of successive answers to the question "How?" first to

---

19. Here I pass over the difficult question of Freudian-style explanations of actions. They seem to me to present a special and rather complicated case, requiring a different sort of treatment.

20. Anscombe, "Practical Inference," 5.

21. Admittedly, the idea of a practical form of reasoning is a very difficult one and I do not here attempt to provide anything remotely like a theory of practical reasoning. But hopefully, my modest remarks will be enough to make plausible the connection Anscombe finds between the practical knowledge involved in explanations of action and the structure of practical reasoning. For her most developed remarks on the form of such reasoning, see her "Practical Inference."

pouring boiling water into a cup, then down to the action of turning on the fire under the kettle. Read the chain the other way, starting from the concluding action of turning on the fire, up through the premises to the objective of making tea, and you have the series of answers to the question "Why?" posed of the actions specified at each step. If the explanations given above for this man's intentionally turning on the fire hold, then his action can also be justified with this argument.

This recasting of our explanation as an argument will only be possible if the explanation that we consider possesses the feature that fits it to serve as an answer to the special sense of the question "Why?" It must be known without observation by the agent so acting. If the order registered in our explanations were opaque to the agent in the way that would require speculation or observation on his part to uncover it, then this identity with the practical syllogism could not hold; for what would be the point of representing the order present in action as recommended by reasoning if it were reasoning that did not represent the considerations on which the agent was in fact acting? In that case the argument might show why the agent *ought* to perform the action, or why it *would have been a good thing* if he had performed it, but it is difficult to see how it could explain the actual performance of the action, given that the agent acting does not appreciate the force of these considerations. Such an argument might display some reasons for performing this action, but they would not be *his* reasons, the reasons why *he* undertook this action. In light of this fact, it seems that if the explanations in question are not knowable without observation then the link with reasons for action, and so too with practical reason, is lost.

With these remarks about solitary action in mind, let us return to the collective case. Let us explore for a moment the difference between the solitary and collective forms of explanation by starting—as Anscombe does—with the question "Why?" For the forms of explanation we have been discussing may be used to define a sense of the question "Why?" differently from the sense discussed by Anscombe.

To see how this is so, consider the following case. Suppose I come upon several men pushing a car: first up a hill and then left down the next street toward the gas station. If I ask one of them, "Why are you pushing the car up the hill?" I might get different sorts of answers depending on in what sense he takes the question. Perhaps he will say, "To get it to the gas station." But perhaps he will say, "To get some exercise, that's why I'm helping out at any rate."

Suppose he takes the second line. Then it is quite possible that I will correct him: "No, but why are you all pushing the car?" Or again, "No, but why did you turn the car left at this particular street?" Perhaps he'll say, "It's just how we get exercise" and that will be one kind of case. But he might say, "Oh, well, we're pushing it to the gas station; it's out of gas. That's why we turned left here." If this is how he answers, then it shows that he originally misunderstood my question: what I was after was not information about how his action relates to what it is that he in particular wants, or is up to, but rather, information about how his action fits into what the group is up to. What I was interested in was not the agent's personal motivation for participating in the actions of the group, but rather the significance of his action in relation to the actions of his peers. In short, he mistook my question for one with Anscombe's sense.[22]

Now consider under what conditions the question "Why?"—understood in the special collective action sense—is refused application. It is definitely refused application if the agent queried is unaware that he is performing the action in question. In that case the action is straightforwardly unintentional; it would also be refused application if taken in Anscombe's sense. But even if the agent is performing an intentional action, the question will be refused application if he does not know that he is acting as part of a group. For example, if he says, "My God! Are there other people pushing this car too?" then the question will have been refused application in this sense.

Interestingly, the question is *not* necessarily refused application when an individual agent does not know without observation the explanation of his action; for, in cases of collective action, we sometimes find a sort of epistemic deferment, especially when either authority relations or relations of trust are involved. For example, those at the bottom end of authority relations are not necessarily privy to the reasoning engaged in by their superiors, and so may not know exactly what collective purposes their actions serve, even as they act together with others to achieve a goal. But note that even in cases like this,

22. Notice that both sorts of explanation can be true of one and the same action; the legitimacy of the one does not impugn the legitimacy of the other. Indeed, in the case above it would be possible for my original question to have been intended the other way. If he answered "To get it to the gas station," I might have corrected him, "No, but why did *you* do it? What were *you* after?" These are two different sorts of interest that we can take in the contributions of an agent to a collective action. We can treat such an action as that of an individual *as an individual,* or of an individual *as a member of the group.*

some suitably placed person(s) must know without observation what purposes the group is pursuing. A group cannot be said to ɸ intentionally, if none of its members knows that it is ɸ-ing, or even if some do but only through observation.

So, although it is more complicated than in the case of solitary action, it is clear from the conditions under which the collective action question is refused application that the answers to this question are also manifestations of self-consciousness. If an agent does not know without observation that he is performing the action in question, or does not know that he is performing it for the sake of some action being undertaken by the group, then the question is refused application. And even where an agent does not know exactly why he is performing a certain action, the epistemic buck will have to be passed to some other suitably placed member of the group who does.

For this reason, the first-person pronoun plays an important role in the collective forms of explanation of action as well. Thus far, the forms of explanation and attributions of action we have been discussing have been cast in the third person. The subjects of our sentences have either been dummy names ("A" and "B") or expressions impersonally referring to some group ("the band" or "the pair"). I have spoken of cases where the explanation of an individual's action is given through a reference to the action of a group, but by sticking to the third person I have obscured a connection between the subjects of each of these actions. If I am acting together with others, then the group the action of which provides a unitary explanation of what we are doing must be a group to which we belong. In collective action the subjects (group and individual) of the judgments we are considering cannot be unrelated: the one must include the other; and the agents in question must be aware of this connection.

This fact can be brought out if we switch gears by moving from the third person into the first. Instead of considering explanations proffered by some disinterested third party, we must imagine the question "Why?" put to the agents in question, and an answer given in their own voice. "Why are you cracking the safe?"—"Because we're knocking over Mellon Bank." "Why are you scanning the streets?"—"Because we're knocking over Mellon Bank." That is, each of the judgments from (2a), with a shift into the first person, can be given in the following way.

> I'm cracking the safe because we're knocking over Mellon Bank.
> I'm scanning the rooftops because we're knocking over Mellon Bank.

Here we have the action of the agent named by the first-person singular being explained by the action of the agent named by the first-person plural.[23] The fact that each is in the first person makes clear that the two subjects are related, and also that the individual agent acting is cognizant of the explanation for his action. The number of the pronouns, on the other hand, makes clear that we have a case of collective action, the hallmark of which, I have been arguing, is the explanation of the singular by the plural.

With all of this in place, the definition of collective action I provided in section 3 can be recast—in high Anscombian fashion—as a definition in terms of a special sense of the question "Why?" different from the sense that defines solitary action. An individual is acting as part of some group if and only if his action is subject to the special collective action sense of the question "Why?" A group of people are acting together if and only if (1) their individual, first-person-singular actions are all subject to the special collective action sense of the question "Why?" and (2) the same answer holds in each case, consisting of an appeal to an action with a first- person-plural subject.

But what about the connection to the practical syllogism that is so central to Anscombe's account in the solitary case? We have already noted that individual agents may not be aware of the rationalizations for their actions in cases when authority relations or relations of trust are involved. We can add further that when a group is acting, the members of the group usually, each focused on his own actions, will have no very clear idea how his compatriots are prosecuting their various tasks. Given this epistemic compartmentalization, can we find, between the actions of diverse individual agents, the same kind of rational connections that are exhibited in a practical syllogism? Don't we rather have bits and pieces of practical knowledge spread all over the place, without necessarily being combined in any conclusive way that could

---

23. The role of the first-person plural in collective action is the centerpiece of Margaret Gilbert's account of collective agency. She argues that there is a special sense of "we" that underwrites the possibility of plural subjects. But she defends this claim by considering social situations where using the first-person plural would be presumptuous or rude (see especially her example involving the inappropriate dinner party guest). I agree with her conclusion, but would argue for it on different grounds. As I see it, this special sense of "we" has nothing to do with norms of etiquette or with conversational implicature about how I am intimately connected with other people, but rather with its aptness to serve in answer to the special sense of the question "Why?" that goes with collective action. See Margaret Gilbert, *On Social Facts* (Princeton, N.J.: Princeton University Press, 1989), 167–203.

be represented by a practical syllogism? In that case, although we have gone a long way toward an Anscombian account, one crucial element would seem impossible to produce in the collective case. The idea that we can shed light on collective action by considering a form of explanation that can be expressed with a practical syllogism will then be lost.

In reply, I would like to say that although there may be no one person who has the whole picture in view all at once, when we have a group performing an intentional action, it is possible to piece together what the different agents know. Once we have assembled the pieces, I think that something on the order of a practical syllogism can be seen as displaying the same rational connections that link the actions of the members to one another.

For instance, when a certain action is being taken by a ship during a storm, we may imagine that an order is relayed by the captain to the first mate, and several orders (of which the captain is unaware) in the service of that order are relayed to individual crew members, who do things of which the first mate is unaware. There will, throughout, be knowledge without observation of what the group is doing. The captain will have knowledge of what the ship is doing through the order he has given, and the first mate through his several orders, and the individual crew members through their individual intentional actions. Sometimes the people performing a particular action may not know why they're performing it, and sometimes the people who know the end that ultimately explains what everyone is doing may not know what particular actions are serving that end. But everyone will know something and this will be enough to satisfy the analogue of Anscombe's claims about non-observational knowledge that holds in the case of collective action.

We could, for instance, race around the deck of the ship asking the question "Why?" and noting down our results: first of the captain, "Why are you giving this order?" Then, leaving the captain behind, we could follow the first mate, posing this same question as he gives his various orders. Then, racing from crew member to crew member we could ask, leaning over their shoulders, "What are you doing?" and "Why are you doing it?" Afterwards, if we were not swept overboard, or made to walk the plank, we could review our notes over a hot cup of tea. Reading backwards from the bottom of a page to the top, we would have a chain of questions and answers no different in form from (although very much more complicated than) Anscombe's case of the tea-maker. Here the explanatory connections between actions would be clearly displayed, and we could read each step as an answer to the question "Why?" posed of its predecessor.

Reading these notes down instead of up, we would be able to see how certain considerations recommended various actions in the light of the objectives of the ship. From the captain's intention in issuing his order, through the orders given by the first mate, and down to the actions and decisions of the crew members, we could set out the notes in the form of a bit of reasoning, recommending the particular actions undertaken by the crew members. In this case we would view each step as an answer to the question "How?" posed of its predecessor. (Our chain of premises here would follow the chain of command.) So the order revealed by the "Why?" questions asked on the deck of the ship could also be displayed as a practical syllogism answering a corresponding set of "How?" questions.

The unity of action represented in the form of explanation considered in section 3 is, seen from another angle, the unity of knowledge represented in the practical syllogism. The same rational transitions that serve to link the elements of the action together into a single explanatory order at the same time serve to justify the action.

5. A Reason to Be Skeptical?

Notice that I have made the case that a collective agent is a subject of a practical syllogism without so much as mentioning the collective agent's mind. Scenting a weakness here, proponents of the standard approach are likely to rush in, insisting that far from avoiding pernicious circularity, I have precisely smuggled in what needs to be explained; for surely, whatever we may believe ourselves to have cobbled together, it cannot be a real practical syllogism unless it has a unitary subject who possesses the relevant practical knowledge of the connections represented. But in the collective case, this requirement cannot be met, precisely because there is no single group mind to be the subject of the knowledge represented in the different premises. Therefore, either the account is an elaborate distraction, leaving mysterious what it is to share an intention, or—even worse!—it is committed to the existence of a mythological group mentality: the dreaded hive mind, rightly dismissed at the outset by proponents of the standard view as superstitious claptrap.

With the materials of our investigation ready to hand, I will attempt to defuse this worry with the help of an analogy. A campus, I suppose, is a geographical-institutional unity of buildings.[24] The buildings that compose a campus are clearly physical things, possessing walls, doors, windows, and roofs, and are the subjects of various physical predicates, e.g., size, shape, and location. The campus, by contrast, does not (or need not) have its own separate roof, doors, and windows. Nonetheless, it is still the subject of various physical predicates, having e.g., a determinate location on a map and definite aesthetic properties. It does this, not by being a giant building to which physical predicates apply, but rather by being a geographical-institutional unity of such buildings. There is obviously nothing superstitious or arcane in this.

Keeping the campus in mind, let us turn to collective agents. A collective agent is a unity of individual agents. Individual agents are embodied, occupying a definite space and possessing limbs, a head, a torso, and so on. They are the unproblematic subject of physical predicates, and interact with the physical world in straightforward ways, by moving about and changing things. A collective agent need not, however, have yet another body in addition to this in order to be a perfectly respectable subject of physical predicates, and bring about changes in the world.[25] For example, if I ask where the band of robbers is, someone might tell me "In Moon Township," or give a more complex answer like, "A, B and C are in Moon Township, but D and E are still at the hideout." But the question is not refused application, and this shows that collective agents are, for example, spatiotemporally located. Similarly, the band can act so as to change the world, e.g., painting the word "action" on a hillside, not by moving a giant set of arms, but rather through the movements made by its members. This claim is no more mysterious than the analogous claim about campuses.

Of course the objection we are considering is concerned with the mental aspect of collective agents, not the physical. But, although the issue is more difficult here, I believe that we might plausibly treat the mental case as paral-

24. I take the example from Gilbert Ryle who uses it to explain what it is to make a category mistake. See Gilbert Ryle, *The Concept of Mind* (Chicago: University of Chicago Press, 1949), 16.

25. Although it might. When I was a child I used to watch a Japanese cartoon named "Voltron," in which Voltron, a giant robot, was formed, in times of crisis, out of five smaller robots. As they were forming Voltron each smaller robot would declare its role in the whole, ending with the declaration of the last robot: "And I'll be the head!" This case is, needless to say, rather outré.

lel to the physical case, at least up to a point. Individual embodied agents are the straightforward subjects of mental predicates, thinking, feeling, and knowing various things—most importantly for our argument, what they are doing and why. So if a collective agent is a unity of individual agents, then it is a unity of knowing subjects. In that case, it need not itself have yet another mind—much less a brain!—in order to be the subject of mind-involving predicates, knowing and being aware of various things. It can do this by being a unity of agents who know and are aware, just as it can be a subject of physical predicates, although not having a body, by being a unity of embodied agents.

In light of this, why not say that a collective agent knows what it is doing, and why, without observation? After all, while it sounds very strange to say that the band of robbers has a group mind, it doesn't sound especially strange to say that the band knows, or is aware, or cognizant, of this or that fact. On the surface of it there is no mystery about the attribution of such mental predicates to a group.[26] Given this fact, consider further that "knowledge without observation" is a philosopher's phrase, being a term that Anscombe coined in the course of her philosophical investigation of intention. If it seems to have a point in this context, why withhold it? So perhaps we can unproblematically speak of groups knowing without observation what they are doing. In this way we would straightforwardly have a unitary knowing subject of the practical syllogism in the collective case.

But even if it is laying it on a bit thick to speak in this way, it doesn't really matter. It is enough that the same order displayed in collective action explanation can also be represented as a set of rational transitions justifying the actions undertaken by members of a group in light of a shared objective. In this way, whether or not there is strictly speaking a unitary knowing subject of the whole action, we can still see the actions in question as recommended by reasoning. This reasoning will not, of course, occur through the exercise of a separate practical reason possessed by the group, but rather through the reasoning of the individual members as they execute their shared objective. We might sum up this point by saying that just as a collective agent can only act through the actions of its individual members, it can

26. No doubt many questions arise about when and in what way we can attribute mental predicates to a group on the basis of the holding of mental predicates of its members. All my argument here requires is that in the relevant cases of collective we can make this transition.

only know through their knowing, and reason through their reasoning. In this way, even without a mind of its own, it can be the subject of a practical syllogism.

It seems then that an Anscombian approach to collective action cannot be dismissed out of hand. In that case, it surely deserves our serious consideration.

Contributors

ANTON FORD is Assistant Professor of Philosophy at the University of Chicago. He works in the philosophy of action, ethics, and political philosophy.

ADRIAN HADDOCK is Lecturer in Philosophy at the University of Stirling (United Kingdom). His research is primarily in the philosophy of mind and action. His recent publications include *The Nature and Value of Knowledge: Three Investigations* (Oxford University Press, 2010) and a number of essays on Kantian themes.

JENNIFER HORNSBY is Professor of Philosophy at Birkbeck College, London, and Co-Director of the Centre for the Study of the Mind in Nature at Oslo. Her main interests are in philosophy of action, mind and language, metaphysics, and feminism in philosophy; she has published work in all these areas.

BEN LAURENCE is Assistant Professor of Philosophy at the University of Chicago. He works primarily on political philosophy and the history of ethics.

JOHN MCDOWELL is Distinguished University Professor at the University of Pittsburgh. His recent publications include *Having the World in View: Essays on Kant, Hegel,* and *Sellars* and *The Engaged Intellect: Philosophical Essays* (both Harvard University Press, 2009). His areas of interest include metaphysics and epistemology, philosophy of action, Kant, and Hegel.

RICHARD MORAN is the Brian D. Young Professor of Philosophy at Harvard University. He is the author of *Authority and Estrangement: An Essay on Self-Knowledge* (Princeton University Press, 2001) and numerous articles on topics such as practical knowledge, metaphor, imagination, and emotion. Recently he has been working on speech, intersubjectivity, and testimony, and on the concept of beauty in Kant and Proust.

ANSELM WINFRIED MÜLLER studied with Elizabeth Anscombe and Anthony Kenny in Oxford. After various positions he was, from 1979 to 2007, Professor of Philosophy at the University of Trier (Germany). His publications are mainly in ethics and philosophy of action and include *Produktion oder Praxis? Philosophie des Handelns am Beispiel der Erziehung* (Ontos, 2008) and "Acting Well," in Anthony O'Hear, ed., *Modern Moral Philosophy* (Cambridge University Press, 2004).

SEBASTIAN RÖDL is Professor of Philosophy at the University of Basel. He is the author of *Self-Consciousness* (Harvard University Press, 2007) and *Categories of the Temporal* (Harvard University Press, forthcoming), as well as of articles in epistemology, philosophy of mind, and philosophy of action.

KIERAN SETIYA is Associate Professor of Philosophy at the University of Pittsburgh. He works mainly in ethics, action theory, and epistemology, and is the author of *Reasons without Rationalism* (Princeton University Press, 2007).

MARTIN J. STONE is Professor of Law at the Cardozo Law School of Yeshiva University and Visiting Professor of Philosophy at the New School Graduate Faculty (both in New York City). His areas of research and publication include philosophy of law, Wittgenstein, philosophy of action, theory of interpretation, and tort law.

FREDERICK STOUTLAND is Professor of Philosophy Emeritus at St. Olaf College (Minnesota) and was Permanent Visiting Professor of Philosophy at Uppsala University (Sweden). His areas of interest include philosophy of action, of mind, and of language. He has published numerous articles in those areas and edited *Philosophical Probings: Essays on von Wright's Later Philosophy* (VIP Press, 2008).

MICHAEL THOMPSON is Professor of Philosophy at the University of Pittsburgh. His areas of interest are ethics, action theory, and practical philosophy generally, especially in their logical and metaphysical aspects. He has published a number of papers in those areas and is the author of *Life and Action* (Harvard University Press, 2008).

Index to Anscombe's *Intention*

Index